THE LONG LIFE GOURMET COOKBOOK

by Barry Herman

Former Chef and Food Services Manager,
PRITIKIN LONGEVITY CENTER

with Bill Lawren

SIMON AND SCHUSTER · NEW YORK

Copyright © 1984 by Barry Herman and Bill Lawren
All rights reserved
including the right of reproduction
in whole or in part in any form
Published by Simon and Schuster
A Division of Simon & Schuster, Inc.
Simon & Schuster Building
Rockefeller Center
1230 Avenue of the Americas
New York, New York 10020
SIMON AND SCHUSTER and colophon are registered trademarks of
Simon & Schuster, Inc.
Designed by Eve Kirch
Manufactured in the United States of America

1   3   5   7   9   10   8   6   4   2

Library of Congress Cataloging in Publication Data
Herman, Barry.
The long life kitchen.

Includes index.
1.Low-fat diet—Recipes.   I.Lawren, Bill.
II.Title.
RM237.7.H46   1984   641.5′638   83–16183
ISBN 0-671-47000-0

Foreword

A frequent question asked me as a cardiovascular surgeon by my patients and friends is "How important is diet in the prevention and treatment of coronary heart disease?" Having participated in the care of several thousand patients undergoing coronary-artery bypass operations. I can say without question that in conjunction with other major factors, including exercise, smoking, and stress, diet does indeed play a significant role in the development, prevention, and possible regression of coronary-artery disease. Through the opportunity of working professionally with Chef Barry Herman in the care of several of my patients, I have determined his dietary principles, which he acquired during his association with Nathan Pritikin, to be sound and medically correct. Chef Herman's recipes, with their emphasis on greatly reduced intake of fats and sodium, and their increased proportions of such beneficial dietary elements as fiber and complex carbohydrates, represent a sound contribution toward a healthy diet. His tasteful recipes change eating a low-fat, high–complex-carbohydrate diet from a sometimes drab endeavor into a delightful gourmet experience.

I am thoroughly convinced that these diet principles as so creatively woven together into gourmet delights by Barry Herman can, in a significant number of cases, not only prevent but also result in regression of atherosclerotic coronary heart disease when followed rigorously and concurrently with a vigorous aerobic-exercise program, cessation of smoking and other use of nicotine, and the more difficult, but also attainable, reduction of continuous stress.

Readers of this book will be delighted at how enjoyable and tasteful healthful eating can be.

Don C. Wukasch, M.D.
Director, Houstonian Preventive
Medicine Center
Houston, Texas

Acknowledgments

Writing a book, any book, is always an act of shared labor. This book is certainly no exception. I would like to thank the following friends, new and old, for their help in making *The Long Life Kitchen* a reality:

For valued nutritional information and invaluable moral support, Janet Segal, R.D., and Jacqueline Susan Miller.

For turning three years of scrawled notes into a manuscript, Marilyn Winn.

For helping turn the manuscript into a clear, logical, and readable book, my editor, Kennie Lyman.

For their hearty appetites and discerning palates, Sam and Paula Douglass, and Ana Maria and Daniel Lawren.

For Michele, Zoe, and Dena

In memory of William K. Herman, M.D.

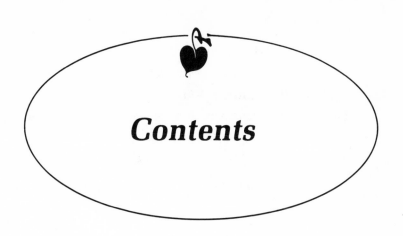

Contents

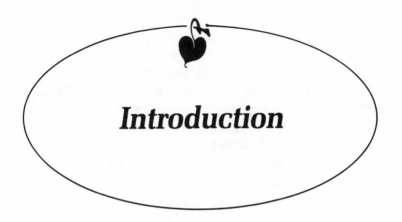

Introduction

Our country is currently in the process of what amounts to a health revolution, a revolution so profound that it promises to make us the fittest, longest-lived population that has ever walked the earth. We are trimming down, shaping up, and in general being good to our bodies in a way that for many of us is both entirely new and unexpectedly satisfying. And scientific evidence is beginning to show that our efforts are being rewarded: our average life-spans are constantly increasing. Recent studies show that during the period from 1968 to 1977, deaths in America from heart disease alone declined by as much as 27 percent!

At the heart of this health revolution lies a greatly increased awareness of the relationship between disease and diet. This awareness began after World War II, when exhaustive research by Dr. Ancel Keys of the University of Minnesota showed that in countries like ours, where the traditional diet was high in animal protein, cholesterol, and saturated fats, heart-disease rates tended to be significantly higher than in countries where intakes of those substances were low.

The researchers realized immediately that they were on to something important. They began to look more closely at atherosclerosis, the buildup of fatty deposits called "plaques" on the interior walls of the arteries. These plaques ultimately cause the arteries to harden and narrow, so that the heart has to work that much harder to deliver blood to the rest of the body. Ultimately the heart is taxed beyond its capability, with resulting angina and potentially fatal heart attacks.

As scientists continued to narrow in on these cardiovascular diseases, they began to pay special attention to the role of cholesterol in the blood. The famous Framingham Heart Study, a National Institutes of Health research program which has followed residents of Framingham, Massachusetts, for the past thirty-five years, has found that men with elevated blood cholesterol levels have heart-attack rates *three times as high as* men whose blood content of that substance is in the normal range. The Framingham findings have since been confirmed many times over by other studies.

Despite all this evidence linking cholesterol with heart disease, it still remained to be shown that the amount of cholesterol in the *blood* had anything to do with the amount found in the diet. In an article, "Diet and Heart Disease," published in its May 1981 issue, *Consumer Reports* asserted that "animal experiments show conclusively that taking in large amounts of cholesterol and fat raises [blood] serum cholesterol in susceptible animals and eventually leads to effects on the arteries. In turn, rigidly controlled studies conducted in hospital or institutional settings suggest that a similar progression is possible for humans."

The connection between dietary cholesterol and that found in the blood was further strengthened in the Western Electric Study published in the prestigious *New England Journal of Medicine*. After monitoring the employees of a Western Electric plant near Chicago for twenty years, the report concluded that "overall fat composition of the diet affects serum cholesterol concentration and the risk of coronary death."

Still, despite their awareness of the scientific conclusions, many Americans remain confused in the dust of what has become "the great diet derby." What, they wonder, is the difference between fats and carbohydrates? What do fats and carbohydrates have to do with cholesterol, and how are they related to risk factors in disease? Why is one kind of protein better than another? What about those strange new substances called "lipoproteins"? What about salt? What about fiber?

Well, without trying to turn what is basically a cookbook into a treatise on diet, I'll try to explain some of these terms and concepts, so that you'll have a better understanding of the basis for the recipes in this book. Let's start with *fats,* since they're usually singled out as diet's most vicious villains. Basically, fats are a type of acid molecule that can be found either in solid form—animal fat, butter, most cheeses, shortening, and lard are some examples—or in such liquids as cooking and salad oils, milk, and cream. *Saturated* (animal) fats are known to be dangerous because of their effect on blood serum cholesterol. While the sorts of unsaturated fats found in vegetable oils are thought to be "healthier," we have stayed on the safe side in this book by keeping *all* fats to an absolute minimum.

Next, let's talk about *carbohydrates,* which may be the most misunderstood of all the food components. Carbohydrates—which under the name of "starches" often appear on the forbidden lists of old-fashioned diets—are actually one of the most important foods we eat, especially in terms of providing the cells with necessary energy. But there is an important difference between *simple* carbohydrates—refined sugars, "brown" sugars, even honey—and *complex* carbohydrates, such as those found in fruits, vegetables, breads, cereals, and yes, even potatoes. When complex carbohydrates enter the bloodstream they are metabolized at a much more slow and even rate than simple carbohydrates, so that the body is not subject to the rapid ups and downs that occur with fast-burning simple carbohydrates. According to Dr. Dennis Sprung, who writes regularly on diet for such national magazines as *Vogue,* complex carbohydrates "can actually help to *decrease* serum cholesterol levels." (Emphasis mine.)

Proteins are for most people the most familiar of all food components. The important thing about proteins is that they contain *amino acids,* which have been called "the building blocks of life." These acids are needed to help our genes regulate metabolism, growth, and resistance to disease. For Americans, the traditional major source of protein has been red meat, principally beef and pork. The problem with these meats is not the proteins themselves, which are just as beneficial as those from other sources, but the fact that the meats themselves are laden with fats. The more fat, the more serum cholesterol. The more serum cholesterol, the greater the risk of heart disease and early death. For that reason, most of the protein found in these recipes comes from nonanimal sources, such as beans and legumes.

Perhaps the most confusing thing for the health-conscious public is the relationship between cholesterol and the substances known as *lipoproteins.* Actually, these proteins act as carriers for the cholesterol in the blood, and they come in two basic varieties: low-density lipoproteins (LDLs) and high-density lipoproteins (HDLs). The LDLs are cholesterol carriers, and scientists have found an increase in LDLs in people who follow a high-cholesterol diet.

On the other hand, HDLs seem to provide some protection against atherosclerosis. At present the relationship between diet and HDLs is not well understood, but there is some evidence that one can increase one's HDL levels through regular strenuous exercise—which should in any case be an important aspect of any health program.

Fiber has attracted a great deal of attention in recent dietary studies. Fiber is basically what your mother used to call "roughage," the indigestible elements of such foods as bran, whole grains, nuts, and some forms of vegetables. Recent scientific work has shown that people whose diets are high in some kinds of fiber tend to have lower serum-cholesterol counts, possibly because the roughage enhances "drainage" of cholesterol into the stool.

The role of *sodium* in such cardiovascular ailments as hypertension (high blood pressure) is well known. Most of us get most of our dietary sodium in the form of table salt, or in the salt included in many processed foods. While some recent studies have shown that people who do not suffer from hypertension may be able to eat more salt than their less fortunate counterparts, we'll stick with the advice of Dr. Myron Winick, Director of the Institute of Human Nutrition at Columbia University: "Since we know that salt is linked with hypertension," Dr. Winick says, "it is important to reduce the amount of salt in the diet."

Of course, heart disease is not the only illness associated directly with diet. The way we eat also affects our chances of getting adult-onset diabetes, hypoglycemia, gout, gallstones, ulcers, and a host of other debilitating ailments. Needless to say, our diet also affects us in less tangible but equally important ways—our energy level, for example; our disposition; our outlook on life; even the level of our sexual activity.

In light of all these realizations, the American Heart Association began years ago to recommend diets in which animal protein, cholesterol, saturated fats, simple carbohydrates, and sodium were reduced, and with a great increase in the intake of fiber and complex carbohydrates. The AHA was ultimately joined in these recommendations by the office of the Surgeon General of the United States, the U.S. Department of Agriculture, and the Department of Health, Education, and Welfare (now Health and Human Services); by a great many individual physicians; and by such diet experts as Nathan Pritikin, the author of *The Pritikin Program for Diet & Exercise,* and Dr. Arnold Fox, author of the *Beverly Hills Medical Diet* (not to be confused with the Beverly Hills Diet made popular by Judy Mazel).

The value of these diets for health and longevity has been shown over and over again, not only in scientific studies, but in the testimonials of people who have changed their eating habits along these newer, more healthful lines. During the years I spent as Chef and Food Services Manager at the Pritikin Center in Santa Monica, California, I saw with my own eyes the often astonishing changes brought about by adherence to this sort of diet. Time and time again, people with long histories of declining health, people whose lives had been riddled by heart attacks, angina, hypertension, and other diet-associated diseases, were within the space of a few months almost totally resurrected. Limp, sagging bodies became trim and strong, full of stamina and youthful energy, while outlooks long dulled by fear suddenly brightened.

When I left the Center, I decided to write a cookbook in which the recipes (all of them brand-new, by the way, and developed after I had left the Center's employ) would incorporate all these dietary principles—de-emphasis on fats, animal protein, salt, and simple carbohydrates; emphasis on complex carbohydrates and fiber. Rather than peg the book to one specific diet, I decided to formulate the recipes so that they could be applied to *any* diet that endorsed the same general principles, whether it be the AHA diet, the American Health Foundation Diet (published in *Health* magazine), the Beverly Hills Medical Diet, or the Pritikin Diet itself.

The strictest of these do not merely limit such dangerous dietary elements as red meat, oils, sugar, and salt: in effect, they forbid them (except for occasional use of meat or poultry stocks) completely. So that this book would be useful for followers of such a regimen, my recipes include very, very little in the way of salt, animal protein, oil, or sugar, and no egg yolks (the high-cholesterol portion of eggs).

This immediately presented a great problem, one that applies to all diets of this type: the problem of taste. Basically, I wanted to take the undeniably healthful but unfortunately bland food recommended by these diets and transform it into a series of exciting, easy-to-prepare, and flavorful menus, meals and dishes to which the word "gourmet" could be applied without the slightest hesitation.

The first problem I confronted can be stated in one word: oil. How to cook without oil or butter and still impart both flavor and richness to the food? Luckily, I was able to solve that problem by using stocks. I made up huge batches of vegetable and defatted chicken stocks—which most diets, even Pritikin, allow for cooking purposes—and used them as the liquid medium for stir-frying vegetables.

Fat-free chicken stock also replaced butter as a cooking medium, and I later learned how to make a flavorful fat-free chicken-stock spread that took to toast as though butter had never been invented. For salt I substituted garlic and other aromatic spices, finding that they enhanced the flavor of food rather than killing it, as salt tends to do. (For those who simply can't do without salt, or whose diet regimen allows it, salt or salt substitutes can be added to most of these recipes. But remember Dr. Winick's advice and keep it to a minimum.) You'll also find that many of the recipes in this book call for the use of soy sauce, which does contain some salt. But you can decrease the amount of salt in the recipe simply by diluting the soy sauce with water before using it.

For a sugar substitute I learned to use frozen apple-juice or raisin-juice concentrates, which contain natural fructose instead of refined "table" sugars. I found that these concentrates allowed me to do some surprisingly sophisticated baking.

Yogurt can be used as a replacement for cheese, for cream, and even for mayonnaise, so that salad dressings and sandwiches are not only possible, but actually quite tasty, with all the richness and smoothness of egg-thickened sauces.

This is not to say that every one of my new experiments was a great success. I had a few notable failures along the way too, failures that seem comical in retrospect but which were on the shattering side at the time. I think the use of buttermilk as a sauce ingredient was probably the most horrible of these disasters. I had thought that buttermilk would make an interesting thickener, that it would turn out a smooth and creamy sauce. So I combined it with some spices and poured it over a batch of vegetables that was steaming. Three minutes later I opened the steamer and saw something that looked like a sponge from Mars, a big wad of curdled milk that looked . . . well, less than appetizing.

Luckily, recovery from these setbacks was swift. As time went on and I continued to receive encouraging reports from clients and friends, I began to get a bit bolder. I played with flavored vinegars and marinades, and I even managed to come up with an eggless Hollandaise sauce, which opened up a whole new world of possibilities for true gourmet cooking. And as a masterstroke, I developed that wonder of wonders, the fat-free French fry!

Thus *The Long Life Kitchen*. With this book the reader can take advantage of my experience and instantly begin to prepare wholesome and flavorful meals of all kinds, within the confines of a restricted diet but without any of the trial-and-error that can be so discouraging. All these recipes are low in calories, of course; and to make things even easier, they have calculations of relative amounts of fat, protein, and complex carbohydrates already built in. In other words, you don't have to go through the complex and tiresome business of calculating which foods you can eat and in which amounts—all that figuring has been done for you.

If you're not on a regimen that prohibits them, you may want to "touch up" these recipes with meat, oils, eggs, sugar, even salt (unless your doctor has you on a salt-restricted diet, in which case salt substitutes may be permissible)—*as long as you do it in the moderate amounts recommended by your particular diet.* By doing so, you'll be able to adopt a diet style that will be filling and satisfying—and delicious—without worrying about gaining weight, raising your blood pressure, or clogging your arteries. You'll feel lighter, healthier, more energetic; and you'll be surprised how your view of yourself and the world in general will brighten. And most important, you might even find yourself adding years to your life in the bargain.

Bon appétit!

Kitchen Setup

The basic utensils for cooking low-fat meals are simple and special at the same time. Since no oils are used, all the frying pans, baking dishes, cookie sheets, and so on, must have nonstick surfaces such as Teflon® or Silverstone®. I suggest the following as basic cooking tools:

Stove-Top Pots and Pans

> one nonstick 9- or 10-inch frying pan
> one nonstick 12- or 14-inch frying pan
> one 1½- or 2-quart cooking pot or saucepan with lid, preferably stainless steel
> one 2½- or 3-quart cooking pot or saucepan with lid, preferably stainless steel
> one 12- or 14-quart stockpot with lid. This can be stainless steel, since a nonstick surface is not required for making stock.

Baking Dishes

one or two 9 × 5 × 4-inch nonstick loaf pans
one 9-inch nonstick pie pan
two 9-inch nonstick round cake pans
two 14 × 16-inch nonstick cookie sheets
one 2-quart Pyrex or Corning Ware covered casserole or
  baking dish
one 3-quart Pyrex or Corning Ware covered casserole or
  baking dish
one 8-inch-square shallow Pyrex baking dish or cake pan
one 8½ × 13-inch shallow Pyrex baking dish
one nonstick muffin tin

Utensils

mixing bowls ranging in size from 1 pint to 2 quarts
a liquid-measuring cup
a set of dry-measuring cups
a set of graduated measuring spoons
a wire whisk
wooden spoons
a large strainer
a small strainer
two rubber or plastic pot scrapers
one nylon pancake turner
one grater with coarse and fine grating surfaces

Appliances

a blender or food processor

Other

aluminum foil
waxed paper
cheesecloth

Basic Shopping List

If you're new to this sort of diet, you may want to stock your kitchen with a ready supply of foods that are low in fat, sodium, and cholesterol and high in unrefined carbohydrates and fiber. It may surprise you to find that your neighborhood supermarkets stock these foods in great quantity. For items you have trouble finding there, shop your health-food store.

The following list will supply you with just about everything you need to prepare the recipes in this book. Naturally, you'll want to buy such perishable items as produce and dairy products on an as-needed basis to prevent spoilage.

Produce

Available the year around

bananas	green vegetables
apples	yellow or white
oranges	vegetables
lemons	carrots
onions	celery

garlic   cucumbers
potatoes (baking)   tomatoes
pears   pineapple

Seasonal

peaches   nectarines
apricots   pomegranates
cherries   kiwi fruit
strawberries   grapes
plums   melons

Note: In most diets of this type, there is no such thing as a forbidden fruit. One caution, however: dried fruits have higher concentrations of sugar per weight than fresh fruits. For this reason, dried fruits should be used in moderation.

Frozen Foods

apple-juice concentrate   artichoke hearts
cut corn   strawberries
peas   blueberries
Chinese snow peas

When you're buying canned goods, it is essential to read the list of ingredients on the label. By law, the ingredients must be listed in the order of volume in which they occur; in other words, those ingredients listed first are those found in the highest volume. So watch for products in which salt, fats, and sugar appear high on the list of ingredients—these should be used, if at all, only in minimal amounts. Be aware that some manufacturers attempt to disguise the amount of sugar in a product by listing it under the name of "corn syrup," "corn sweetener," "fructose," or "sucrose." If you find more than one of those terms on the list—no matter how far down it appears—the product may well be prohibitively high in sugar. This also applies, of course, to such dried products as packaged cereals. Canned fruits are often packed in heavy syrup, which is especially high in sugar, yet the word "sugar" does not even appear on the label!

On the other hand, there are many canned products you don't have to worry about. Examples are tomato paste and fruits or vegetables packed in water. Usually dietetic products are salt- and sugar-free.

Canned Goods

    crushed tomatoes in heavy puree (no salt if possible)
    tomato paste (no salt, preservatives)
    hearts of palm
    artichoke bottoms, packed in water
    evaporated skim milk
    tuna, packed in water

Dry Goods

    pinto beans
    navy or Great Northern beans
    lima beans
    lentils
    garbanzos
    red beans
    whole-wheat spaghetti noodles*
    whole-wheat lasagne noodles*
    whole-wheat fettuccine noodles*
    whole-wheat flour
    arrowroot powder
    cornstarch

* All noodle products should be made with semolina flour. Noodles made of bleached white flour and egg noodles are unacceptable, as are noodles made with salt or preservatives.

baking powder (low-sodium if available)
baking soda
corn flour or rice flour
tapioca flour
nonfat dry milk
Grape-Nuts cereal (the nuggets, not the flakes)

Most low-fat diets permit some use of cheese. Even the
Pritikin Diet makes some room for cheeses, as long as their fat
content is 1 percent or less. (Read the label—it'll tell you the
fat content of the product.)

Cottage cheese is especially useful in low-fat diets, and
you'll find it making an appearance in a number of these recipes. To reduce the amount of fat in store-bought cottage
cheese to an absolute minimum, strain it and rinse it with cold
water, allowing the curd to remain. This produces the "dry
cottage cheese" referred to throughout this book.

A note: Commercial dry cottage cheese goes by different
names in different areas of the country. In the East, for example, you may find it called "pot-style" cottage cheese, while in
California it may go under the name of "hoop cheese." And in
New Orleans, it's—what else?—"Creole cheese." The point is
that any of these products should be acceptably low in fat.

Dairy

nonfat or skim milk
nonfat or low-fat yogurt
cottage cheese
eggs

Bread

Pritikin bread (wheat and/or rye)
sourdough bread
corn tortillas
whole-wheat tortillas (chapaties)

Herbs, Spices, and Flavorings

basil	gumbo filé
bay leaves	fennel seed
ground cardamom	ground nutmeg
celery seed	oregano (whole leaves)
chili powder	rosemary
ground cinnamon	sage
ground cloves	Tabasco
coriander	tamari or soy sauce*
cumin	tarragon
dill	thyme
turmeric	vanilla extract

From the Health-Food Store

In addition to the list below, look here for salt- and sugar-free products you can't find in the supermarket.

chapaties
whole-wheat noodles
dried beans (all)
herb teas
long-grain brown rice
millet
kasha (buckwheat groats)
raw sesame seeds
rice crackers (no oil, no salt)
whole-wheat crackers (no oil, no salt)
bulgur
whole grains and flakes (rolled oats, bran flakes, cracked wheat, and the like)
low-sodium baking powder

* Soy sauce contains about 20 percent salt. As it occurs in a number of the recipes in this book because of the flavor it imparts to certain foods, you may want to reduce its salt content by diluting it with water—the more water, the less salt. For those on entirely salt-free diets, soy sauce should be omitted from any recipe where it appears.

Snacks

Popcorn, to be made in a hot-air popcorn machine or microwave oven, both of which are available at major appliance stores. Popcorn may be seasoned with lemon juice, minced garlic, Tabasco, and any combination of herbs.

Chips

corn tortillas
whole-wheat tortillas
Tortillas may be cut, like a pie, into six or eight slices, placed on a nonstick baking sheet, and baked in a 350° oven (preheated) for 12–15 minutes or until toasty and crisp.

Leftovers

such as salads,
soups,
stir-fried vegetables

Fresh Fruit

Chilled Sliced Vegetables

    such as carrots,
      celery,
      broccoli,
      cauliflower

Spoon-Size Shredded Wheat

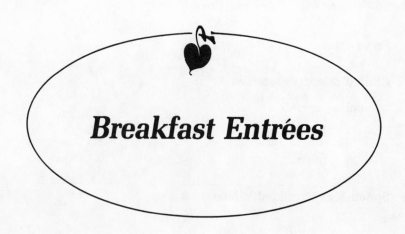

Breakfast Entrées

Nutritionists tell us that breakfast is the most important meal of the day. Yet the typical American breakfast can be downright dangerous. Eggs, with yolks full of cholesterol, are cooked in oil or butter, which are loaded with fat. Traditional breakfast meats—ham, bacon, and sausage—are extremely high in fats and cholesterol.

Most breakfast cereals take essentially healthful whole grains, which supply needed fiber, complex carbohydrates, and vitamins, then bleach and refine them until very little is left in the way of real nutrients.

In contrast, the recipes in this chapter use real, unrefined whole grains, fruit sugars instead of refined sugars, and at the same time little or no fat. In that they provide a full complement of essential proteins, complex carbohydrates, vitamins, and minerals, they all conform to the traditional nutritionist's concept of the "balanced breakfast." If you want to add a piece of fruit or melon, and complete the meal with a cup of herb tea, so much the better.

Hot Cereals

Hot cereals have long been appreciated for their nourishment and for a "stick-to-the-ribs" feeling that gives a person his vital morning energy. The recipes in this section can be served with fresh fruits—peaches and apricots, for example, in spring and summer; apples and bananas the year around— or sweetened with moderate amounts of partially thawed frozen juice concentrates. You might even want to try sweetening breakfast breads and cereals with the fruit preserves that appear later in the book; but since cooked fruits contain somewhat more sugar, it's best to do this only in moderation.

Any airtight container will serve for storing the dry grains used for these cereals. I recommend the old-fashioned Mason jars simply because they tend to be serviceable and somewhat less expensive than fancier containers.

In too much of a hurry to cook cereal in the morning? No problem. All these cereals can be prepared at leisure the night before. For the oatmeal, cracked-wheat, or seven-grain cereals, just put the grains in a thermos, add boiling water, and close the thermos tight. In the morning you'll have your cereal hot, ready, and waiting. This method needs no attention and avoids danger of burning.

◦§ OATMEAL

Serves 2–4

1 cup rolled oats
2½ cups water

Place the oats in a pot with the water. Bring the cereal to a boil; then reduce the heat and simmer for 20 minutes.

❧ CRACKED-WHEAT CEREAL

Serves 2–4

1 cup cracked wheat
2½ cups water

Place the cracked wheat and water in a pot, and bring to a boil. Reduce the heat and simmer for 30 minutes. Serve with sliced banana, cinnamon, and nonfat milk.

❧ SEVEN-GRAIN CEREAL

½ cup oat berries
½ cup rye berries
½ cup wheat berries
½ cup pearl barley
½ cup hulled buckwheat
½ cup brown rice
½ cup millet
½ cup unprocessed miller's bran

Mixing the grains in the proportions above will supply you with a long-lasting bulk of seven-grain cereal. To prepare a hearty breakfast for 2 to 4 people, add 1 cup of the mixed grains to 4½ cups of water. Bring this mixture to a boil. Lower the heat and let simmer for 30 minutes.

Note: If you want to add variety to your seven-grain cereal, simply vary the proportions of the grains used in each mixture.

✑ WHOLE-GRAIN-FLAKE CEREALS

Serves 2–4

Use the chart below to make fast-cooking whole-grain cereals.

CEREAL FLAKES	WATER	COOKING TIME
1 cup wheat flakes	2½ cups	8 minutes
1 cup barley flakes	2½ cups	6 minutes
1 cup rye flakes	2½ cups	16–20 minutes
1 cup rice flakes	2½ cups	3–5 minutes

Combine the cereal flakes with the water, bring to a boil, reduce the heat, and simmer gently for the time indicated.

✑ GRITS

An old Southern favorite!

Serves 2–4

1 cup grits
2 cups water
1 teaspoon salt-reduced soy sauce or 1 tablespoon frozen apple-juice concentrate

Place the grits in a pot and add the water. Bring to a boil, reduce the heat, and simmer for approximately 15 minutes. Season with soy sauce or partially thawed frozen apple-juice concentrate.

Cold Cereals

When you buy a packaged cereal from your local market, you're usually getting a product which has been stripped of essential nutrients by the refining process, and in which the main ingredient is refined sugars. These cereals, like the hot ones presented in the last section, are made with nothing but unrefined whole grains and sweetened only with natural fruit sugars.

Some whole grains, like rolled oats and grits, can be found in conventional supermarkets. Others can be bought at health-food stores or through "organically" oriented food co-operatives.

An unusual serving hint: Try pouring apple or cranapple juice over these cereals instead of nonfat milk.

◄§ "EASY" HOMEMADE CEREAL

Serves 4–6

**4 cups rolled oats
2 cups rye flakes
cinnamon**

Place the oats and the rye flakes in a colander and dampen with water. Drain well. Lay the mixture in a thin layer in a shallow baking dish or on a nonstick cookie sheet. Place in a preheated oven at 325° and toast for 20 to 30 minutes, stirring occasionally to avoid browning. During the last 5 minutes of the toasting, sprinkle with cinnamon. Cool the cereal and store it in a dry place. Serve with hot or cold nonfat milk and slices of fresh fruit. This also makes a good snack, to be eaten dry like peanuts.

◆§ DATE GRANOLA

Serves 4–6

10 dates
1½ cups rolled oats
1½ cups wheat flakes
1½ cups Grape-Nuts
½ cup whole-wheat flour

Place the dates in a cup of hot water, soak for 30 minutes, and drain thoroughly. Then remove pits and chop the dates. Mix the dry ingredients in a large bowl. Puree the dates in a blender and pour them over the dry mixture. Mix thoroughly. Crumble this mixture in a thin layer on two nonstick cookie sheets. Bake in a 350° oven for 10 minutes. Reduce the heat to 250° and bake for an additional 30 minutes or until dry.

◆§ APPLE GRANOLA

Serves 4–6

3 cups uncooked rolled oats
2 cups Grape-Nuts
¾ cup nonfat dry milk
1½ teaspoons cinnamon
2 large apples, peeled and grated
⅓ cup frozen apple-juice concentrate
1 teaspoon coconut extract
1 tablespoon pure vanilla extract

Combine all the ingredients in a large bowl. Place the mixture on a nonstick cookie sheet, spreading it evenly to make a thin layer. Bake in a 375° oven for 45 minutes or until it is dry and crumbly. Store the granola in an airtight container.

Egg Dishes

The egg has long been the standard ingredient in the American breakfast. So that the egg-lovers among you will not feel entirely abandoned, I've included a number of egg and omelette recipes that I think you'll find not only satisfying, but surprisingly tasty. The main thing I've done is remove the yolks, which are high in dangerous cholesterol, and replace them with the whites.

Egg whites, you see, are what I'd call a "good deal" from a nutritional point of view. They have no fat, no cholesterol, and very few calories. At the same time, they contain a healthy amount of an important amino acid that can't be found in such nonanimal protein sources as beans and legumes.

There's only one problem with egg whites: they have a nasty habit of sticking to any pan they're cooked in—even Teflon or Silverstone. To avoid this, simply place one drop of vegetable oil in a heated pan, then spread the hot oil over the surface of the pan with a paper towel or a clean dry cloth. This is known as "seasoning" the pan, and will crop up in the cooking instructions for any of my recipes that include egg whites.

◄§ PREMIERE OMELETTE

I cooked this dish once for a man whose favorite dish was omelettes, but who had had to deny himself because of his extremely restrictive low-cholesterol diet. The poor fellow was in a real bind, not only because he liked omelettes so much, but because they were the only thing he knew how to cook. Well, after he finished eating this one, he came up to me, and I could almost see the tears starting to form in his eyes as he thanked me profusely. "Barry," he said, "if you were a girl I'd kiss you."

Serves 2

6 egg whites
¼ teaspoon turmeric (optional)
1 drop vegetable oil
¼ teaspoon salt-reduced soy sauce
1 tablespoon nonfat yogurt (See recipe page 72)
½ teaspoon frozen apple-juice concentrate

Beat the egg whites with the turmeric until stiff. (The turmeric will add flavor and an appealing yellow color to the omelette.) Add the soy sauce, yogurt, and apple-juice concentrate. Season the pan with the drop of oil (see page 38). Pour the mixture into the pan and cook over low heat for approximately 2 minutes on each side; then fold in half and serve. Garnish with slices of fresh tomato.

◄§ CHEESE OMELETTE

Serves 2

¼ pound dry cottage cheese
2 tablespoons nonfat yogurt (See recipe page 72)
1 tablespoon chopped parsley
6 egg whites
¼ teaspoon turmeric
½ teaspoon salt-reduced soy sauce
½ teaspoon frozen apple-juice concentrate
1 drop vegetable oil

Place the cottage cheese and 1 tablespoon of yogurt in a blender, and blend until smooth. Mix in the parsley. Beat the egg whites with the turmeric and soy sauce until stiff. Fold in the apple-juice concentrate and 1 tablespoon of yogurt. Season the pan (See page 38). Pour the egg whites into the pan and cook over low heat for approximately 2 minutes. When the omelette is cooked on one side, turn it over and pour the cheese blend into the center. Cook 4 minutes and fold in half. Garnish with finely chopped scallions.

⊷§ MUSHROOM OMELETTE

Serves 2

½ pound mushrooms, sliced
1 tablespoon onion, chopped fine
1 teaspoon bell pepper, chopped
6 egg whites
¼ teaspoon turmeric
1 teaspoon dill
½ teaspoon salt-reduced soy sauce
1 tablespoon nonfat yogurt
½ teaspoon frozen apple-juice concentrate
1 drop vegetable oil

In a frying pan, sauté the mushrooms, onion, and bell pepper in 1 tablespoon water for 5 minutes or until the mushrooms are tender. Drain all liquid and remove. Beat the egg whites until stiff with the turmeric, dill, and soy sauce. Fold in the yogurt and apple-juice concentrate. Season the pan (See page 38). Pour the egg whites into the pan. When the omelette is cooked on one side, turn it over and place the sautéed mushroom mixture in the center of the omelette. Cook 2 minutes, fold in half, and serve. Leona's Sour Cream (page 71) makes a great garnish. For an even livelier and spicier flavor, serve with Spanish Sauce (page 257).

⤳ GARDEN OMELETTE

Serves 2

½ cup sliced mushrooms
½ cup broccoli florets, finely chopped
½ cup cauliflower florets, finely chopped
1 tablespoon chopped onion
2 cloves garlic, minced fine
6 egg whites
¼ teaspoon turmeric
½ teaspoon frozen apple-juice concentrate
2 tablespoons nonfat yogurt

In a frying pan, sauté the mushrooms, broccoli, cauliflower, onion, and garlic in a little water for 7 minutes or until tender. Drain off the liquid. Beat the egg whites with the turmeric until stiff. Fold in the apple-juice concentrate and yogurt. Heat a nonstick pan, place 1 drop of vegetable oil in the heated pan, and wipe around the entire pan with a paper towel or a clean dry cloth. Pour the egg whites into the pan. When the omelette is cooked on one side, turn it over and place the sautéed vegetable combination in the center of the omelette. Cook 2 to 3 minutes, fold in half, and serve. Garnish with Leona's Sour Cream (page 71).

ᴥ§ BAKED EGG CASSEROLE

Serves 2

    8 hard-boiled egg whites, grated coarse
    ½ cup brown rice
    ½ cup millet
    2 cups nonfat chicken stock (See recipe page 86)
    1 cup sliced mushrooms
    1 bell pepper, chopped
    ½ onion, sliced thin
    1 clove garlic, minced fine
    1 teaspoon celery seed
    1 teaspoon chopped chervil or parsley

Combine all the ingredients in a 1-quart casserole dish and mix thoroughly. Bake for 1 hour at 350°. Serve this casserole with Italian Sauce (page 251) or Spanish Sauce (page 257).

Pancakes

The pancake has often been unjustly maligned in old-fashioned diets as being high in "starches" and low in nutrients. Actually, when they're made with whole-grain flours, pancakes not only are healthful and nutritious, but have a robust flavor that makes a great day-starter.

For making pancakes, several cooking hints are in order. First of all, pancake batter should not be thoroughly beaten, but mixed lightly, so that it retains a slightly lumpy texture. This will turn out a lighter, more delicate pancake. It's also important to have your pan or griddle at exactly the right temperature: too hot, and the pancake will burn; too cool, and the batter will stick to the pan in a gooey mess. To test the pan or griddle for correct temperature, simply sprinkle a few drops of water on the hot surface. If the drops just lie there, the pan's not hot enough. If they evaporate immediately, it's too hot. But when they seem to dance along the surface of the pan, that's when the temperature's just right.

Now: how to tell when a pancake is ready to turn. That one's easy: when the bubbles that form on the batter are just starting to pop, turn her over. When the pancake is turned, the center will rise and steam will appear. When the center falls and steaming subsides, she's done!

❧ WHOLE-WHEAT PANCAKES

Makes 6–8 pancakes

1 cup whole-wheat flour
1 teaspoon baking powder
½ teaspoon baking soda
1 tablespoon frozen apple-juice concentrate
1 teaspoon pure vanilla extract
dash cinnamon (optional)
⅓ cup evaporated skim milk
⅓ cup nonfat milk

Sift the flour, baking powder, and baking soda together into a mixing bowl. Add all the other ingredients and mix, but do not beat. Two to three tablespoons of batter will make a 3-4-inch pancake. Cook approximately 3 minutes on each side. Serve with fresh fruit or with the fruit syrups and Yogurt Cream Topping on pages 316–319.

❧ BUCKWHEAT PANCAKES

Makes 6–8 pancakes

1 cup buckwheat flour
1 teaspoon baking powder
½ teaspoon baking soda
1 tablespoon frozen apple-juice concentrate
1 teaspoon pure vanilla extract
a dash of cinnamon (optional)
⅓ cup evaporated skim milk
⅓ cup nonfat milk

Sift the flour, baking powder, and baking soda into a mixing bowl. Mix in all the other ingredients. Add water to thin batter, if needed, 1 teaspoon at a time. Two to 3 tablespoons of batter will make a 3–4-inch pancake. Cook approximately 3 minutes on each side. Serve with fresh fruit or with the fruit syrups on pages 316–317. (Serve with Yogurt Cream Topping.)

❧ OATMEAL PANCAKES

Makes 6–8 pancakes

½ cup whole-wheat flour
1 teaspoon baking powder
½ teaspoon baking soda
a dash of cinnamon (optional)
1 cup cooked oatmeal (See recipe page 33)
⅓ cup evaporated skim milk
⅓ cup nonfat milk or nonfat yogurt (page 72)
1 tablespoon frozen apple-juice concentrate
1 teaspoon pure vanilla extract

Sift the flour with the baking powder, baking soda, and cinnamon (optional). Add the rest of the ingredients and mix lightly. If the batter needs thinning, add water, 1 teaspoon at a time. Test the frying pan to be sure it is ready (See page 42). Two to 3 tablespoons of batter will make a 3–4-inch pancake. Cook approximately 3 minutes on each side. Serve with sliced fruit or Yogurt Cream Topping (See recipe page 319).

✑ APPLE-WHEAT PANCAKES

Makes 6–8 pancakes

1 cup whole-wheat flour
1 teaspoon baking powder
½ teaspoon baking soda
1 tablespoon frozen apple-juice concentrate
1 teaspoon pure vanilla extract
dash cinnamon (optional)
⅓ cup evaporated skim milk
⅓ cup nonfat milk
1 apple, peeled, cored, and chopped
¼ cup raisins (optional)

Sift the flour, baking powder, and baking soda into a bowl. Add the remaining ingredients and mix. Do not beat. Two to 3 tablespoons of batter will make a 3–4-inch pancake. Cook approximately 3 minutes on each side. Serve with fresh fruit, fresh fruit syrup (page 316), or Yogurt Cream Topping (page 319).

✒ BANANA-RAISIN PANCAKES

Makes 6–8 pancakes

1 cup whole-wheat flour
2 teaspoons baking powder
1 teaspoon baking soda
1 tablespoon frozen apple-juice concentrate
1 teaspoon pure vanilla extract
dash of cinnamon (optional)
⅓ cup evaporated skim milk
⅓ cup nonfat milk or nonfat yogurt
1 banana, cut into small chunks
¼ cup raisins

Sift the flour with the baking powder and baking soda into a mixing bowl. Mix in the rest of the ingredients. Do not beat. Add water to thin batter, if needed, 1 teaspoon at a time. Two to 3 tablespoons of batter will make a 3–4-inch pancake. Cook approximately 3 minutes on each side. Serve with fruit or Yogurt Cream Topping (page 316).

✒ CORN FRITTERS

If you want a fritter with a light, cakelike texture, use a fine cornmeal. A coarser cornmeal will turn out a fritter with a full-bodied, crunchy texture.

1 cup yellow or white cornmeal
1 cup whole-wheat flour
2 teaspoons baking powder
1 teaspoon baking soda
1 cup frozen cut corn, defrosted and drained
2 green onions, chopped
1 teaspoon sweet basil
1 tablespoon frozen apple-juice concentrate

⅔ cup evaporated skim milk
⅔ cup nonfat milk
dash Tabasco (optional)

Combine all these ingredients in a mixing bowl. Do not beat. Heat the nonstick frypan or nonstick grill to 375–400°F.—until a drop of water "dances" and turns to steam. Two to 3 tablespoons of batter will make a 3–4-inch fritter. After a few minutes, bubbles will appear on the fritter surface. After the bubbling and popping stops, flip the fritter. Cook approximately 3 minutes on each side. When the fritter is turned, the center will rise and steam will appear. When the fritter falls back and steaming subsides, it is ready. Serve with applesauce (See recipes pages 311, etc.)

Lunch and Sandwich Spreads

When you first went on your low-fat diet, you probably thought you'd have to give up that staple of the American lunch, the sandwich. How, you demanded of yourself, can I make a sandwich without butter, without mayonnaise, and without meat? Well, not only is it possible to do all those things, but you can actually make some amazingly sophisticated sandwiches, spreads, and dips without worrying in the least about fats—lunch and snack foods that you'll be proud to serve even at your most formal midday luncheons.

Try the spicy cheese spread or creamy salmon cheese. You can even do a mock chicken liver, using mushroom chunks, a reduced chicken stock, and spices. (I once tried this on a luxury cruise of the Caribbean, and it turned out to be an enormous hit!) Keep your refrigerator stocked with these pâtés and spreads, and I'll bet you'll soon forget the salamis and burgers that you once thought were indispensable.

To thin the consistency of these spreads, add 1 teaspoon nonfat milk.

Note: Many of these recipes call for "dry" cottage cheese. This is made from any store-bought cottage cheese (low-fat, of course), which is then placed in a strainer and rinsed with cold water. The remaining curd is the "dry" cottage cheese.

CREAM CHEESE

Here it is, a "cream" cheese that has all the flavor and versatility of the packaged varieties, but with practically no fat (less than 1 percent)! Use it combined with sliced or chopped vegetables to make a delicious sandwich spread. Fold it into an omelette, use it as a cake or cookie topping, spread it on English or sweet muffins . . . the possibilities are practically endless.

Makes 1½ pints

- 1 **pound dry cottage cheese**
- ½ **cup nonfat** *dry* **milk**
- 1 **cup nonfat milk or nonfat yogurt (page 72)**
- ½ **tablespoon vanilla extract**
- 2 **tablespoons frozen apple-juice concentrate**

Place all ingredients in a blender; blend until smooth. Chill.

SPICY CHEESE SPREAD

Makes 1½ pints

- 1 **pound dry cottage cheese**
- 2 **cucumbers, peeled and cut into chunks**
- 2 **cloves garlic, minced fine**
- ½ **cup nonfat milk or nonfat yogurt**
- 2 **tablespoons chopped pimento**
- 1 **chili pepper with seeds removed, chopped**
- ¼ **teaspoon celery seed**
- **dash cayenne or Tabasco (optional)**

Place all ingredients in a blender. Blend until smooth. For sandwiches, serve on whole-wheat bread or Rye Bread (page 300).

⋖§ MUSTARD-GINGER CHEESE

Makes 1½ pints

1 pound dry cottage cheese
2 tablespoons grated fresh ginger
2 tablespoons frozen apple-juice concentrate
1 teaspoon Dijon mustard
½ teaspoon celery seed
1 clove garlic, peeled and cut into chunks

Place all ingredients in a blender and blend until smooth. Serve on brown rice crackers. For sandwiches, serve on whole-wheat bread, Easy Herb Bread (page 301), or Sesame Rolls (page 305).

⋖§ CURRIED BEAN SPREAD

Makes 1½ pints

2 cups Great Northern (navy) beans cooked in beef stock, chicken stock, or water until tender
1 tablespoon curry
1 teaspoon basil
1 teaspoon paprika
1 jalapeño chili pepper, seeds removed
1 tablespoon frozen apple-juice concentrate
1 clove garlic, peeled and chopped fine
1 tablespoon tamari or soy sauce
½ onion, peeled and chopped fine
1 cup defatted chicken stock (page 86) or water

Place all these ingredients in a blender or food processor and blend until smooth. For sandwiches, serve on whole-wheat bread or Raisin Bread (page 302).

◆§ CREAMY ARTICHOKE SPREAD

Makes 1½ pints

1 pound dry cottage cheese
1 small can artichoke hearts packed in water
1 tablespoon lemon juice
1 teaspoon sweet basil
2 cloves garlic, chopped coarse
1 tablespoon frozen apple-juice concentrate
½ teaspoon celery seed

Place all ingredients in a blender or food processor and blend until smooth. For sandwiches, serve on whole-wheat bread or Zucchini Bread (page 303).

◆§ CREAMY BEET SPREAD

Makes 1½ pints

1 pound fresh or drained canned beets, peeled and sliced
2 tablespoons frozen apple-juice concentrate
1 pound dry cottage cheese

Steam the fresh beets, if used, for 30 minutes. Place steamed beets, apple-juice concentrate, and cottage cheese in a blender or food processor and blend until smooth. For sandwiches, serve on whole-wheat bread or Easy Herb Bread (page 301).

◆§ CREAMY CARROT-APPLE CHEESE

Makes 1½ pints

2 carrots, scraped and cut into 1-inch chunks
1 apple, peeled, cored, and cut into 1-inch chunks
1 pound dry cottage cheese
½ teaspoon cinnamon
½ cup frozen apple-juice concentrate
1 tablespoon orange rind

Place all ingredients in a blender or food processor and blend until smooth. For sandwiches, serve on whole-wheat bread or Raisin Bread (page 302).

◆§ CREAMY CUCUMBER CHEESE

Makes 1½ pints

2 cucumbers, peeled and cut into 1-inch chunks
1 pound dry cottage cheese
1 tablespoon grated lemon rind
1 scallion, chopped
1 teaspoon dillweed
1 clove garlic, peeled and chopped coarse
1 cup nonfat dry milk
2 tablespoons frozen apple-juice concentrate
1 tablespoon tamari or soy sauce

Place all ingredients in a blender or food processor. Blend until smooth. For sandwiches, use whole-wheat bread; or for a delicious variation, try this spread on Onion-Garlic Rolls (page 304).

◂§ GARDEN CHEESE

Makes 1½ pints

1 pound dry cottage cheese
1 cup broccoli florets
½ onion, peeled and cut into chunks
1 carrot, scraped and cut into chunks
1 cup cauliflower florets
1 clove garlic, peeled and cut into chunks
1 stalk celery, cut into 1-inch chunks
¼ cup raisins
1 cup nonfat yogurt
½ teaspoon basil
½ teaspoon oregano
dash Tabasco

Place all these ingredients in a food processor or blender and blend until smooth. For sandwiches, serve on whole-wheat bread or Easy Herb Bread (page 301).

◂§ MOCK CHICKEN LIVER

Serves 4–6

2 cups mushrooms, chopped
3 scallions, chopped
6 egg whites, hard-boiled and grated coarse
4 cups defatted chicken stock (page 86)
1 cup whole-wheat bread crumbs
1 tablespoon soy sauce
2 cloves garlic, minced fine
½ teaspoon celery seed

Place all the ingredients in a 1½–2-quart pot. Simmer over a medium-low flame for about 30 minutes, or until all the liquid has cooked off. Serve warm on whole-wheat-toast triangles, or chilled on a lettuce leaf with finely sliced onion.

✎§ SALMON SPREAD

Makes 1½ pints

1 pound dry cottage cheese
10–12-ounce can red salmon packed in water
2 scallions (white part only) or ½ onion, cut into chunks
dash Tabasco
dash paprika
¼ cup pimento

Drain salmon thoroughly; remove all bones and skin. Place all ingredients in a blender or food processor and blend until smooth. For sandwiches, serve on Rye Bread (page 300) or whole-wheat bagels with a slice of onion or tomato.

✎§ SWEET TUNA-AND-CHEESE SPREAD

Makes 1½ pints

1 pound dry cottage cheese
6½–8-ounce can tuna packed in water, drained
1 stalk celery, chopped
1 apple, peeled, cored, and cut into chunks (optional)
½ cup nonfat milk or nonfat yogurt
¼ onion, peeled and cut into chunks (optional)
1 tablespoon capers
dash Tabasco

Place all ingredients in a blender or food processor and blend until smooth. For sandwiches, serve on whole-wheat bread or Zucchini Bread (page 303).

✑§ SPICY TUNA-AND-CHEESE SPREAD

Makes 1½ pints

1 pound dry cottage cheese
6½–8-ounce can tuna packed in water, drained
1 stalk celery, chopped
½ cup nonfat dry milk
1 small green chili, seeds removed (optional)
½ cup nonfat milk
2 scallions, green removed

Place all ingredients in a blender. Blend until smooth. For sandwiches, serve on whole-wheat bread or Onion-Garlic rolls (page 304).

Salads

I once worked as private chef for a lady whose figure was as petite as her bankbook was immense. Her major goal in life was to be able to eat like a thoroughbred and still be able to wear her whole Size 5 wardrobe. The trick to keeping her happy in that regard turned out to be salads. This is because for women in general, a major weight problem is their tendency to retain water. Well, such vegetables as green beans and green or yellow squashes—which are delicious in salads—act as diuretics, helping the body shed excess water and unwanted pounds.

The problem is that when you say the word "salad," most people conjure up an image of a plateful of shredded lettuce dotted with a few tomatoes and smothered with a fatty oil- or mayonnaise-based dressing. But for those concerned with health on the one hand and creative cookery on the other, this concept simply won't do. The following group of recipes will show that it's possible to make fresh, interesting, and lively salads without compromising your low-fat diet. And most of them, by the way, can be used either as accompaniments to entrées or as meals in themselves—just vary the serving size as necessary.

✑ ANNROSE QUEEN OF HEARTS SALAD

Serves 4-6

1 can artichoke hearts packed in water *or* 1 pound frozen artichokes, thawed
1 green bell pepper, seeded and sliced thin
1 medium-sized red onion, peeled and sliced thin
2 tomatoes, quartered, then cut crosswise into eighths
¼ cup pimento, cut into strips
½ cup lemon juice
1 tablespoon capers (optional)
1 teaspoon oregano
1 teaspoon sweet basil
½ teaspoon celery seed
dash Tabasco (optional)
1 tablespoon tamari or soy sauce

Drain the artichokes, and cut them into quarters. Mix them with the pepper, onion, and tomatoes in a large bowl. Mix the lemon juice, oregano, basil, and celery seed separately. Add the pimento, capers, Tabasco, and tamari. Pour the dressing over the vegetables, toss, and chill. Allow to marinate for 1 hour. Serve cold.

CAUTION: Because of the use of pimento, capers, Tabasco, and tamari, this recipe is not recommended for people on totally salt-restricted diets.

✥ GREEN BEANS VINAIGRETTE

Serves 4–6

1 pound fresh or 2 packages frozen green beans, ends removed, cut in half
1 small can artichoke hearts packed in water (or ½ pound frozen artichoke hearts)
1 fresh red bell pepper *or* 1 can pimento, rinsed in cold water, chopped
4 cloves garlic, minced fine
1 cup red wine vinegar or rice vinegar
1 teaspoon oregano
1 teaspoon thyme
1 tablespoon Dijon mustard
2 tablespoons frozen apple-juice concentrate
1 tablespoon tamari or soy sauce

Unlike many salad recipes, in which the salad and the dressings must be prepared separately and then combined, with this one you can simply mix all the ingredients in a large bowl, then chill and serve cold.

✥ TANGY GREEN BEAN SALAD

Serves 4–6

1 pound fresh or 2 packages frozen green beans, ends removed and cut into 1- to 2-inch pieces
1 bell pepper, seeds and stem removed, sliced thin
2 cloves garlic, minced fine
1 tablespoon frozen apple-juice concentrate
juice of 1 lemon
1 tablespoon tamari or soy sauce
½ cup chopped parsley leaves

Steam the green beans in 2 inches of boiling water for 5 minutes. Drain. Mix all the ingredients in a large bowl. Chill and serve.

✌§ MARINATED BEET SALAD

Serves 4–6

8 fresh beets
1 red onion, sliced thin
2 cucumbers, peeled and sliced thin (optional)
1 tablespoon frozen apple-juice concentrate
juice of 1 lemon
a few leaves of escarole

Boil the beets in water to cover for 40 minutes. Cool and peel. Cut into ¼-inch slices. Mix all ingredients together. Chill and serve on escarole.

✌§ BROCCOLI-FLORET SALAD

Serves 4–6

2 bunches broccoli with florets cut into 2-inch lengths
½ pound dry cottage cheese
1 clove garlic, minced fine
pinch celery seed
½ cup nonfat milk
1 tablespoon tamari or soy sauce
a few pimento slices for garnish

Place broccoli in a pot with 1 inch water. Cover and steam for 5 minutes; then drain and allow the broccoli to cool. Combine the cheese, spices, and milk in a blender. Blend until smooth. In a large bowl mix steamed broccoli and cheese dressing. Chill and serve. For color, garnish with pimento slices.

⋖§ CARROT SALAD WITH ROSEMARY

Serves 4–6

  8 medium carrots, scraped and sliced into thin sticks (julienne)
  6 stalks celery, sliced thin
  1 teaspoon rosemary
  ¼ teaspoon cinnamon
  2 cloves garlic, chopped fine
  1 tablespoon cornstarch dissolved in ½ cup cold water
  1 cup defatted chicken stock (page 86) or water

Steam carrots and celery in 1½ inches boiling water for 10 minutes. Place rosemary, cinnamon, garlic, and cornstarch solution in a saucepan with 1 cup chicken stock or water. Bring to a boil. Remove from heat and mix with steamed vegetables. Chill and serve.

⋖§ CARROT DELIGHT

Serves 4–6

  6 carrots, scraped and cut into ¼-inch slices
  2 apples, peeled, cored, and chopped into ½-inch chunks
  2 tablespoons frozen apple-juice concentrate
  juice of 1 lemon
  a pinch of cinnamon
  orange slices for garnish (optional)

Mix all the ingredients in a large bowl. Chill and serve. Garnish with orange slices if desired.

ও SUMMER CARROT SALAD

Serves 4-6

8 carrots, scraped and sliced thin
2 tablespoons frozen apple-juice concentrate
juice of ½ lemon
½ teaspoon cinnamon
½ cup raisins (optional)
orange slices for garnish (optional)

Mix all the ingredients together in a large bowl. Chill and serve. Garnish with orange slices if desired.

ও CAULIFLOWER-AND-CARROT SALAD

Serves 4-6

1 head cauliflower, stem removed, cut into 1-inch florets
1 carrot, scraped and sliced thin
1 bell pepper, seeds and stem removed, chopped into small chunks
½ cup lemon juice or vinegar
½ bunch fresh parsley leaves, minced
2 cloves garlic, minced fine
3 scallions (white part only), sliced fine

In a covered pot, steam the cauliflower, carrot, and bell pepper in 2 inches of boiling water for 8 minutes. Cool and drain. Combine the lemon juice, parsley, garlic, and scallions in a small bowl. Mix the vegetables and dressing together in a large bowl. Chill and serve.

◄§ SIMPLE CUCUMBER-AND-ONION SALAD

Of all the salads I ever made, this one was not only the simplest, but the most widely accepted and enjoyed.

Serves 4-6

3 cucumbers, peeled and sliced thin
1 red onion, sliced thin
juice of 1 lemon

Mix all ingredients. Chill for 1 hour and serve.

◄§ ITALIAN EGGPLANT SALAD

Serves 4-6

1 eggplant, peeled and cut into 1-inch cubes
6 tomatoes, cut into quarters, or 1 12-ounce can tomatoes in heavy puree
8 cloves garlic, minced fine
1 teaspoon sweet basil
1 teaspoon whole oregano
1 tablespoon reduced-salt tamari or soy sauce
1 pound fresh mushrooms, sliced
toasted sesame seeds for garnish (optional)

Steam the eggplant in 1 inch of boiling water for 8 minutes. Cook the tomatoes, garlic, and spices for 10 minutes in a saucepan over a medium flame. Add the steamed eggplant and mushrooms. Cook for 2 minutes more, mixing constantly. Chill and serve. Garnish with toasted sesame seeds if desired.

✅ MARINATED MUSHROOM SALAD

Serves 4–6

1 pound mushrooms, rinsed in cold water
1 pound fresh bean sprouts, rinsed and drained
3 cloves garlic, minced
a pinch of sweet basil
a pinch of oregano
½ cup rice or red wine vinegar
leaves of butter lettuce or romaine

In a covered pot, steam the mushrooms in 2 inches of boiling water for 3 minutes. Drain thoroughly and cool. Mix all the rest of the ingredients together in a large bowl. Fold in the cooled mushrooms, mix, chill, and serve on a leaf of butter lettuce or romaine.

✅ PICKLE SALAD

Serves 4–6

1 pound pickled cucumbers, sliced ½ inch thick
½ bunch fresh dill (flowers only), chopped, or 2 tablespoons
  dry dillweed
½ cup rice or red wine vinegar
4 cloves garlic, chopped fine
1 tablespoon tamari or soy sauce
1 small chili pepper, seeds removed, chopped fine
chopped pimento for garnish

Mix all the ingredients in a large bowl and allow them to marinate for 1 hour. Chill for 2 hours and serve. Garnish with chopped pimento.

✑ CREAMY POTATO SALAD

Serves 6–8

6 medium new potatoes, peeled and cut into chunks
½ pound dry cottage cheese
1 tablespoon Dijon mustard
1 teaspoon celery seed
4 cloves garlic, minced
2 tablespoons frozen apple-juice concentrate
1 tablespoon tamari or soy sauce
a dash of cayenne
1 bell pepper, chopped into small chunks
1 carrot, scraped and grated

Using a 2-quart pot, boil the potatoes in water to cover for 40 minutes. Combine the cottage cheese, mustard, celery seed, garlic, apple-juice concentrate, tamari, and cayenne. Blend in a blender until smooth. Put the potatoes and the rest of the vegetables in a large bowl, pour on the dressing, and mix gently. Chill and serve garnished with a dash of paprika, or surrounded by stalks of parsley.

✑ SUMMER SLAW

Serves 4–6

1 head green cabbage, shredded
½ head red cabbage, shredded fine
2 carrots, scraped and grated
1 bell pepper, seeds and stem removed, sliced thin
½ red onion or 3 scallions, sliced thin
3 cloves garlic, chopped fine
½ cup rice or red wine vinegar
2 tablespoons frozen apple-juice concentrate
1 tablespoon tamari or soy sauce

½ teaspoon celery seed
½ teaspoon dillweed
½ teaspoon sweet basil

Mix the cabbage, carrots, bell pepper, onion, and garlic in a large bowl. In another bowl mix the vinegar, apple-juice concentrate, soy sauce, and herbs. Combine the vegetables with the dressing, chill for 1 hour, and serve.

✑ SANTA MONICA COLE SLAW

Serves 4–6

1 head green cabbage, shredded
1 carrot, scraped and shredded
½ green onion, sliced
1 apple, diced into small chunks
1 bell pepper, seeded and sliced thin
½ pound dry cottage cheese
2 tablespoons frozen apple-juice concentrate
2 cloves garlic, minced fine
1 teaspoon celery seed
1 tablespoon tamari or soy sauce

Mix cabbage, carrot, onion, apple, and pepper in a large bowl. Place cottage cheese, apple-juice concentrate, garlic, and celery seed in a blender. Blend until smooth. Mix dressing with vegetables, chill, and serve.

⋘ CREAMY COLE SLAW

Serves 4–6

1 head cabbage, sliced thin
1 carrot, scraped and grated
3 scallions (green included), chopped fine
4 cloves garlic, minced fine
½ pound dry cottage cheese
1 bell pepper, seeds and stem removed, cut into chunks
leaves of ½ bunch parsley (for a zingier flavor, try cilantro
   leaves)
1 tablespoon grated orange rind
1 apple, seeds and core removed, cut into chunks

Mix the cabbage, carrot, scallions, and garlic in a large bowl. Combine the cottage cheese, bell pepper, parsley, orange rind, and apple in a blender. Blend until smooth. Pour this dressing over the cabbage mixture in the bowl and mix thoroughly. Chill and serve.

⋘ COLE SLAW VINAIGRETTE

Serves 4–6

1 head green cabbage, sliced thin
½ head red cabbage, sliced thin (optional)
1 bell pepper, seeded and chopped fine
3 scallions (white part only), chopped fine
3 cloves garlic, minced fine
½ small jar pimento, rinsed in cold water and cut into strips
1 teaspoon celery seed
1 cup rice vinegar or juice of 1 lemon
1 apple, peeled and chopped fine
1 carrot, scraped and grated
1 teaspoon tamari or soy sauce

Mix all the ingredients together in a large bowl. Chill and serve.

ᨳ SWEET SQUASH SALAD

Serves 4-6

1 acorn squash
2 zucchini squash (unpeeled), sliced thin
2 crookneck squash (unpeeled), sliced thin
juice of 1 lemon
¼ teaspoon cinnamon
2 tablespoons frozen apple-juice concentrate

Wrap the acorn squash in aluminum foil and bake for 1 hour at 350°. Remove squash from oven and allow to cool for 20 minutes. Remove foil. Cut the squash in half and remove the seeds. Scoop out the flesh with a large spoon and cut into chunks. Mix the chunks of acorn squash with all the other ingredients in a large bowl. Chill and serve. For an attractive serving suggestion, scoop out the pulp from ½ grapefruit and fill the shell with the salad.

ᨳ SPANISH TOMATO SALAD

Serves 4-6

6 fresh tomatoes, cut into quarters, core removed
½ bunch fresh cilantro, chopped *or* 2 tablespoons dry cilantro
4 scallions, sliced small
1 fresh chili pepper (red or green) with seeds removed, chopped fine
juice of 1 lemon
1 tablespoon tamari or soy sauce

Mix all the ingredients together in a large bowl. Chill and serve. Garnish with cilantro leaves.

↩§ CHIP SALAD

Serves 4–6

> 4 large turnips (or, where available, 3 jicama), peeled and
> sliced into thin chips
> 3 scallions, sliced thin
> 4 cloves garlic, chopped fine
> dash cayenne (optional)
> 1 orange, sliced thin
> ½ bunch parsley or fresh mint (leaves only), chopped fine

Mix all the ingredients in a large bowl. Allow the salad to marinate for 1 hour. Chill and serve on a bed of orange slices dipped in fine-chopped parsley.

Salad Dressings

Most of us think of salad dressing as the salad's "better half," and it's certainly true that the dressing gives the salad most of its flavor and appeal. Also, since a diet high in complex carbohydrates means you'll be eating a great many more salads than you may have eaten in the past, I've gone out of my way to provide enough different dressing recipes—incorporating what I think is a wide and tantalizing variety of flavors—so that even something as simple as a hearts-of-lettuce salad can be "decorated" with an interesting spectrum of tastes. In this section I'll show you how to start with such basics as "mayonnaise" and "sour cream" made from dry cottage cheese or yogurt, and I'll give you a tangy basic vinaigrette. Then we'll move on to more complex and even more exciting dressings: French dressing, for example, made from sweet potatoes and lemon juice; or delightful Italian dressings out of herbs, flavored vinegars, and frozen apple-juice concentrate.

Since yogurt is a basic ingredient in many of these recipes, a word is needed to explain why I prefer homemade yogurt (You'll find my recipe on page 72) to the store-bought varieties. For one thing, it's cheaper. About a dollar's worth of nonfat milk will make a quart of yogurt, which costs twice that much or more in the supermarket. For another, most commercial yogurts contain sugar and at least some fat, while my yogurt is almost entirely sugar- and fat-free. Finally, it's about as simple to make yogurt my way as it is to pick a carton of it out of a supermarket case.

A few words about storage: Vinaigrette dressings will store indefinitely in the refrigerator. Vegetable dressings store for ten days to two weeks when refrigerated, and three to six months when frozen. Creamy dressings, on the other hand, are highly perishable. They'll keep three to five days in the refrigerator—any longer than that, and you'll find them going sour.

Another thing: Many of these salad dressings can be used as cold sauces for certain appetizers and entrées. For example, the Spicy Tomato Dressing (page 81) can be a delightful pick-me-up for steamed rice. The vinaigrettes, on the other hand, can be heated and used as sauces for main dishes, and they also make a good medium for stir-frying vegetables.

◄§ SLENDER MAYONNAISE

Makes 1½ pints

> 2 **cups defatted chicken stock (See recipe page 86)**
> 2 **cups nonfat yogurt (recipe page 72) or dry cottage cheese**
> **(See page 48)**
> **a dash of sage**
> ½ **teaspoon grated fresh ginger**
> 1 **tablespoon frozen apple-juice concentrate**
> 1 **teaspoon lemon juice**

Boil the chicken stock until it is reduced by half. Blend together with all the rest of the ingredients until smooth. Chill. Serve over half a steamed artichoke, or steamed vegetable salad. For sandwiches, use it just as you'd use a normal mayonnaise.

✑§ LEONA'S SOUR CREAM

This recipe is dedicated to my mother, for whom it is named. My mom's background, you see, is Hungarian, and in Hungary sour cream is as vital to good cooking as pasta is to the Italians. My mom used it at almost every meal—on fresh fruit for breakfast, on salads for lunch, in hot and cold soups, on baked potatoes, and in her delicious desserts. In fact, when I first started cooking for low-fat diets, I went home and went on a crusade to "clean up" my mother's refrigerator. I threw out just about everything that had any kind of fat or sugar in it. But when I got to the sour cream, she put her hand on my arm and said, "What are you going to do with that?" I patiently explained that the stuff was full of fat and was eventually going to kill her. She looked at me, and her eyes turned just as iron-hard as the grip she had on my arm. She said, "Son, without sour cream, life's not worth living."

So Mom, this one's for you. . . .

1 **pound dry cottage cheese**
2 **ripe bananas, broken into pieces**
2 **teaspoons pure vanilla extract**
2 **tablespoons frozen apple-juice concentrate**
1 **cup nonfat milk**

Blend all the ingredients until smooth.

Leona's Sour Cream can be used every way my mom used it and more: mixed with brown rice, as a topping for steamed fresh vegetables or Guacamole sin Aguacate (page 109), as a garnish for bean soups or borscht, and in many kinds of baking.

✌§ YOGURT

When the "health-food movement" first hit this country, yogurt suddenly became a household item. And well it should be, for the lactobacillus cultures it contains are known to be very good for the digestion. Some people, in fact, even use it as a sort of preventive medicine when traveling in other countries and eating foods to which they are unaccustomed. Beyond that, yogurt has a universe of uses in low-fat cooking: as a base ingredient for salad dressings, for making sauces rich and creamy, for fruit and dessert toppings, even as a replacement for milk with breakfast cereals.

Makes 1 pint

   1 **quart skim milk**
   ⅓ **cup nonfat dry milk (for a fuller-bodied yogurt add ⅔ cup more)**
   1 **tablespoon unflavored low-fat yogurt**

Mix the milk and dry milk thoroughly in a saucepan. Heat, stirring constantly, to 120°F., using a candy thermometer to measure the temperature. DO NOT BOIL. Remove from heat and pour into a crock or a stainless steel bowl. Stir in the yogurt and place in oven. Leave oven door ajar so that oven light bulb acts as warming agent. DO NOT ACTUALLY TURN THE OVEN ON. Takes about 12 hours. If your oven doesn't have a light, leave the yogurt in a warm place, but do not put it directly on a heat source.

⋑ HERB VINAIGRETTE DRESSING

This is the traditional dressing served on the basic mixed green salad. It's also excellent on raw vegetables and fresh sliced tomatoes. My personal favorite, though, is to use it as a light sauce over steamed brussels sprouts.

Makes 1½ pints

    1 medium-size carrot, scraped and chopped
    1 celery stalk, chopped
    2 scallions, chopped
    2 cups rice vinegar
    1 teaspoon Dijon mustard
    2 tablespoons frozen apple-juice concentrate
    1 teaspoon oregano
    1 teaspoon basil
    ½ teaspoon rosemary
    ½ teaspoon celery seed
    2 tablespoons lemon juice
    1 tablespoon reduced-salt tamari or soy sauce

Steam the carrot and celery in ½ cup water for 5 minutes. Place all the ingredients in a blender. Blend until smooth, chill, and serve.

⋑ TANGY YOGURT DRESSING

Makes 1½ pints

    1 cucumber, peeled and chopped
    ¼ teaspoon celery seed
    1 bell pepper, seeded and chopped
    2 cups nonfat yogurt (page 72)
    1 tablespoon lemon juice
    1 tablespoon frozen apple-juice concentrate

Place all ingredients in a blender or food processor. Blend until smooth. Chill. Serve over a salad made of mixed sliced squashes.

✌§ SPICY YOGURT DRESSING

Makes 1½ pints

2 cups nonfat yogurt (page 72)
2 scallions, chopped
1 clove garlic, peeled and minced fine
½ cup pimento, rinsed, drained, and chopped
1 teaspoon chili powder
1 tablespoon tomato paste *or* 1 ripe tomato
a dash of cayenne or Tabasco
1 tablespoon reduced-salt tamari or soy sauce

Place all the ingredients in a blender or food processor. Blend until smooth. Chill. Serve over a salad of zucchini and crookneck squash.

✌§ ITALIAN YOGURT DRESSING

Makes 1½ pints

2 cups nonfat yogurt (page 72)
1 zucchini (unpeeled), cut into chunks
½ onion, peeled and chopped
1 clove garlic, peeled and minced fine
½ teaspoon sweet basil
½ teaspoon oregano
a dash of rosemary
1 tablespoon reduced-salt tamari or soy sauce

Place all ingredients in a blender. Blend until smooth. Chill. Serve over sliced cold asparagus salad.

✑ CURRIED YOGURT DRESSING

Makes 1½ pints

2 cups nonfat yogurt (page 72)
1 cup carrot, scraped and cut into small chunks
1 apple, peeled, cored, and cut into chunks
2 tablespoons frozen apple-juice concentrate
¼ teaspoon cinnamon
1 clove garlic, peeled and minced fine
1 teaspoon curry powder
1 scallion, sliced
a dash of cayenne (optional)

Place all the ingredients in a blender or food processor. Blend until smooth. Chill. Serve over shredded carrots or jicama.

✑ TROPICAL YOGURT DRESSING

Makes 1½ pints

2 cups nonfat yogurt (page 72)
1 apple, peeled, cored, and cut into chunks
1 tablespoon lemon juice
½ cup fresh pineapple *or* 1 small can pineapple packed in water (no added sugar)
1 tablespoon frozen apple-juice concentrate
1 tablespoon grated orange peel

Place all the ingredients in a blender or food processor. Blend until smooth. Chill. Serve over fresh-fruit salad.

⋘ GARDEN YOGURT DRESSING

Makes 1½ pints

2 cups nonfat yogurt (page 72)
1 zucchini (unpeeled), cut into chunks
1 carrot, scraped and cut into chunks
1 stalk celery, cut into chunks
½ onion, peeled and chopped
½ bell pepper, seeds and stem removed, chopped fine
1 clove garlic, peeled and minced
1 tablespoon reduced-salt tamari or soy sauce

Place all ingredients in a blender or food processor. Blend until smooth. Chill. Serve with broccoli-tip salad.

⋘ EASY ITALIAN DRESSING

Makes 1½ pints

1 cup rice vinegar
1 cup lemon juice
1 cup frozen apple-juice concentrate
2 cloves garlic, minced fine
1 tablespoon basil
1 tablespoon oregano
1 tablespoon reduced-salt tamari or soy sauce

Combine all the ingredients. Chill and serve over mixed green salad.

⇜§ TANGY ITALIAN DRESSING

Makes 1½ pints

2 cups rice vinegar
½ cup frozen apple-juice concentrate
2 tablespoons capers, chopped fine
½ cup fresh lemon juice
2 teaspoons oregano
2 teaspoons sweet basil
4 cloves garlic, peeled and minced fine
½ teaspoon rosemary
1 tablespoon reduced-salt tamari or soy sauce
a dash of tarragon (optional)
a dash of Tabasco (optional)

Mix all the ingredients together thoroughly. Chill and serve over sliced cucumbers and cherry tomatoes.

⇜§ ITALIAN HERB DRESSING

Makes 1½ pints

2 cups red vinegar
2 tablespoons frozen apple-juice concentrate
1 teaspoon sweet basil
2 cloves garlic, minced fine
2 tablespoons pimento, chopped fine
½ teaspoon oregano
½ teaspoon thyme
½ teaspoon rosemary
1 tablespoon grated lemon or orange peel
1 scallion, chopped

Place all ingredients in a blender or food processor. Blend until smooth. Chill. Serve over mixed green salad.

✥ ITALIAN VEGETABLE DRESSING

Makes 1½ pints

1 zucchini, cut into 1-inch chunks
1 carrot, scraped and cut into 1-inch pieces
1 bell pepper, seeds and stem removed, chopped fine
½ onion, peeled and chopped
1 stalk celery, chopped
1 cup red wine vinegar
2 cloves garlic, peeled and minced fine
1 teaspoon sweet basil
1 teaspoon oregano
½ teaspoon ground cardamom
2 tablespoons frozen apple-juice concentrate
2 tablespoons lemon juice

Place all ingredients in a blender. Blend until smooth.
Serve over a salad made with fresh green beans.

✥ ISLAND FRENCH DRESSING

This recipe was the result of one of those happy accidents
that can make cooking such an agreeable surprise. I had
cooked a large batch of yams for a special banquet—so many
yams, in fact, that I found myself with a refrigerator full of
leftovers. Well, when I opened the refrigerator the next
morning, my nose was piqued by an aroma that smelled
vaguely like French dressing. So I started experimenting—a
little lemon juice here, some vinegar there, spices, and so
on—and soon I had a rich, full French dressing that's one
hundred percent fat-free!

2 large red yams
½ cup lemon juice
½ cup rice vinegar

2 scallions (white part only), chopped
2 cloves garlic, minced fine
2 tablespoons tomato paste
1 tablespoon reduced-salt tamari or soy sauce
2 cups water
2 tablespoons frozen apple-juice concentrate

Bake yams 1 hour at 350°. Remove skins and cut the yams into chunks. Place all the ingredients in a blender or food processor. Blend until smooth. Chill and serve over a mixed green salad with whole-wheat croutons.

✑§ CREAMY GARLIC DRESSING

Makes 1½ pints

2 cups nonfat yogurt (page 72)
1 cup nonfat milk or nonfat (strained) buttermilk
1 teaspoon dill
6 cloves garlic, minced fine
1 cucumber, peeled and chopped
1 tablespoon reduced-salt tamari or soy sauce
1 tablespoon frozen apple-juice concentrate
a dash of Tabasco (optional)

Place all the ingredients in a blender or food processor. Blend until smooth. Chill and serve. For a varied texture, reserve ¼ of the chopped cucumber and stir it into the blended dressing.

CREAMY MUSTARD DRESSING

Makes 1½ pints

2 cups nonfat yogurt (page 72)
1 tablespoon grated orange peel
1 tablespoon grated lemon peel
2 tablespoons frozen apple-juice concentrate
2 tablespoons Dijon mustard
½ teaspoon dillweed (optional)
1 tablespoon reduced-salt tamari or soy sauce
a dash of Tabasco (optional)

Place all ingredients in a blender or food processor. Blend until smooth. Chill. Serve over tossed hearts of romaine.

CREAMY GINGER DRESSING

Makes 1½ pints

2 cups nonfat yogurt (page 72)
1 banana, peeled and broken into pieces
1 tablespoon chopped fresh ginger
1 tablespoon grated orange peel
1 tablespoon frozen apple-juice concentrate
1 teaspoon lemon juice

Place all ingredients in a blender or food processor. Blend until smooth. Chill. Serve over a salad of Chinese bean sprouts and snow peas.

◄§ SPICY TOMATO DRESSING

Makes 1 pint

4 fresh tomatoes, cut into small chunks *or* 1 16-ounce can crushed tomatoes in heavy puree (no added salt)
½ onion, chopped
2 cloves garlic, minced fine
1 teaspoon coriander
1 teaspoon chili powder *or* 1 small fresh chili, seeds removed, chopped fine
½ teaspoon basil
½ teaspoon oregano
1 tablespoon reduced-salt tamari or soy sauce

Place all the ingredients in a blender or food processor. Blend until smooth. Serve over sliced cucumbers or steamed rice.

◄§ CUCUMBER DRESSING

Makes 1½ pints

3 cucumbers, peeled and cut into chunks
2 cloves garlic, peeled and minced fine
½ onion, peeled and cut into chunks
¼ bunch fresh mint *or* 1 tablespoon dry mint
½ teaspoon dillweed
1 tablespoon reduced-salt tamari or soy sauce
1 teaspoon basil
½ teaspoon celery seed
juice of 1 lemon
a dash of Tabasco (optional)

Place all the ingredients in a blender or food processor. Blend until smooth. Chill. Serve over sliced tomatoes.

❧ CREAMY LEMON-CUCUMBER DRESSING

Makes 1½ pints

2 cups nonfat yogurt (See recipe, page 72)
2 cucumbers, peeled and chopped
2 tablespoons frozen apple-juice concentrate
2 tablespoons lemon juice
1 cup nonfat milk or buttermilk
½ teaspoon celery seed
a dash of Tabasco (optional)

Place all the ingredients in a blender or food processor. Blend until smooth. Chill. (Incidentally, this same recipe makes a delicious, tangy cold soup.)

❧ TOMATO-EGGPLANT DRESSING

Makes 1½ pints

1 eggplant, peeled and cut into chunks
2 fresh tomatoes, chopped *or* 1 12-ounce can tomatoes in heavy puree (no salt added)
1 pound mushrooms, cleaned thoroughly
1 onion, peeled and sliced thin
6 cloves garlic, chopped fine
1 teaspoon basil
1 teaspoon oregano
1 tablespoon reduced-salt tamari or soy sauce
juice of 1 lemon

Sauté all the ingredients except the lemon juice for 15 minutes or until eggplant is thoroughly cooked. Add lemon juice. Place in a blender or food processor and puree until smooth. Chill and serve over spinach salad or cooked sweet corn.

✑ CREAMY PALM SALAD DRESSING

I made this recipe for a lady from Brazil, where hearts of palm (or "palmito") are commonly used in cooking. Here she was, stuck in this strange country, homesick and on a diet at the same time. This dressing seemed to cheer her up so much that I thought it should be shared.

Makes 1½ pints

- **1 pound dry cottage cheese**
- **½ cup nonfat (strained) buttermilk**
- **1 clove garlic, chopped coarse**
- **½ can hearts of palm, drained, rinsed with cold water, and cut into chunks**
- **1 tablespoon tamari or soy sauce**
- **½ teaspoon celery seed**
- **2 tablespoons capers**
- **dash Tabasco (optional)**
- **1 tablespoon frozen apple-juice concentrate**
- **1 teaspoon cardamom**

Place all the ingredients in a blender or food processor. Blend until smooth. Chill.

In any dressing such as this one, where exotic and unusual ingredients make a strong appearance, you might want to reserve and chop part of the main ingredient to add to the pureed dressing. This will add an even more interesting texture to the recipe.

SPICY CHEESE DRESSING

Makes 1½ pints

1 pound dry cottage cheese
1 green bell pepper, seeds removed, chopped fine
2 scallions (white part only), chopped
1 cup nonfat buttermilk
½ cup frozen apple-juice concentrate
1 small can pimento, rinsed in cold water
1 small can mushrooms, rinsed in cold water
1 teaspoon chili powder
1 teaspoon Dijon mustard
a dash of Tabasco (optional)
1 tablespoon reduced-salt tamari or soy sauce

Place all ingredients in a blender or food processor. Blend until smooth. Chill and serve over steamed carrots or raw zucchini.

Stocks and Soups

As far as I'm concerned, the first thing one should do in learning how to cook for a low-fat diet is to begin making stocks. They become the essential medium for cooking, replacing oil and butter. Plus they give an immediate and distinctive flavor to the dishes in which they're used.

You'll notice that in these stocks meat puts in its first appearance. Here it's important to remember that it's not meat itself that clogs the arteries with cholesterol, it's the *fat* found in most meats. Well, there's no fat in a well-strained meat stock. So the flavor stays—along with the protein value and beneficial gelatin from the meat bone—but the fat is gone, and so is the danger.

Since I didn't want to have to make stocks every day (and I'm sure you don't either), necessity forced me to find a convenient and workable way to store them. For storing small amounts, I use ice-cube trays—which in effect gives me homemade frozen bouillon cubes. For larger amounts, I use Styrofoam cups, cover them tightly, and store them in the freezer.

A note of caution: Most commercial bouillon cubes are to be avoided because of their high salt content. The same is true for canned stocks and for all but a few (very expensive) frozen stocks.

Now as to soups:

Long considered a mere appetizer, soups are now making a strong showing as meals in themselves. And the best news is that you need sacrifice none of the heartiness of soups in order to stay within the confines of a low-fat diet. Pureed vegetables and nonfat dry milk can be blended to give your soups a smooth, rich texture—try the recipes for cream of fresh pea, or cream of mushroom, and you'll see what I mean. With browned onions, garlic, and defatted meat stock, you can make a fantastic onion soup. Once you develop a spirit of adventure, you'll find yourself trying the recipes for bouillabaisse and such cold soups as gazpacho and borscht—all delicious, and all delightfully low in fats.

All these soups have a refrigerator life of up to three days and a freezer life of up to three months.

Note: Recipes that contain beans, legumes, or grains are somewhat higher in calories than the vegetable or "creamed" soups.

⊸§ DEFATTED CHICKEN STOCK

Makes 4–6 quarts

2 whole chickens (2–3 pounds each)
6 celery stalks with heel and leaves, cut into 1-inch chunks
4 carrots, cut into 1-inch chunks (make sure greens are removed, or stock will turn black)
2 large onions, cut into quarters, skin remaining intact
1 whole head of garlic, smashed, skins intact
1 bell pepper, quartered, seeds removed
2 jalapeño peppers, seeds removed, quartered

1 bunch parsley, rinsed clean
6 shallots, smashed, skins intact
1 cup dry sherry
2 tablespoons sweet basil
1 tablespoon oregano
2 tablespoons sage
4 bay leaves, crushed
2 teaspoons thyme
2 teaspoons rosemary
1 teaspoon whole cloves
1 teaspoon dillweed (optional)
½ teaspoon nutmeg
½ teaspoon cinnamon

Remove and discard the skin and any fat from the chicken. Discard the giblets and cut the breast meat from the bone, reserving it for use as an entrée (See recipes, pages 183–203). Place the breastbones, the rest of the chicken, and all the other ingredients in a 12–14-quart stockpot, and fill the pot with water up to 1 inch of the top. Bring to a boil, reduce to a simmer, and cover. The pot should be very lightly steaming. Continue cooking for 2 to 3 hours. Turn off heat and allow to stand overnight or until cool. Strain the stock through a fine sieve or cheesecloth. The stock may be frozen in ice-cube trays or 1-pint Styrofoam cups with lids. Once the stock is frozen, any remaining fat can be removed from the top just before use.

✒§ DEFATTED BEEF STOCK

Makes 4–6 quarts

3 pounds beef bones with a very small amount of meat
2 small (3-bone) short ribs
whole-wheat flour for dusting
paprika
6 celery stalks with heel and leaves, cut into 1-inch chunks
4 carrots (greens removed), cut into 1-inch chunks
2 large unpeeled onions, cut into quarters
1 whole unpeeled head of garlic, smashed
2 bell peppers, seeds removed, quartered
2 jalapeño peppers, seeds removed, quartered
1 bunch parsley, rinsed clean
6 unpeeled shallots, smashed
1 cup Marsala wine or Burgundy
2 tablespoons sweet basil
1 tablespoon oregano
2 tablespoons sage
4 bay leaves, crushed
2 teaspoons thyme
2 teaspoons rosemary
1 teaspoon fennel seed
1 teaspoon nutmeg
1 teaspoon cinnamon
1 teaspoon dillweed (optional)
½ teaspoon aniseed (optional)

Dust the bones and short ribs thoroughly with whole-wheat flour. Sprinkle them with paprika and place them on a large nonstick baking dish, two if necessary, arranging them so that they do not touch each other. Place them in an oven at 500°F. for 35 to 45 minutes, turning after 20 minutes, until they are totally browned. Place the bones and all the other ingredients in a 12–14-quart stockpot and fill the pot with water up to 1 inch of the top. Bring to a boil, reduce the heat until the liquid is simmering gently, and cover. The pot should be very lightly steaming. Continue cooking for 2 to 3 hours. Turn off the heat and allow the stock to stand overnight or until cool. Strain the stock through a fine sieve or cheesecloth. Store in the freezer in ice-cube trays or 1-pint Styrofoam cups with lids. Once the stock is frozen, any remaining fat can be removed from the top just before use.

✑ FISH STOCK (COURT-BOUILLON)

Makes 4–6 quarts

3 pounds fish heads, backbones, and tails
whole-wheat flour for dusting
paprika
6 celery stalks with heel and leaves, cut into 1-inch chunks
4 carrots (greens removed), cut into 1-inch chunks
2 unpeeled onions, cut into quarters
1 whole unpeeled head of garlic, smashed
1 bell pepper, seeds removed, quartered
2 jalapeño peppers, seeds removed, quartered
1 bunch parsley, rinsed clean
6 shallots, skins intact, smashed
1 cup dry sherry
1 tablespoon sweet basil
1 tablespoon dillweed
6 bay leaves, crushed
1 teaspoon whole cloves
1 teaspoon tarragon

Dust fish heads, backbones, and tails with whole-wheat flour. Sprinkle paprika moderately over the tops. Arrange the bones on a large nonstick baking dish so they are not touching each other. Place them in an oven at 500°F. for 20 minutes. Place the bones and all the other ingredients in a 12–14-quart stockpot and fill the pot with water up to 1 inch of the top. Bring to a boil, reduce the heat until the liquid simmers gently, and cover. The pot should be very lightly steaming. Continue cooking for 2 to 3 hours. Turn off the heat and allow the stock to stand overnight or until cool. Strain through a fine sieve or cheesecloth. This stock may be stored in the freezer in ice-cube trays or 1-pint Styrofoam cups with lids.

∽§ VEGETABLE (GARDEN) STOCK

Don't be surprised if this stock makes no further appearances in the soup section. It's used primarily for sauces (for example, see Zucchini Sauté Italian Style, page 228) and as a medium for stir-frying.

Makes 4–6 quarts

4 carrots (greens removed), cut into 1-inch chunks
6 celery stalks with heel and leaves, cut into 1-inch chunks
2 unpeeled onions, cut into quarters
1 whole unpeeled head of garlic, smashed
2 bell peppers, seeds removed, quartered
½ pound fresh green beans
½ pound fresh zucchini or yellow squash, cut into 1-inch chunks
1 bunch parsley, rinsed clean
2 jalapeño peppers, seeds removed, quartered
½ bunch cilantro (optional)
½-inch chunk of fresh ginger, smashed
½ pound fresh mushrooms *or* 1 ounce dried mushrooms
1 tablespoon basil
1 tablespoon oregano
2 teaspoons celery seed
1 teaspoon coriander
1 teaspoon whole cloves
1 teaspoon marjoram

½ teaspoon nutmeg
½ teaspoon cinnamon
½ lime
1 cup sherry or Sauterne

Place all the ingredients in a 12–14-quart stockpot, and fill the pot with water up to 1 inch of the top. Bring to a boil, reduce the heat until the liquid simmers gently, and cover. The pot should be very lightly steaming. Continue simmering for 2 to 3 hours. Turn off the heat and allow the stock to stand overnight or until cool. Strain completely through a fine sieve or cheesecloth. Store in the freezer in ice-cube trays or 1-pint Styrofoam cups with lids.

✑§ CREAM OF ASPARAGUS SOUP

Serves 4–6

1 pound fresh asparagus *or* 1 package frozen asparagus
½ pound mushrooms, sliced thin
1 onion, chopped fine
½ teaspoon rosemary (optional)
4 cloves garlic, minced
1 teaspoon basil
1 teaspoon dillweed
½ teaspoon celery seed
2 cups nonfat dry milk
2 tablespoons tamari or soy sauce
1 teaspoon cornstarch dissolved in ½ cup cold water
4–6 cups defatted chicken stock (page 86) or water

Steam the asparagus in a covered pot with 2 inches of boiling water for 12 minutes. Put the steamed asparagus in a blender and puree until smooth. Sauté the onion, garlic, and dill in a frying pan with ½ cup of the stock or water until

brown. Add the mushrooms and sauté 3 minutes longer. Boil
4–5 cups of the stock or water in a 2-quart pot. Add the
pureed asparagus and the sautéed condiments. Then add the
nonfat dry milk and the cornstarch solution, stirring vigorously for 10 seconds. Simmer 5 minutes. Garnish with
chopped parsley and serve.

➛§ ALL-BEAN SOUP

Serves 4–6

> ½ package frozen green beans
> 1 bell pepper, seeded and diced
> 2 fresh tomatoes, quartered
> 6 cloves garlic, minced
> 1 onion, sliced thin
> 5–6 cups defatted chicken stock (page 86) or water
> 1 cup dried lentils
> 1 cup dried navy beans
> ½ cup dried yellow split peas
> 1 teaspoon basil
> 1 teaspoon celery seed
> 1 16-ounce can crushed tomatoes in heavy puree (no salt
> added)
> 1 tablespoon tamari or soy sauce
> a dash of cayenne or Tabasco
> parsley for garnish

Place the green beans, pepper, fresh tomatoes, garlic, and
onions in a 2½–3-quart pot and simmer in 1 cup chicken stock
or water for 10 minutes. Add the dried beans and peas, the
herbs, the canned tomatoes, and the rest of the chicken stock
or water. Cook over low flame, covered, for 1 hour or until the
beans are tender. Add the tamari or soy sauce and Tabasco.
Serve with parsley garnish.

✑ LENTIL SOUP

Serves 4–6

1 pound dried lentils
1 onion, peeled and chopped
2 carrots, scraped and sliced
4 cloves garlic, peeled and chopped
2 stalks celery, cut into 1-inch slices
2 fresh tomatoes, quartered and cored
½ bunch parsley
2 tablespoons reduced-salt tamari or soy sauce
Leona's Sour Cream (page 71) for garnish

Place all the ingredients in a 2-quart pot. Cover with water up to 1 inch of the rim (about 6 cups). Cook over a low flame for 1 hour. Serve garnished with Leona's Sour Cream.

✑ BABY LIMA BEAN SOUP

Serves 4–6

2 cups dried baby lima beans
1 onion, peeled and chopped fine
1 carrot, scraped and sliced
4 cloves garlic, peeled and chopped
1 stalk celery, cut into 1-inch chunks
1 small can crushed tomatoes in heavy puree (no salt added)
½ bunch parsley
2 tablespoons reduced-salt tamari or soy sauce

Place all the ingredients in a 2-quart pot, fill with water up to 1 inch below the rim, and cover. Bring to a boil. Reduce the heat and simmer for 1 hour or until the beans are tender.

❧ NAVY BEAN SOUP

Serves 4–6

1 pound dried navy beans
1 onion, peeled and chopped
2 carrots, scraped and sliced
4 cloves garlic, peeled and chopped
2 stalks celery, cut into 1-inch slices
2 fresh tomatoes, quartered and cored
½ bunch parsley
2 tablespoons reduced-salt tamari or soy sauce
chopped scallions for garnish

Place all ingredients (except the scallions) in a 2-quart pot. Cover with water up to 1 inch of the rim of the pot (about 6 cups). Cook over low flame for 1 hour. Garnish with chopped scallions.

❧ BORSCHT—HOT OR COLD

Serves 4–6

2 potatoes, peeled and cut into quarters (for hot soup only)
8–9 cups defatted chicken stock (page 86) or water
8 fresh medium-size beets *or* 1 10- to 12-ounce can of beets, drained and rinsed
1 cup sliced cabbage
1 onion, sliced thin
1 cup dietetic tomato juice
4 cloves garlic, minced
2 tablespoons frozen apple-juice concentrate, partially thawed
juice of 1 lemon
1 tablespoon reduced-salt tamari or soy sauce
Leona's Sour Cream (page 71)

Boil the potatoes, if used, for 30 minutes in 3 cups of de-fatted chicken stock or water. Peel the beets and slice thin. Using a covered 2½–3-quart pot, steam the beets in 2 cups chicken stock or water for 20 minutes or until tender. Add the remaining stock, cabbage, onion, tomato juice, garlic, and apple juice. Cook, covered, over low heat for 20 minutes, steaming lightly. Add the lemon juice and tamari. To serve hot, place 2 pieces of potato in the bottom of each soup bowl. Pour the borscht over them and top with Leona's Sour Cream. For cold soup, chill in the refrigerator for several hours, then pour into individual bowls, and top with Leona's Sour Cream.

⤢§ BOUILLABAISSE

Serves 6–8

> 4 cloves garlic, peeled and minced fine
> 1 onion, chopped
> 1 bell pepper, seeds removed, chopped
> 1½ quarts fish stock (page 89)
> ½ pound fresh fish (white meat), cut into 1-inch cubes
> ½ pound uncooked shrimp, shelled and deveined
> 6 fresh tomatoes or 1 35-ounce can crushed tomatoes
>   (no salt added)
> 1 tablespoon reduced-salt tamari or soy sauce
> dash Tabasco or cayenne
> 1 cup dry sherry

Simmer the garlic, onion, and bell pepper in 1 cup fish stock for about 15 minutes, or until the vegetables are thoroughly cooked. Add the fish, the shrimp, and the rest of the stock. Then add the crushed tomatoes, the soy sauce, and Tabasco or cayenne to taste. Finally, add the sherry and sim-mer for 10 minutes. Serve with sourdough bread or whole-wheat toast.

⋙ BROCCOLI BISQUE

Serves 4–6

    1 quart defatted chicken stock (page 86) or water
    2 cups nonfat dry milk
    1 tablespoon salt-reduced soy sauce
    ½ onion, chopped fine
    4 cloves garlic, minced
    2 tablespoons cornstarch dissolved in ½ cup cold water
    2 bunches broccoli
    shredded carrots for garnish

Reserve 1 cup of the chicken stock or water. Bring the rest to a boil in a 2½–3-quart pot. Add the nonfat dry milk and soy sauce and stir. Turn off the heat. Simmer the onion and garlic in the reserved cup of chicken stock or water until brown. Add to the broth. Stir in the cornstarch solution. Steam the broccoli for 8 to 10 minutes in 1 cup water. Puree in a blender and add to the soup. Garnish with shredded carrots.

⋙ CABBAGE SOUP

Serves 4–6

    1 head green cabbage, sliced
    2 onions, peeled and sliced
    2 carrots, scraped and sliced
    2 zucchini, sliced
    2 fresh tomatoes, quartered *or* 1 small can tomato paste (no
        salt added)
  5–6 cups defatted chicken stock (page 86) or water
    6 cloves garlic, peeled and chopped fine
    2 teaspoons basil
    1 teaspoon oregano
    a dash of Tabasco
    1 tablespoon tamari or soy sauce

Steam all the vegetables for 15 minutes in a covered 2½- or 3-quart pot in 1 cup of chicken stock or water. Add the herbs and spices, the soy sauce, and the rest of the stock or water. Cover and cook another 15 minutes. Serve with a parsley garnish.

◀§ SWEET-AND-SOUR CABBAGE SOUP

Serves 4–6

> 1 head green cabbage, cut into 1-inch-wide strips
> 2 carrots, scraped and sliced thin
> 1 onion, peeled and sliced thin
> 2 fresh tomatoes, cored and quartered
> 1 bell pepper, seeds removed, sliced thin
> 3 stalks celery, sliced
> 6 cloves garlic, peeled and chopped fine
> 1 teaspoon sweet basil
> 1 teaspoon dill
> 2 tablespoons fresh or dried parsley
> 5–6 cups defatted chicken stock (page 86) or water
> 1 10- to 12-ounce can crushed tomatoes in heavy puree (no salt added)
> juice of 1 lemon
> 3 tablespoons frozen apple-juice concentrate, partially thawed
> 2 tablespoons rice vinegar (optional)
> 1 tablespoon tamari
> lemon wedges for garnish

Place all the vegetables (except the tomatoes) and spices along with 5–6 cups chicken stock or water in a 2-quart pot. Cover and cook over low heat, simmering lightly for 20 minutes. Add the tomato puree, lemon juice, apple juice, vinegar, and tamari. Simmer 5 minutes longer. Serve with fresh lemon-wedge garnish.

◄§ CREAMED CARROT CHOWDER

Serves 4–6

    8 carrots, scraped and sliced thin
    ½ package frozen cut corn
    ½ package frozen green beans
    2 stalks celery, sliced thin
    1 bell pepper, seeded and chopped fine
    ½ teaspoon celery seed
    ½ teaspoon rosemary
    1 tablespoon minced fresh ginger
a pinch of cayenne
a pinch of cinnamon
    1 tablespoon frozen apple-juice concentrate
5–6 cups defatted chicken stock (page 86) or water
    1 tablespoon reduced-salt tamari or soy sauce
    2 cups nonfat dry milk
    1 tablespoon cornstarch dissolved in ½ cup cold water
pimento for garnish

Place all the ingredients except the dry milk and cornstarch in a 2½–3-quart pot. Bring to a boil; then reduce the
heat and simmer 20 minutes. Add the nonfat dry milk and the
cornstarch solution. Simmer 2 more minutes, stirring until
thickened, and serve. Garnish with thin strips of pimento.

◄§ CREAM OF CAULIFLOWER SOUP

Serves 4–6

    1 head cauliflower (stem removed), cut into florets
    3 scallions, sliced very thin
    ½ onion, peeled and chopped fine
    4 cloves garlic, peeled and chopped fine
    1 stalk celery, minced fine

  1 cucumber, peeled and chopped fine
  1 teaspoon basil
  ½ teaspoon thyme
a dash of cayenne
4–6 cups defatted chicken stock (page 86) or water
  2 cups nonfat dry milk
  1 teaspoon cornstarch dissolved in ½ cup cold water
chopped parsley for garnish

Steam the cauliflower for 12 minutes in a covered 2-quart pot with 2 inches of boiling water. Place in a blender and puree. Simmer the onions, garlic, celery, and cucumber with the herbs and spices in ½ cup chicken stock or water for 10 minutes. Combine this sauté with the pureed cauliflower in a 2-quart pot; add the remaining stock or water. Add the nonfat dry milk and cornstarch solution, stirring vigorously. Simmer 5 minutes. Serve with a garnish of chopped parsley.

❧ CREAM OF CUCUMBER SOUP

Serves 4–6

  6 cucumbers, peeled and sliced
  2 stalks celery, sliced thin
  ½ bell pepper, seeds removed, sliced thin
  4 cloves garlic, chopped fine
  1 teaspoon basil
  2 scallions (white part only), sliced
  ½ teaspoon celery seed
  2 cups nonfat buttermilk, strained to remove buds *or* 1 cup nonfat yogurt (page 72)
  ½ cup defatted chicken stock or water
  2 tablespoons frozen apple-juice concentrate
  1 tablespoon reduced-salt tamari or soy sauce
parsley and yogurt for garnish

Place half the cucumbers in a blender with 1 cup buttermilk or ½ cup yogurt. Blend until smooth. Sauté vegetables and spices in a 2-quart pot for 10 minutes, using ½ cup chicken stock or water as liquid medium. Add blended mixture and the remaining cucumbers along with 1 cup buttermilk or ½ cup yogurt. Chill and serve with parsley and a dollop of yogurt for garnish.

◄§ GAZPACHO

Serves 4–6

- 8 fresh medium-size tomatoes, quartered *or* 8 whole dietetic canned tomatoes (no salt added)
- 4 scallions, sliced thin
- ½ bell pepper, seeded and cut into chunks
- ½ onion, peeled and cut into chunks
- 1 cucumber, peeled and chopped
- ½ cup cilantro or fresh mint leaves
- juice of 1 lemon
- 4 cloves garlic, chopped fine
- 2 stalks celery, chopped
- 1 small green or red chili, seeded and chopped fine
- 2 tablespoons reduced-salt tamari or soy sauce
- lemon slices for garnish

Put the tomatoes in a blender and blend until smooth. Add all other ingredients (except the lemon slices). Chill for one hour and serve with lemon slices floating on the top.

CREAM OF MUSHROOM SOUP

Serves 4–6

- 1 pound fresh mushrooms, sliced thin
- 1 onion, chopped fine
- 1 tablespoon pimento, rinsed in cold water and chopped fine
- 4 cloves garlic, peeled and minced fine
- 4 shallots or scallions, minced fine
- 1 cucumber, peeled and chopped fine
- 1 carrot, chopped fine
- 1 teaspoon dill
- 2 cups nonfat dry milk
- 1 tablespoon cornstarch dissolved in ½ cup cold water
- 4–6 cups defatted chicken stock (page 86) or water
- pinch of dill for garnish

Put the onion, pimento, garlic, shallots, cucumber, and carrot in a frying pan with ½ cup of the chicken stock or water. Sauté for 10 minutes. Boil the remaining stock or water in a 2-quart pot. Add the sautéed vegetables and the mushrooms. Stir in the nonfat dry milk and the cornstarch solution. Simmer for 5 minutes. Serve with a pinch of dill.

FRENCH ONION SOUP

Serves 4–6

- 8 onions, sliced
- 8 cloves garlic, chopped
- 1 quart defatted beef stock (page 88) or water
- 2 bell peppers, seeded and sliced thin
- 1 carrot, sliced thin
- 2 tablespoons reduced-salt tamari or soy sauce
- 1 tablespoon cornstarch dissolved in ½ cup cold water
- 2 slices whole-wheat bread, toasted and cut into squares

Sauté the onions and garlic in a pan with 1 cup stock or water until browned. Place all the ingredients except the cornstarch and bread in a 2½–3-quart pot with a lid. Cover and simmer over low heat for 1 hour. Stir the cornstarch solution into the soup. Crown the soup with the toasted bread squares.

✎§ CREAM OF PALM SOUP

Serves 4–6

>   2 tablespoons whole-wheat flour
>   1 onion, chopped fine
>   4 cloves garlic, minced fine
>   1 small red or green chili, seeds removed, minced fine
> 4–6 cups defatted chicken stock (page 86) or water
>   1 10–12-ounce can hearts of palm, drained and cut into ¼-inch pieces
>   2 tablespoons reduced-salt tamari or soy sauce
>   2 cups nonfat dry milk
>   1 tablespoon cornstarch dissolved in ½ cup cold water
> fresh mint for garnish

Toast the flour by sliding it around in a saucepan over a high flame for approximately 1 minute. Add the onions, garlic, and chili pepper. Sauté over low heat in ½ cup chicken stock or water until the onions are browned. In a 2½–3-quart pot add hearts of palm and the sautéed mixture to 4–5 cups boiling water or chicken stock and the tamari. Stir in the dry milk and cornstarch solution. Simmer until thickened. Serve immediately, garnished with fresh mint.

✔§ CREAM OF FRESH-PEA SOUP

Serves 4–6

  1 pound fresh peas *or* 1 package frozen peas
  1 potato, peeled and cut into small cubes
  1 onion, sliced thin or chopped fine
  4 cloves garlic, minced fine
  1 carrot, cut into small cubes
  1 teaspoon basil
  1 teaspoon thyme
  ½ teaspoon oregano
  1 teaspoon curry powder
  2 tablespoons reduced-salt tamari or soy sauce
a pinch of cayenne
  4–6 cups defatted chicken stock (page 86) or water
  2 cups nonfat dry milk
  1 tablespoon cornstarch dissolved in ½ cup cold water

Put all the ingredients except the nonfat dry milk and the cornstarch mixture in a 2-quart pot. Cook for 30 minutes, covered, over low heat until the potato is tender. Test by piercing the cubes with a fork. Strain the soup, return the liquid to the cooking pot, and blend the vegetables in a blender or food processor. Return the blended vegetables to the pot with the liquid and add the nonfat milk and cornstarch mixture. Bring to a boil, stir, and serve.

⋖§ SPLIT-PEA SOUP

Serves 4–6

> 2 carrots, sliced thin
> 1 onion, chopped fine
> 2 stalks celery, cut into chunks
> 1 bay leaf
> 2 teaspoons basil
> 2 teaspoons oregano
> 4 cloves garlic, minced
> ½ teaspoon rosemary
> 5–6 cups defatted chicken stock (page 86) or water
> 2 cups dry split peas, placed in a strainer and rinsed with cold water
> 2 tablespoons reduced-salt tamari or soy sauce
> dash Tabasco or cayenne
> parsley for garnish

Using a 2-quart cooking pot, sauté the carrots, onion, celery, and herbs in ½ cup chicken stock or water for 10 minutes. Add the split peas and 4 to 6 cups chicken stock or water. Cook over a low flame for 1 hour or until the peas have become very soft. Just before serving, add the tamari and Tabasco or cayenne. Serve with parsley garnish.

⋖§ DELECTABLE VEGETABLE SOUP

Serves 4–6

> 2 carrots, scraped and sliced thin
> 2 fresh tomatoes, cored and quartered
> 2 stalks celery, sliced julienne
> ¼ head cauliflower (or ½ package frozen cauliflower), cut into florets; slice the core thin and include
> 1 bell pepper, seeds removed, sliced thin

   8 fresh green beans or ⅓ package frozen green beans
   ½ pound mushrooms, quartered
   ½ head cabbage, cut into cubes
   ⅓ package frozen cut corn
   6 cloves garlic, peeled and minced fine
   1 onion, peeled and sliced thin
5-6 cups defatted chicken stock (page 86) or water
   2 teaspoons basil
   1 teaspoon oregano
   1 teaspoon thyme
   ½ teaspoon rosemary
a dash of cayenne or Tabasco
   1 tablespoon reduced-salt tamari or soy sauce
juice of 1 lemon
lemon for garnish

Place the vegetables, garlic, and onion in a 2½–3-quart pot along with 1 cup water or chicken stock. Cover and sauté over low heat, stirring occasionally, for 20 minutes. Add the seasonings and the remaining water or stock. Cover and simmer for 5 minutes. Serve with lemon-wedge garnish.

~§ CHINESE HOT-AND-SOUR SOUP

Serves 4–6

    1 pound bean sprouts, rinsed in cold water
    1 bell pepper, seeds removed, cut into squares
    1 onion, sliced thin
    1 small can bamboo shoots, rinsed in cold water
    2 scallions (white part only), sliced lengthwise into 1-inch
      strips
    ½ head bok choy (Chinese cabbage), chopped
    1 small green or red chili, seeded and chopped fine
    6 cloves garlic, peeled and chopped fine
    1 small can water chestnuts, rinsed in cold water and sliced
      thin
  4–6 cups defatted chicken stock (page 86) or water
    1 tablespoon grated fresh ginger
    2 tablespoons rice vinegar
  juice of ½ lemon
    ¼ pound tofu (soybean curd), cut into cubes
    1 tablespoon cornstarch dissolved in ½ cup chicken stock
      or water
  lemon wedges and cilantro for garnish

Sauté all the vegetables, the garlic, and the water chestnuts in a 2-quart pot for 10 minutes, using ½ cup chicken stock
or water as the liquid medium. Add the ginger, vinegar, lemon
juice, tofu, and remaining stock and simmer for 5 minutes.
Add the cornstarch mixture and stir to thicken. Serve with
lemon wedges and cilantro.

⌥ ORIENTAL VEGETABLE SOUP

Serves 4–6

  ½ pound fresh or canned bean sprouts, rinsed in cold water
  ½ pound fresh snow peas *or* ½ package frozen snow peas
  2 cups chopped bok choy (Chinese cabbage)
  1 small can bamboo shoots, rinsed in cold water
  1 bell pepper, seeds removed, sliced thin
  2 fresh tomatoes, quartered
  1 16-ounce can crushed tomatoes in heavy puree (no salt added)
  4 cloves garlic, chopped fine
  1 tablespoon minced fresh ginger
4–6 cups defatted chicken stock (page 86) or water
  1 teaspoon basil
  ½ teaspoon celery seed
  1 teaspoon chili powder
  2 teaspoons reduced-salt tamari or soy sauce
a dash of Tabasco
cilantro for garnish

Put the vegetables, garlic, and ginger in a 2-quart pot. Sauté 10 minutes in ½ cup chicken stock or water. Add all other ingredients along with the remaining stock or water. Simmer 10 minutes. Serve with cilantro garnish.

Note: If you want to convert this soup to an Oriental Egg Drop soup, simply float 2 stirred egg whites, 1 teaspoon at a time, over the top of the hot soup just before serving.

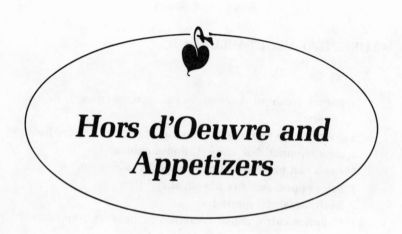

Hors d'Oeuvre and Appetizers

Good news: you no longer have to heave a sigh and throw your diet out the window when party time comes around. In fact, now you'll be able to lay out a party spread that not only conforms to your diet, but is tasty and pretty enough to rate a color photo feature in the London *Sunday Times,* as one of my layouts did.

The variety possible in appetizers and party foods is truly amazing: from vegetable pâtés to stuffed cherry tomatoes to hot hors d'oeuvre like cheese puffs, miniature pizzas, and mini-blintzes. Believe it or not, I'll even show you how to make mock sweet-and-sour meatballs using eggplant instead of ground beef! So if you thought your home had had to drop out of the party circuit forever, consider this chapter the reprieve you've been waiting for.

Note: Some of these recipes contain animal protein, so it is recommended that these foods be eaten in moderation. Some recipes contain soy sauce, so they should be reviewed carefully by persons on salt-restricted diets.

⋅⧽ GUACAMOLE SIN AGUACATE (WITHOUT AVOCADO)

Most low-fat diets severely restrict the use of avocados because they contain about 80 percent fatty oils.

½ package frozen peas
½ package frozen asparagus
1 eggplant, peeled and cut into chunks
1 green or red chili, seeded and cut into chunks
½ onion, peeled and cut into chunks
½ teaspoon chili powder
2 cloves garlic, chopped fine
1 tablespoon reduced-salt tamari or soy sauce

Place all the ingredients in a blender or food processor and blend until smooth. Serve with toasted corn tortilla chips, or roll dollops of guacamole in leaves of butter lettuce and tie with ribbons of pimento.

⋅⧽ GARLIC-CHEESE CELERY STICKS

Makes 24 servings

½ pound dry cottage cheese
1 small cucumber, peeled, seeded, and cut into chunks
2 cloves garlic, minced
½ green bell pepper, quartered
1 scallion, sliced
1 tablespoon frozen apple-juice concentrate
1 teaspoon tamari
¼ teaspoon celery seed
¼ teaspoon sweet basil
¼ teaspoon dillweed
8 celery stalks, cut into 3-inch lengths
paprika for garnish

Place all the ingredients except the celery stalks and paprika in a blender or food processor and blend until smooth. Spoon this cheese mixture into the celery stalks, mounding it generously. Dust with paprika and serve chilled. For a more decorative effect, a pastry tube with a large star tip may be used to fill the celery stalks.

❧ STUFFED ZUCCHINI

Makes 24–30 rolls

- ½ **pound dry cottage cheese**
- 1 **cup mushrooms**
- 2 **scallions, sliced**
- 1 **clove garlic, minced**
- ½ **teaspoon celery seed**
- ½ **teaspoon oregano**
- ¼ **teaspoon Tabasco (optional)**
- 1 **teaspoon tamari**
- 6 **medium zucchini, sliced into 1½-inch lengths**

Place all the ingredients except the zucchini in a blender or food processor and blend until smooth. With a teaspoon, scoop a ½-inch cup out of the center (seeded part) of each zucchini chunk. Place 1 tablespoon of the cheese mixture in each zucchini "cup," mounding the cheese to form a dome. The Stuffed Zucchini may be served chilled, or they may be placed on a nonstick baking sheet, placed in a 350°F. oven for 10 minutes, and served warm.

❧ STUFFED MUSHROOMS ITALIANA

Serves 3–4

- 1 **dozen large mushrooms, rinsed in cold water**
- ¼ **pound dry cottage cheese**
- ½ **teaspoon sweet basil**

½ teaspoon oregano
½ teaspoon thyme
12 small pieces of pimento (optional)
½ teaspoon baking soda
¼ teaspoon fennel seed (optional)
escarole lettuce

Carefully separate the stems from the caps of the mushrooms. Place the mushroom stems, cheese, and herbs in a blender or food processor and blend until smooth. Add ½ teaspoon baking soda to this mixture and mix in thoroughly. Place about 1½ teaspoons of the cheese filling in each mushroom cap so that it is mounded up and not spilling over the edges of the cap. Put ½ cup water in a baking dish. Place the mushrooms in the dish and garnish each with a pimento chip (optional). Bake in a 350°F. oven for 15 minutes. Serve hot on a bed of escarole.

⊸§ CONTINENTAL STUFFED MUSHROOMS

Serves 3–4

 1 dozen large mushrooms, rinsed in cold water
 2 cloves garlic, minced fine
¼ bell pepper, minced fine
¼ onion, minced fine
 1 teaspoon tamari
½ teaspoon marjoram
 2 slices of whole-wheat or sourdough bread
12 small pieces of pimento (optional)
¼ cup tiny canned shrimp (optional)
a dash of Tabasco (optional)
Bibb lettuce or endive

Remove the stems from the mushrooms, being careful not to damage the caps; chop the stems fine. Sauté the mushroom stems, garlic, bell pepper, onion, tamari, Tabasco, and marjoram in a little water until the onion is clarified. Place this mixture in a strainer and drain until all the liquid has come off. Allow the mixture to cool. Toast the bread and crumble it into this mixture, blending thoroughly. Add the shrimp if used. Fill each mushroom cap with stuffing so that it is mounded up and not spilling over the edges of the cap. Put ½ cup water in the bottom of a baking dish. Put the stuffed mushrooms in the baking dish, garnish each with a pimento chip (optional), and bake in a 350°F. oven for 15 minutes. Serve hot, surrounded by a border of Bibb lettuce or endive.

►§ CALIFORNIA SUSHI ROLL

Makes 8

> 1 package nori (dark brown Japanese seaweed that is rolled into flat sheets)
> 1 cup brown rice
> 1 teaspoon rice vinegar (no sugar)
> 1 tablespoon frozen apple-juice concentrate
> a dash of marjoram
> 1 whole pimento, cut lengthwise into ¼-inch strips
> 1 small jar capers
> 1 small can artichoke bottoms, drained and sliced into strips
> ¼ cup raw sesame seed

Put the brown rice, vinegar, apple juice, and majoram in a 1½-quart pot. Add 2¼ cups water, bring to a boil, and cover. Reduce heat until only light steam escapes from under the lid. Cook for 45 minutes. When the steaming stops, the rice is done.

Take one sheet of nori (it will measure approximately 4 inches wide and 10 inches long) and set it in front of you. Place approximately 2 heaping tablespoons of the rice on one of the 4-inch ends. Put one line of pimento strip, one single-file line of capers, and one line of artichoke slices on the rice. Place approximately 2½ tablespoons of the rice on top of this. Roll up the nori, pressing firmly, until the whole strip is used. Moisten the end with water to secure. Repeat with the remaining ingredients. You should make 4 rolls. Cut the rolls diagonally and dust with raw sesame seed. Serve chilled. The sushi may be served with wasabe (Japanese mustard powder to which water is added) and tamari diluted half and half with water.

⋖§ SUSHI CANAPÉ

Makes 8

1 **package nori (dark brown Japanese seaweed that is rolled into flat sheets)**
1 **cup brown rice**
1 **teaspoon rice vinegar (no sugar)**
1 **tablespoon frozen apple-juice concentrate**
a **dash of marjoram**
1 **carrot, scraped and cut into thin strips, 2 inches long**
1 **cucumber, peeled, seeded, and cut into thin strips, 2 inches long**
4 **hearts of palm, cut into quarters lengthwise**
¼ **cup raw sesame seed**

Put the brown rice, vinegar, apple juice, and majoram in a 1½-quart pot. Add 2¼ cups water, and bring to a boil. Cover. Reduce heat until only light steam escapes from under the lid. Cook for 45 minutes. Take one sheet of nori (approximately 4 inches wide and 10 inches long) and place it on a working surface pointing away from you lengthwise. Mound heaping tablespoons of rice along the end nearest you. Line carrot sticks, cucumber sticks, and 2 heart-of-palm sticks on top of the rice. Put 2 heaping tablespoons rice mixture on top of this. Roll the nori away from you, pressing firmly, until the whole piece of nori is used. Moisten the nori with water to secure the roll. Repeat this process until the rice and vegetables are used up. You should be able to make 4 rolls. Cut the rolls in half diagonally and dust with raw sesame seed. Serve chilled. The sushi may be served with wasabe (Japanese mustard powder to which water is added) and tamari diluted by half with water.

◀§ SASHIMI CANAPÉ

Serves 8–10

½ pound filleted fresh tuna, sea bass, salmon, or other solid
   fish
1 cup brown rice
1 teaspoon rice vinegar (no sugar added)
1 tablespoon frozen apple-juice concentrate, partially
   thawed
a dash of marjoram
apple and orange slices for garnish
a few sprigs of parsley for garnish

Place the brown rice, vinegar, apple juice, and marjoram in a 1½-quart pot. Add 2¼ cups of water, bring to a boil, and cover. Reduce heat until the liquid is steaming lightly and cook for 45 minutes. Cut the filleted fish into 1-inch strips. Slice diagonally ¼ inch thick. Moisten your hands with cold water. Take 2 tablespoons of the rice mixture and press into an egg-shaped form with your hands. Set on a flat surface and lay one slice of fish over the rice; may be picked up with hands to mold into rice patty. Repeat this until the rice and fish are used up. Arrange the sashimi on a wooden board with alternating slices of apple and orange as a border, and a garnish of parsley florets. Serve chilled. The sashimi may be served with wasabe (Japanese mustard powder to which water is added) and tamari diluted by half with water.

~§ ONION-CHEESE-PUFF ROLLS

Makes 12 rolls

1 **pound dry cottage cheese**
½ **onion, minced**
1 **clove garlic, minced fine**
1 **tablespoon frozen apple-juice concentrate**
1 **teaspoon arrowroot powder**
½ **teaspoon baking soda**
1 **teaspoon tamari**
1 **dash Tabasco (optional)**
6 **slices whole-wheat or sourdough bread**

Place all the ingredients except the bread in a blender and puree. The mixture should be very thick, but if it is too dry, slowly add 1 tablespoon nonfat milk. Remove the crust from the bread and flatten each slice with a rolling pin or the side of a glass. Spread the cheese mixture generously on the bread. Roll up the bread; from the side it will look like a pinwheel. Place on a nonstick baking sheet and toast at 375°F. for 15 minutes. Cut the rolls in half and serve warm.

⇜§ BAKED SALMON ROLLS

Makes 16 rolls

- 1 1-pound can red salmon packed in water
- ¼ cup pimento
- 2 cloves garlic, minced fine
- 2 scallions, chopped
- 1 teaspoon Dijon mustard (no salt)
- 1 teaspoon arrowroot powder or cornstarch
- ½ teaspoon celery seed
- ¼ teaspoon Tabasco (optional)
- 8 slices whole-wheat or sourdough bread

Place the salmon with all the other ingredients except the bread in a blender and blend until smooth. Remove the crust from the bread. Flatten each slice with a rolling pin or the side of a glass. Spread the salmon mixture generously on each slice of bread. Roll up the slices of bread and place on a non-stick baking sheet. Bake in a 350°F. oven for 20 minutes. Cut the rolls in half and serve warm. Any remaining salmon mixture may be used as a dip with vegetable chips. Variation: Water-packed solid white tuna may be substituted for the salmon.

⇜§ MINIATURE COCKTAIL PIZZAS

Makes 24 pieces

Cheese Mixture

- ½ pound dry cottage cheese
- 1 clove garlic, minced fine
- ½ bell pepper, chopped fine
- 1 teaspoon frozen apple-juice concentrate, partially thawed
- 1 teaspoon reduced-salt tamari or soy sauce

½ teaspoon sweet basil
½ teaspoon oregano
½ teaspoon thyme

Place these ingredients in a mixing bowl and mash with a fork until thoroughly mixed.

SAUCE MIXTURE

1 8-ounce can crushed tomatoes in heavy puree *or* 2 fresh tomatoes, cored and chopped fine
½ teaspoon basil
½ teaspoon oregano
1 teaspoon tamari
a dash of Tabasco (optional)

Place all the ingredients in a mixing bowl and mix thoroughly.

CRUST

8 slices whole-wheat or sourdough bread

Flatten each slice of bread with a rolling pin or the side of a glass. Remove the crust.

To assemble the pizza, place approximately 2 tablespoons of the sauce on each slice of bread. Top it with two tablespoons of the cheese mixture. Place the pizzas on a nonstick baking sheet and bake at 375°F. for 15 minutes. Just before serving, cut into quarters.

Note: A variety of toppings can be added to these pizzas, depending on your taste in flavors and colors. If you like a meaty flavor and chewy texture, top with mushrooms. Chopped onions will add a touch of spicy zest. Brighten it up with strips of pimento, or for an added dash of color and an unusual fruity flavor, try chopped pineapple.

❧ MINIATURE BLINTZES

Makes 18–24 blintzes

¾ pound dry cottage cheese
1 tablespoon frozen apple-juice concentrate
½ teaspoon reduced-salt tamari or soy sauce
½ teaspoon cinnamon
a dash of nutmeg (optional)
1 recipe crêpes (see page 294)
1 teaspoon baking soda

Preheat the oven to 350°F. Place the cottage cheese, apple-juice concentrate, tamari, cinnamon, and nutmeg in a blender and puree. Make the crêpes, using 3 tablespoons batter for each, so that they are approximately 4 inches in diameter. Add 1 teaspoon baking soda to the cheese mixture. Place approximately 1½ tablespoons cheese mixture in the middle of each crêpe.

With your fingertips, lift two opposing outside edges of the crêpe and fold in toward the center approximately half the width of the crêpe. Now take the remaining outside edge closest to you and fold in toward the center of the crêpe, placing the edge over the cheese and covering the crêpe approximately by ⅓. Now lift the whole folded portion and allow to cover the remaining edge. Place on a nonstick baking sheet, cover with aluminum foil, and bake for 15 minutes.

SAUCE

2 apples, peeled, cored, and sliced
2 tablespoons frozen apple-juice concentrate
¼ teaspoon cinnamon

Put the apples in a saucepan with the apple-juice concentrate and the cinnamon. Simmer for approximately 15 minutes or until the apples are tender. Put the mixture in a blender and puree. Serve hot or cold.

Stack the blintzes in a spiral pattern on a plate. Surround the plate with small bowls of sauce and of such colorful condiments as Leona's Sour Cream (page 71) or Fruit Topping (page 317).

⋐ COCKTAIL CANNELLONI

Makes 12–16

½ **pound dry cottage cheese**
6 **medium mushrooms, chopped fine**
1 **clove garlic, chopped**
½ **teaspoon basil**
¼ **teaspoon oregano**
a dash of thyme (optional)
1 **teaspoon baking soda**
1 **teaspoon frozen apple-juice concentrate**
1 **teaspoon tamari**
1 **recipe crêpes (See page 294)**

Place all the ingredients except the crêpes in a blender or food processor and puree. Make the crêpes, using 3 tablespoons of batter for each, so that they are approximately 4 inches in diameter. Place 1 tablespoon of the cheese mixture on each crêpe and roll it up. Place the crêpes in a nonstick baking dish.

SAUCE

1 cup sliced mushrooms
1 clove garlic, minced fine
½ teaspoon celery seed
2 cups defatted chicken stock (page 86)
1 teaspoon arrowroot powder or cornstarch dissolved in 2
tablespoons cold water
2 tablespoons chopped parsley for garnish

Place the mushrooms, garlic, celery seed, and stock in a saucepan. Bring to a boil and continue to boil for 5 minutes. Add the arrowroot or cornstarch solution to the boiling sauce and stir until it thickens. Pour the sauce over the crêpes and place in a 375°F. oven for 15 minutes. Serve warm with a garnish of chopped parsley.

⊸§ LASAGNE SQUARES

Makes 12–16 squares

½ package whole-wheat lasagne noodles
½ pound dry cottage cheese
1 teaspoon sweet basil
1 teaspoon oregano
½ teaspoon thyme
1 clove garlic, peeled and minced
1 teaspoon arrowroot powder or cornstarch

Boil the lasagne noodles as directed on the package for 10 minutes. Drain and spread on a dish towel to cool. Place the cheese, the herbs, and the arrowroot or cornstarch in a blender or food processor and blend until smooth. Place in a bowl and chill in the refrigerator.

SAUCE

> 1 16-ounce can crushed tomatoes in heavy puree *or* 2 fresh
> tomatoes, quartered
> 1 teaspoon sweet basil
> ½ teaspoon rosemary
> ½ teaspoon fennel seeds (optional)
> 2 cloves garlic, minced fine
> 1 teaspoon tamari
> a dash of Tabasco (optional)

Place all the ingredients in a saucepan, bring to a boil, and simmer for 10 minutes. Reserve about ½ cup of sauce and keep it warm. Set aside the rest and allow it to cool.

Place ⅓ of the cooled sauce mixture in the bottom of a 3-quart rectangular baking dish. Place one layer of noodles on top of the sauce. Place ½ the cheese mixture on top of this, spreading it evenly down the center of each noodle. Add a second layer of noodles, and spread ⅓ of the cooled sauce mixture over them. Place the remaining cheese mixture down the center of the noodles as before. Add a third layer of noodles and cover with the remaining cooled sauce. Cover the baking dish with aluminum foil and place in a 350°F. oven for 1 hour. Remove from the oven and let stand sealed for 15 minutes. Cut the lasagne into squares the width of the noodles and serve warm in a chafing dish with a dollop of the reserved sauce on each square.

◄§ SWEDISH-STYLE EGGPLANT BALLS

Makes 24–30 balls

1 **medium eggplant**
2 **pieces whole-wheat or sourdough bread**
2 **garlic cloves, minced fine**
1 **teaspoon sweet basil**
½ **teaspoon oregano**
¼ **teaspoon celery seed**
1 **stalk celery, minced fine**
½ **onion, minced fine**

Wrap the eggplant in aluminum foil and bake for 1 hour at 350°F. Cool and remove the skin, placing the eggplant meat in a mixing bowl. Toast the two slices of bread and crumble into the bowl. Mix in the balance of the ingredients. If the mixture is too moist to form into balls, add one more slice of toasted and crumbled bread. Moisten your hands with cold water and form the mixture, one tablespoon at a time, into balls. Place these balls on a nonstick baking sheet and bake in a 375°F. oven for 20 minutes.

SAUCE

1 **8-ounce can crushed tomatoes in heavy puree** *or* **2 fresh medium tomatoes, chopped**
1 **teaspoon Dijon mustard (salt-free)**
1 **clove garlic, minced fine**
1 **teaspoon reduced-salt tamari or soy sauce**
½ **teaspoon basil**
¼ **teaspoon celery seed**
a dash of Tabasco (optional)
1 **tablespoon dry sherry (optional)**
escarole for garnish

Place all these ingredients in a saucepan and bring to a boil. Reduce the heat and simmer for 15 minutes. If sherry is added, simmer an additional 5 minutes. Serve the sauce warm in a separate chafing dish for dipping the eggplant balls. Serve the eggplant balls in a bowl garnished with escarole. Have frilled toothpicks available for dipping.

⤚§ SWEET-AND-SOUR ZUCCHINI BALLS

Makes 24–30 1-inch balls

- **4 medium zucchini, chopped**
- **3 cloves garlic, minced fine**
- **½ onion, minced**
- **½ bell pepper, minced**
- **1 jalapeño pepper, seeds removed, chopped**
- **1 teaspoon sweet basil**
- **½ teaspoon thyme**
- **1 tablespoon frozen apple-juice concentrate**
- **1 teaspoon tamari**
- **2 slices whole-wheat or sourdough bread**
- **1 egg white**
- **escarole for garnish**

Place all the ingredients except the bread and egg white in a saucepan with ¼ cup water. Stir and simmer over a low flame until the zucchini is tender. Toast the bread. Place the zucchini mixture in a strainer suspended over a bowl and allow the liquid to drain. Set the liquid aside. Place the cool zucchini mixture in a bowl and crumble in the sliced toast. Stir in the egg white. Dip your hands in cold water and form the zucchini mixture into balls. Place on a nonstick cookie sheet and toast in the oven at 375°F. for 15 minutes.

SAUCE

> **liquid drained from cooked zucchini**
> **1 cup crushed pineapple**
> **1 teaspoon lemon juice**
> **1 teaspoon reduced-salt tamari or soy sauce**
> **1 teaspoon arrowroot powder or cornstarch**

Place the reserved zucchini liquid and the pineapple in a saucepan. Add lemon juice and bring to a boil. Put the tamari, arrowroot or cornstarch, and 2 tablespoons water in a cup. Mix thoroughly and pour into the sauce. Simmer for 10 minutes, stirring occasionally. When the sauce thickens, remove it from the heat. Serve the heated sauce in a chafing dish. Serve the zucchini balls in a bowl garnished with escarole. Have frilled toothpicks available for dipping.

⋖§ CHINESE SWEET-AND-SOUR VEGETABLE CAKES

Makes 6–8 cakes

> **1 cup brown rice**
> **1 teaspoon rice vinegar (no sugar)**
> **1 tablespoon frozen apple-juice concentrate**
> **a dash of marjoram**
> **½ small can water chestnuts, quartered**
> **1 cup fresh or frozen peas**
> **½ bell pepper, chopped**
> **2 scallions, sliced**
> **1 cup chopped bok choy (Chinese cabbage)**
> **1 teaspoon grated fresh ginger**
> **1 clove garlic, minced fine**
> **1 egg white**

Place the brown rice, vinegar, apple juice, and marjoram in a 1½-quart pot. Add 2¼ cups water and bring to a boil. Cover and reduce the heat until only light steam escapes from under the lid. Cook for 45 minutes. Don't stir—and don't peek. When no more steam comes out under the lid, the rice is done. Let it cool. Meanwhile, sauté the vegetables, ginger, and garlic in 1 tablespoon water for 8 minutes. Put vegetables in a strainer and allow to cool and drain. Mix with the rice and add 1 egg white, stirring until thoroughly mixed. Take an ice cream scoop dipped in cold water, pack with rice-vegetable mixture, and release on a nonstick baking dish. (A cup dipped in cold water may be used instead of the ice cream scoop.) Be sure to press the rice mixture firmly into the cup or the scoop. The cakes are then baked in a 350°F. oven for 15 minutes. Serve with the selection of Chinese sauces on pages 128–29.

✎§ CHINESE VEGETABLE SKEWERS

Makes 8–10 skewers

   2 **bell peppers, seeded and cut into eighths**
   1 **Bermuda onion, cut into quarters and separated into leaves**
   1 **can water-packed water chestnuts, drained**
  16 **medium-size fresh mushrooms, rinsed in cold water**
  ½ **can bamboo shoots, drained**
   1 **small can water-packed artichoke hearts, drained**
   1 **package bamboo skewers**
   1 **egg white**
   1 **teaspoon reduced-salt tamari or soy sauce**
   1 **tablespoon minced fresh ginger**
   2 **cloves garlic, minced**
   1 **teaspoon rice vinegar (no sugar)**
   1 **slice of whole-wheat or sourdough bread, toasted and crumbled**

Impale the prepared vegetables on skewers, alternating them, until the skewer is full. Place the skewers in a 14×14×2-inch nonstick baking dish. Cover with aluminum foil and crimp the edges securely. Place in a 350°F. oven for 15 minutes. Remove from the oven and remove the foil. Place the egg white (Do not beat) in a bowl and stir in the tamari, ginger, garlic, and vinegar. Paint the skewers with this mixture. Return the skewers to the baking dish, dust with the bread crumbs, and bake, uncovered, at 350°F. for an additional 10 minutes. Arrange the skewers on a round plate like the spokes of a wheel. Serve with a selection of the Chinese sauces found on page 128.

⋐§ ORIENTAL CHICKEN SKEWERS

Makes 8–10 skewers

- ¼ **teaspoon sage**
- 1 **teaspoon tamari**
- 1 **tablespoon minced fresh ginger**
- 2 **cloves garlic, minced fine**
- 1 **teaspoon rice vinegar (no sugar)**
- 1 **chicken breast, cut into 1-inch cubes**
- 2 **bell peppers, seeded and cut into eighths**
- 1 **Bermuda onion, cut into quarters and separated into chips**
- 1 **can water-packed water chestnuts, drained**
- 16 **medium-size fresh mushrooms, rinsed in cold water**
- 1 **can bamboo shoots**
- 1 **package bamboo skewers**
- 1 **egg white**
- 1 **slice whole-wheat or sourdough bread, toasted and crumbled**

Combine the sage, tamari, ginger, garlic, and vinegar in a mixing bowl and marinate the chicken cubes for 1 hour. Impale the prepared vegetables and the marinated chicken cubes (reserve the marinade) on the skewers, alternating the vegetables and chicken, until the skewer is full. Repeat this until all the vegetables and chicken are used. Put the skewers in a 14×14×2-inch nonstick baking dish. Cover with aluminum foil and crimp the edges securely. Place in a 350°F. oven for 15 minutes. Remove from the oven and remove the foil. Mix 1 egg white with the reserved marinade, paint chicken and vegetables with the mixture, and sprinkle them with the bread crumbs. Put the skewers back into the oven and cook uncovered at 350°F. for an additional 10 minutes.

Note: Lobster tails, cut into 1-inch cubes, may be substituted for the chicken.

To serve, cut a grapefruit in half and place it upside down on a plate. Insert the skewers so that they're displayed "porcupine style." Serve with a selection of the Chinese sauces on page 128.

⋖§ CHINESE EGG ROLLS

Makes 24

- 1 pound fresh bean sprouts *or* 1 can, drained
- 1 pound Chinese snow peas *or* ½ package frozen, defrosted and drained
- ½ small can water chestnuts, sliced
- ½ can bamboo shoots, chopped
- 3 scallions, sliced fine
- 1 cup chopped cabbage (use bok choy—Chinese cabbage—if available)
- 1 stalk celery, chopped fine
- 1 yellow crookneck squash *or* 1 zucchini, chopped fine
- 1 cup mushrooms, sliced
- 1 clove garlic, minced fine
- 1 teaspoon fresh ginger, minced fine
- 1 teaspoon tamari
- 2 cups defatted chicken stock (page 86)
- 1 package whole-wheat chapaties (Indian tortillas)

Put all the ingredients except the chapaties in a saucepan, bring to a boil, and simmer for 10 minutes. Place a strainer over a bowl. Pour the vegetable mixture into the strainer, collecting the liquid in the bowl. Allow the vegetables to cool, and reserve the liquid for the sauce. Put the cooled vegetables into a bowl, add 1 egg white, and mix thoroughly. Place one cup of the mixed sautéed vegetables across the center of a chapati. Take one side of the chapati and fold it over the vegetables toward the center, press firmly, and continue rolling until the roll reaches the other edge. Repeat this until the vegetable mixture is used completely. Place the rolls on a nonstick baking sheet and toast in a 350°F. oven for 10 minutes. Remove from the oven and slice into quarters. Turn these quarters vegetable side up and return to the oven for an additional 10 minutes.

SAUCES

These three sauces are recommended for egg rolls. They are also good with Chinese Vegetable Skewers (page 125) and Oriental Chicken Skewers (page 126).

MUSTARD SAUCE

- ½ of the liquid drained from the vegetables
- ¼ cup Dijon mustard (salt-free)
- 1 tablespoon dry sherry
- 1 clove garlic, minced fine
- 2 teaspoons arrowroot powder or cornstarch
- 1 teaspoon frozen apple-juice concentrate (optional)

Place all the ingredients except the arrowroot or cornstarch in a saucepan and simmer for 15 minutes. Dissolve the arrowroot or cornstarch in 2 tablespoons cold water and add to the simmering mustard sauce. Stir until the sauce thickens and remove from the heat. One teaspoon frozen apple-juice concentrate may be added to sweeten the sauce.

SWEET-AND-SOUR SAUCE

> 1 small (8-ounce) can dietetic apricots, drained and pitted
> 1 small (8-ounce) can dietetic plums, drained and pitted
> 2 tablespoons frozen apple-juice concentrate
> ¼ teaspoon reduced-salt tamari or soy sauce
> 1 teaspoon rice vinegar (no sugar)
> 2 teaspoons arrowroot powder or cornstarch

Place all the ingredients except the arrowroot or cornstarch in a saucepan and bring to a boil. Reduce the heat and simmer for 15 minutes. In a separate cup, dissolve the arrowroot or cornstarch in 2 tablespoons of water. Add to the simmering sauce, stir until the sauce thickens, and continue to cook for 5 minutes. Remove from the heat and serve.

POLYNESIAN SAUCE

> 1 small (8-ounce) can dietetic apricots, drained and pitted
> 1 small can crushed pineapple, packed in water
> 1 tablespoon tomato paste
> 1 teaspoon grated fresh ginger
> 1 clove garlic, minced fine
> 2 tablespoons frozen apple-juice concentrate
> 1 teaspoon reduced-salt tamari or soy sauce
> 1 teaspoon rice vinegar (no sugar)
> 2 teaspoons arrowroot powder or cornstarch

Put all the ingredients except the arrowroot or cornstarch into a saucepan and bring to a boil. Reduce the heat and simmer for 15 minutes. In a separate cup, combine 2 tablespoons cold water and the arrowroot or cornstarch and mix until dissolved. Add to the simmering sauce, stir until the sauce thickens, and continue to cook for 5 minutes. Remove from heat.

⊸ POLYNESIAN EGG ROLLS (LOOMPIA)

Serves 4–6

1 cup whole-wheat flour
1 egg white
1 teaspoon baking soda
1 cup defatted chicken stock (page 86)
1 medium onion, sliced thin
2 cups fresh or canned bean sprouts, drained
1 small can bamboo shoots, sliced
1 carrot, scraped and shredded fine
1 clove garlic, minced fine
1 cup chopped fresh pineapple *or* 1 small can water-packed chunk pineapple, drained
¼ cup fresh cilantro, minced

Mix the flour, egg white, and baking soda in a bowl until it forms into a ball. Dust with whole-wheat flour and place in the refrigerator for 1 hour.

In a saucepan, bring the chicken stock to a boil, add the vegetables, garlic, pineapple, and cilantro, and simmer for 10 minutes. Place the mixture in a strainer to drain and cool.

Take the dough from the refrigerator, place on a pastry board or a wooden surface, and dust generously with whole-wheat flour. Roll out the dough with a rolling pin until it is approximately ⅛ inch thick. Cut into 6-inch squares. Place approximately ½ cup of the filling in the center of each square. Bring two opposing outside edges of the dough up to the center, and pinch them together gently and firmly with your fingers. Seal the remaining open ends with a fork. Place the loompia on a nonstick baking sheet and bake for 20 minutes at 350°F. Serve with the Chinese sauces on page 128.

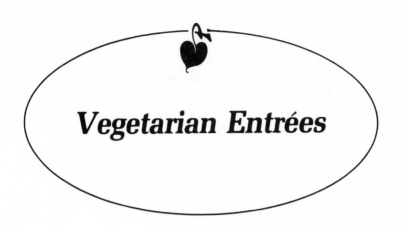

Vegetarian Entrées

The vegetable has traditionally been the stepchild of the American dinner, cooked without flair and presented without imagination. But now, with the popularity of diets that are low in protein and fats and high in complex carbohydrates, the vegetable is on the verge of becoming the star of the dinnertime show. Most vegetables are low in calories yet high in nutritional value, so they can be eaten in appreciable quantities without fear of weight gain or damage to the arteries.

No one seriously doubts that vegetables are "good for us." The question is one of flavor: can these vegetables be made to taste any better to us now than they seemed to when Mother was shoving them down our throats? Well, I suggest you try the Squash Soufflé, or the Eggplant Moussaka à la Grèque—in fact, any of the recipes in the following chapter. I think you'll find them not only fascinating and flavorful, but satisfying and, yes, even filling enough so that you won't even miss the meat entrées they're replacing.

And by the way, vegetable dishes tend to cost about half as much as dishes made with meat.

Note: Some of these recipes call for tamari or other soy-based sauces. For those people whose diets are rigidly salt-free, these sauces should be omitted.

ᵛᵍ CHEESE ENCHILADAS

I was once called on to cook a fat-free dinner for then-California Governor Jerry Brown and his friend Linda Ronstadt. Since I knew they were both great fans of Mexican food (they had met at the famous Los Angeles Mexican restaurant called El Coyote), I challenged myself to come up with a fat-free enchilada. This recipe was the result. (By the way, Jerry and Linda loved it!)

Serves 4–6

8 corn tortillas

SAUCE

- **1 small onion, chopped**
- **2 tablespoons minced fresh jalapeño peppers**
- **3 cloves garlic, minced fine**
- **2 teaspoons chili powder**
- **1 teaspoon cumin**
- **1 teaspoon coriander**
- **1 teaspoon paprika**
- **1 teaspoon basil**
- **1 teaspoon oregano**
- **5 cups defatted chicken stock (page 86) or water**
- **1 small (4½-ounce) can tomato paste**

Sauté the vegetables and spices in 1 cup chicken stock or water until the vegetables are tender and the liquid has nearly disappeared. Add the tomato paste and the rest of the stock and simmer.

CHEESE

 1 pound dry cottage cheese
 ½ cup grated zucchini (optional)
 1 cup chopped tomato
 1 tablespoon arrowroot powder

In a blender or food processor, puree the cheese and zucchini, if used, until smooth. Mix in the tomatoes and arrowroot powder.

Dip each tortilla in the warm sauce and then place ½ cup cheese mixture in the middle, roll up, and place in a nonstick baking dish. Pour the remaining sauce evenly over top of the enchiladas. Cover tightly with a lid or aluminum foil and bake for 30 minutes at 350°F.

⋐§ EGG ROLLS

Serves 4–6

 1 cup bean sprouts, rinsed in cold water
 ½ bell pepper, chopped into small chunks
 ½ onion, sliced thin
 3 scallions, sliced thin
 2 cups sliced bok choy or cabbage
 1 cup fresh or frozen snow peas, cut into ½-inch lengths
 ½ small can water chestnuts, rinsed in cold water and sliced
 ½ small can bamboo shoots, rinsed in cold water and chopped
 ½ cup fresh or canned dietetic pineapple chunks (optional)
 1 cup defatted chicken stock (page 86) or water
 1 tablespoon reduced-salt tamari or soy sauce
 2 tablespoons frozen apple-juice concentrate
 2 egg whites
 6 whole-wheat-flour tortillas
 3 cloves garlic, minced fine
 1 tablespoon grated fresh ginger

Sauté the vegetables (and pineapple, if used) in the chicken stock or water with the tamari, apple-juice concentrate, garlic, and ginger for 8 minutes. Drain thoroughly in a strainer over a bowl, reserving the liquid. When the drained vegetables are cool, put them in a bowl and mix in the egg whites. Place ¾ to 1 cup vegetable mixture on a whole-wheat tortilla. Roll and place on a nonstick cookie sheet. Bake for 10 minutes at 350°F. Then remove from the oven, and with a serrated edge or bread knife cut in half. Return to the 350°F. oven for an additional 5 minutes. Serve with Sweet-and-Sour Sauce (page 129), Mustard Sauce (page 128), or the Basic Tomato Sauce below.

Basic Tomato Sauce

the reserved liquid drained from the cooked vegetables
1 tablespoon Dijon mustard (salt-free)
2 tablespoons tomato paste
1 teaspoon basil

Place all these ingredients in a saucepan and simmer for 15 minutes. Serve hot or cold.

✑ POTATO PANCAKES

Serves 4–6

2 medium-size russet potatoes, peeled and cut into chunks (Keep them in a bowl with water to cover until ready to use, so that they won't discolor.)
1 small onion, peeled and cut into chunks
2 cloves garlic, peeled and minced
1 tablespoon reduced-salt tamari or soy sauce
a dash of Tabasco
2 egg whites

Place all the ingredients in a blender or food processor and blend until smooth. Heat a large nonstick frypan over medium heat. Place a drop of water in the pan, and if it steams and "dances," the pan is ready to use. Spoon ¼ cup of the potato mixture into the hot pan and cook for 3 to 5 minutes, until bubbles form and break open. Turn the pancakes and cook until steaming subsides (3 to 5 minutes). Serve with Leona's Sour Cream (page 71) and/or fresh applesauce.

✒ CHEESE BLINTZES

Blintzes can be served with a variety of toppings. Try nonfat yogurt (page 72) sweetened with 2 tablespoons of partially thawed frozen apple-juice concentrate or fresh or frozen sliced strawberries, for example, or fruit jams or preserves (See pages 312–315). Applesauce is a traditional favorite, as is sour cream (use Leona's, page 71). For an unusual tropical flair, try serving the blintzes with Papaya Cream Topping (page 319).

Serves 4–6

- 3 **cups dry cottage cheese**
- 1 **tablespoon arrowroot powder or cornstarch**
- 1 **banana**
- ½ **cup frozen apple-juice concentrate**
- 1 **cup nonfat yogurt**
- ¼ **teaspoon cinnamon**
- 1 **tablespoon pure vanilla extract**
- 4 **egg whites, beaten until stiff**
- 1 **recipe crêpes (page 294)**

Blend the cottage cheese, arrowroot powder, banana, apple-juice concentrate, yogurt, and flavorings until smooth. Fold in the egg whites. Put about ¾ cup of the mixture in the center of each crêpe. Fold two sides of the crêpe over the filling as if you were folding a letter. Then fold the open ends toward the center and bake, seam side down, in a nonstick baking dish covered with aluminum foil for 20 minutes at 325°F.

◆§ SPICY TAMALE PIE

Serves 4–6

- 1½ cups cornmeal
- 2 carrots, shredded
- 1 bell pepper, sliced thin
- ½ pound mushrooms, sliced
- 1 onion, chopped
- 1 tablespoon chopped pimento (optional—do not use if on a salt-free diet)
- 2 cloves garlic, minced
- 3 cups defatted chicken stock (page 86) or water
- 2 tablespoons chili powder
- 2 tablespoons chopped parsley
- 1 tablespoon tamati or soy sauce
- ½ small can tomato paste (salt-free)
- 1 pound dry cottage cheese
- 6 egg whites, beaten stiff

Bring 3 cups of water to a boil. Combine the cornmeal with 1 cup cold water. Gradually pour into the boiling water, stirring constantly, until the mixture begins to boil again. Reduce the heat and cook, stirring occasionally, until the mixture has begun to thicken and get creamy-looking (about 5 minutes). Chill.

Simmer all the vegetables and the garlic in the water or chicken stock until tender. Then add the chili powder, parsley, tamari, and tomato paste. Cook about 10 minutes, or until the sauce thickens. Line a nonstick casserole with ½ the chilled cornmeal. Mix ¾ of the vegetables with the cottage cheese. Pour this mixture into the casserole. Mix the remaining ¼ of the vegetables with the last ½ of the cornmeal. Fold in the egg whites. Pour this on top of the vegetable-cheese mixture. Cover and bake 20 minutes at 350°F. Uncover and continue baking at 400°F. for 15 minutes or until browned.

⊰§ QUICHE

Supposedly, real men don't eat it, but it's always been a personal favorite of mine. So here's my low-fat entry into The Great Quiche Controversy.

Serves 4–6

½ cup tomato juice
1 cup whole-wheat or sourdough bread crumbs
1 pound dry cottage cheese
1 tablespoon arrowroot or cornstarch
1 cup nonfat yogurt (page 72)
1 carrot, scraped and grated
1 bell pepper, sliced thin
8 mushrooms, sliced
1 tablespoon reduced-salt tamari or soy sauce
¼ cup frozen apple-juice concentrate

Mix the tomato juice and bread crumbs and press into a 9-inch pie tin so as to form a ½-inch crust. Toast in the oven for 15 minutes at 350°F.

Blend the cottage cheese, arrowroot, and yogurt until smooth. Place the carrot, pepper, mushrooms, tamari, and apple-juice concentrate in a 2-quart pot and sauté for 10 minutes. Mix the vegetables with the cheese mixture in a large bowl. Pour into the piecrust and bake for 20 minutes at 350°F.

Note: To make Mushroom Quiche, increase the amount of mushrooms to 1 pound.

CREAMY CABBAGE CURRY

Serves 4–6

1 onion, peeled and chopped fine
4 cloves garlic, peeled and minced fine
1 tablespoon grated fresh ginger
2 teaspoons curry powder
2 cups defatted beef stock (page 88), chicken stock (page 86), or water
1 red bell pepper, seeded and cut into rings
2 carrots, scraped and sliced into ¼-inch lengths
1 head green cabbage, sliced into 1-inch strips
2 zucchini, sliced thin
1 tablespoon reduced-salt tamari or soy sauce
1 tablespoon cornstarch dissolved in ½ cup cold stock or water
2 tablespoons frozen apple-juice concentrate
2 cups nonfat yogurt
shredded carrots for garnish

Place the onion, garlic, ginger, curry powder, and 1 cup of stock or water in a 1½–2-quart pot or wok. Simmer over a low flame for 5 minutes, stirring occasionally. Add the pepper, carrots, cabbage, and zucchini. Cover and simmer for 10 minutes. Add the remaining stock, tamari, and cornstarch solution. Bring to a boil, stirring gently. Reduce the temperature. Add the frozen apple-juice concentrate, cover, and cook for 3 minutes. Turn off the heat, add the yogurt, and stir. Serve with rice or semolina noodles. Garnish with shredded carrots.

⊌§ EGGPLANT MOUSSAKA À LA GRÈCQUE

Serves 4–6

1 teaspoon basil
1 tablespoon oregano
6 cloves garlic, peeled and minced fine
1 tablespoon reduced-salt tamari or soy sauce
juice of 1 lemon
2 tablespoons frozen apple-juice concentrate, partially thawed
1 28–29-ounce can crushed tomatoes in heavy puree (salt-free if possible)
1 pound dry cottage cheese
1 tablespoon arrowroot powder or cornstarch
2 potatoes, peeled and cut into ½-inch slices
1 pound mushrooms, quartered
1 onion, peeled and sliced thin
1 bell pepper, seeds removed, chopped fine
2 eggplants, peeled and cut into 1-inch cubes

In a bowl mix the basil, oregano, garlic, tamari, lemon juice, apple-juice concentrate, and tomatoes. Put the cottage cheese in a blender or food processor along with the arrowroot powder or cornstarch and ½ cup of tomato mixture, and blend until smooth. Place 1 cup of the tomato mixture in a 2-quart nonstick casserole or Pyrex baking dish and spread it around the bottom. Place the potatoes in an even layer on top of this sauce. Spread ½ cup tomato mixture on top of the potatoes and then place the mushrooms, onion, and pepper on top in an even layer. Spread 1 cup of tomato mixture on top of this layer. Pour the cheese mixture on top and spread evenly. Then add a layer of all the eggplant cubes on top of the cheese. Finish by topping with the remaining tomato mixture. Cover with lid or aluminum foil and bake in a 350°F. oven for 40 minutes. Remove from oven and allow to stand, covered, for 15 minutes. Serve hot, with sourdough or garlic toast (page 304).

❧ EGGPLANT CASSEROLE

Serves 4–6

2 stalks celery, chopped
1 onion, chopped
4 cloves garlic, peeled and minced fine
1 bell pepper, seeded and chopped
2 cucumbers, seeded and chopped
1 cup defatted chicken stock (page 86), vegetable stock (page 90), or water
1 eggplant, peeled and cut into cubes
1 16-ounce can tomato puree
⅛ teaspoon cayenne
1 tablespoon reduced-salt tamari or soy sauce
1 cup whole-wheat or sourdough bread crumbs

Sauté the celery, onion, garlic, bell pepper, and cucumber in the stock or water until thoroughly cooked. Add the eggplant, tomato puree, cayenne, and soy sauce. Place the mixture in a casserole and cover with bread crumbs. Cover and bake for 30 minutes at 350°F. Uncover and bake an additional 10 minutes, or until the bread crumbs are toasted.

❧ EGGPLANT ITALIANA

Serves 4–6

6 cloves garlic, minced fine
1 onion, chopped fine
1 cup defatted chicken stock (page 86) or water
4 fresh tomatoes, quartered *or* 1 28- or 29-ounce can crushed tomatoes in heavy puree
2 carrots, scraped and sliced thin

1 bell pepper, seeds removed, cut into strips
3 zucchini, sliced thin
1 pound mushrooms, quartered
2 eggplants, peeled and cut into 1-inch cubes
1 tablespoon reduced-salt tamari or soy sauce

Place the garlic and onion in a 2½–3-quart pot with ½ cup chicken stock or water and cook until browned. Add tomatoes, carrots, bell pepper, and zucchini. Cook until steaming for 10 minutes, stirring occasionally. Add the mushrooms, eggplant, remaining stock or water, and tamari. Cook until tender. Serve over whole-wheat noodles, or semolina-flour noodles, or curried rice.

✍ SQUASH SOUFFLÉ

When most cooks think soufflé, they think about spending the whole day in the kitchen preparing it. Well, this soufflé came out of one of those tight situations in which an equipment failure left me with only about 45 minutes to do the whole thing from start to finish. In fact, if there were an Olympic race in soufflé-cooking, this one would probably be a medal-winner.

Serves 6–8

2–3 pounds banana squash (or any hard-skinned winter squash) with hard skin removed
4 carrots, scraped and cut into 1-inch lengths
1 medium sweet potato, peeled and cut into 1-inch slices
1 clove garlic, peeled and minced fine
½ cup frozen apple-juice concentrate
1 tablespoon arrowroot or cornstarch
1 teaspoon cinnamon
1 tablespoon dry sherry
¾ cup cooked millet (page 245)
3 egg whites, beaten until stiff

Steam the squash, carrots, sweet potato, and garlic in a 1½–2-quart pot with 2 inches of water for 30 minutes. Cool and drain. Put in a blender or food processor with the apple-juice concentrate and cornstarch, and blend until smooth. Add the cinnamon and sherry and mix thoroughly. Spread the millet evenly on the bottom of a 2-quart nonstick or Pyrex baking dish and pat flat. Toast in the oven at 350°F. for 10 minutes. Fold the egg whites into the cooled vegetable mixture and pour over the millet. Bake 20 minutes at 350°F., until top begins to brown.

⌐§ STUFFED ACORN SQUASH

Serves 6

> 3 acorn squash
> 1 cup wild rice
> 1 cup brown rice
> 4½ cups defatted chicken stock (page 86) or water
> 1 carrot, sliced
> ½ onion, chopped
> ½ small can water chestnuts, chopped
> ½ cup fresh or frozen peas
> 1 tablespoon parsley
> 2 tablespoons frozen apple-juice concentrate, partially thawed
> 1 tablespoon reduced-salt tamari or soy sauce

Wrap each acorn squash in aluminum foil and bake them at 350°F. for 30 minutes. Cool. Cut in half lengthwise and remove the seeds.

To make the stuffing, cook all the rice in 4 cups of chicken stock or water. Cool. Sauté the carrot, onion, chestnuts, peas, and parsley in ½ cup chicken stock over a low flame for 10 minutes. Add the apple-juice concentrate and tamari. Fold in the rice.

Put 1 cup stuffing in each half acorn squash. Cover and bake 20 minutes at 325°F.

☙ ZUCCHINI-MUSHROOM PIE

Serves 4–6

FILLING

- **4 medium zucchini (unpeeled)**
- **¼ pound mushrooms, sliced**
- **1 teaspoon arrowroot or cornstarch**
- **½ teaspoon basil**
- **1 13-ounce can evaporated skim milk**
- **2 egg whites, beaten lightly**

Steam the zucchini for 12 minutes, cool, and mash in a large mixing bowl. Add the remaining ingredients and mix together thoroughly.

CRUST

- **1 cup rolled oats**
- **1 tablespoon wheat flakes (optional)**
- **2 tablespoons frozen apple-juice concentrate, partially thawed**

Mix these ingredients together in a bowl until the oats are dampened. Press this mixture to a ¼-inch thickness in a 9-inch nonstick pie pan, and place in a 350°F. oven for 10 minutes until lightly toasted.

Pour the zucchini-mushroom mixture into the piecrust and place in a 375°F. oven for 50 minutes to 1 hour until the top is firm and slightly cracking.

✍§ ZUCCHINI CREOLE

Serves 4–6

3 fresh tomatoes, quartered *or* 1 small can tomato puree
1 onion, cut into ¼-inch slices
4 cloves garlic, chopped fine
1 small green or red chili pepper, seeds removed, chopped fine
1 cup defatted beef stock (page 88) or water
¼ pound mushrooms, sliced
8 zucchini, sliced thin
1 sweet red bell pepper, sliced thin
1 green bell pepper, sliced thin
1 tablespoon frozen apple-juice concentrate
1 tablespoon reduced-salt tamari or soy sauce
fresh parsley for garnish

Sauté the tomatoes with the onion, garlic, and chili pepper in the beef stock or water for 5 minutes. Add the mushrooms, zucchini, and peppers. Stir thoroughly and continue to cook for 5 minutes. Add apple-juice concentrate and tamari and simmer for 3 minutes. Serve over brown rice with parsley garnish.

✍§ COUNTRY BAKED TOMATOES

Serves 4

4 large tomatoes
3 cups defatted chicken stock (page 86), vegetable stock (page 90), or water
½ cup millet
½ cup brown rice
¼ cup lentils
2 cloves garlic, chopped fine

½ **red onion, chopped fine**
½ **bell pepper, chopped fine**
1 **small can water chestnuts, drained, rinsed in cold water, and sliced**
1 **teaspoon basil**
1 **tablespoon tamari or soy sauce**
parsley for garnish

Scoop the insides from the tomatoes, being careful not to damage the tomato shells, and set aside in a bowl. Bring 2 cups stock or water to a boil and add the millet, rice, and lentils. Cover and reduce the heat until only light steam escapes from under the lid. Cook for 45 minutes. Sauté the garlic, onion, bell pepper, tomato pulp, and water chestnuts along with the basil, tamari, and capers in 1 cup chicken stock or water for 15 minutes. Combine with cooked millet mixture and stuff into tomato shells. Place the stuffed tomatoes in a baking dish and pour 1 cup of stock into the bottom of the dish. Cover and bake for 20 minutes in a 325°F. oven. Serve with a parsley garnish.

↩§ PETERJACK ONE-POT CHILI

I created this dish for a close friend who was studying restaurant management and figured he ought to learn how to cook. The trouble was, he had spent less time in a kitchen than you or I spend in Hudson's Bay. As a matter of fact, when I went to survey his kitchen I found that he had only one pot to cook in! Hence this one-pot chili—low fat, of course—which I dedicate in perpetuity to my ambitious but underequipped friend.

Serves 4–6

       3 tomatoes, cut into chunks
       1 onion, sliced thin
       1 cup white-meat chicken, cut into chunks (optional)
       4 summer or crookneck squash (unpeeled), cut into cubes
       1 potato, peeled and cut into cubes
       ½ package frozen cut corn
       1 16-ounce can crushed tomatoes in puree (no salt added)
       2 tablespoons gumbo filé (sassafras)
       4 cloves garlic, minced fine
       1 teaspoon oregano
       2 tablespoons chili powder
       1 teaspoon basil
       1 teaspoon coriander
       1 teaspoon ground cumin
       1 bay leaf
    5–6 cups defatted chicken stock (page 86) or water
       2 tablespoons reduced-salt tamari or soy sauce

Place all the ingredients except the chicken in a 2½–3-quart pot. Cover and simmer lightly 1 hour or until the potato is tender. Add the chicken if desired and continue to simmer for 10 minutes. Serve with corn bread (page 307).

❧ SAM'S TEXAS CHILI

I once worked as chef for a Texas millionaire who spent half his life on his private jet. This chili turned out to be one of his favorites, not only because he was, like all true Texans, a lifelong chili-lover, but because it could be made in advance of a trip, then carried aboard his plane and reheated. In fact, I remember one occasion when a pack of Louisiana oil wells were bought and sold on the plane over steaming bowls of this chili.

Serves 4–6

½ cup pinto beans
½ cup lentils
½ cup garbanzos
2 zucchini or summer squash, cut into ½-inch chunks
1 bell pepper, seeds removed, chopped
1 onion, peeled and chopped
1 jalapeño pepper, seeds removed, chopped
1 tablespoon reduced-salt tamari or soy sauce
2 tablespoons chili powder (1 tablespoon each light and dark if available)
1 tablespoon oregano
1 tablespoon basil
6 cloves garlic, peeled and chopped fine
2 tablespoons gumbo filé
½ cup Ortega chili peppers, chopped
½ small can tomato paste
6 cups defatted beef stock (page 88) or chicken stock (page 86)
2 cups defatted beef stock or chicken stock for second cooking

Put all the ingredients except the final 2 cups of stock in a 2½–3-quart pot and bring to a boil. Reduce the heat and simmer for 2 hours. Turn off the heat and let the chili stand covered for 2 hours. Bring it to a boil a second time and reduce the heat to a simmer, adding an additional 2 cups of stock. Simmer for 1 hour, testing the beans to see if they are tender. Serve with garlic toast (page 304) or corn bread. By the way, this chili is even tastier on the second day.

⇜§ QUICK VEGETABLE STEW

Serves 4–6

1 pint defatted chicken stock (page 86) or water
6 cloves garlic, minced fine
1 onion, peeled and sliced thin
2 carrots, scraped and sliced thin
1 potato, peeled and cut into cubes
½ head green cabbage, core removed and cut into 1-inch cubes
2 tomatoes, cored and cut into chunks
2 turnips, peeled and cut into chips
3 stalks celery, sliced in 1-inch lengths
1 teaspoon sage
1 teaspoon basil
1 tablespoon reduced-salt tamari or soy sauce
1 teaspoon poultry seasoning
1 tablespoon cornstarch dissolved in ½ cup defatted chicken stock or water

Put the chicken stock or water in a 2½– or 3-quart pot. Add the garlic, onion, carrots, and potato. Cover and cook for 5 minutes. Add the cabbage, tomatoes, turnips, and celery, stirring occasionally. Add the sage, basil, tamari, and poultry seasoning. Continue to simmer for 10 minutes. Then slowly stir in the cornstarch solution and simmer and stir until the stew has thickened. Serve with sourdough toast, garlic bread, or corn bread.

✒ VEGETABLES ROSEMARY

Serves 4–6

2 cups defatted chicken stock (page 86) or water
6 cloves garlic, minced
1 tablespoon rosemary
8 carrots, scraped and sliced thin
6 stalks celery, sliced thin
2 cucumbers, peeled and cut into small chunks
3 green onions, sliced thin
2 tomatoes, cut into chunks *or* 1 small basket cherry tomatoes
1 pound mushrooms, cut into quarters
1 tablespoon tamari or soy sauce
2 tablespoons frozen apple-juice concentrate
1 tablespoon cornstarch dissolved in ½ cup cold water

Place the chicken stock or water, the garlic, and the rosemary in a 1½–2-quart pot or wok. Bring to a boil and add the carrots, celery, cucumbers, and onions. Stir well, cover, and cook for 5 minutes. Add the tomatoes, mushrooms, tamari, and apple-juice concentrate, stirring thoroughly. Then mix in the cornstarch solution. Simmer for 2 minutes. Serve.

✑ FETTUCCINE PRIMAVERA

Serves 4–6

1 package whole-wheat or semolina-flour fettuccine noodles
1 cup nonfat yogurt (page 72)
4 cloves garlic, minced fine
1 bell pepper, sliced thin
1 pound mushrooms, sliced thin
1 tablespoon frozen apple-juice concentrate, partially
  thawed
1 tablespoon reduced-salt tamari or soy sauce
2 cups defatted chicken stock (page 86) or water
2 tablespoons cornstarch dissolved in ½ cup cold water

Cook the fettuccine in water until *al dente* (12–15 minutes).

Sauté the garlic, pepper, and mushrooms in the apple juice, tamari, and ½ cup of stock or water for a few minutes. Add the remaining chicken stock or water and cook until the liquid is reduced in volume by one half. Add the yogurt and heat until warm. DO NOT BOIL (use a double boiler if available). Add the cornstarch solution and stir until thick and creamy. Fold the sauce into the noodles and serve.

✑ EGGPLANT BALLS

Makes 24–30 balls

1 medium eggplant
3 slices whole-wheat or sourdough bread, crumbled
4 cloves of garlic, peeled and chopped fine
1 carrot, scraped and grated
2 tablespoons chopped parsley
1 onion, peeled and chopped fine
½ cup diced mushrooms

2 **egg whites, beaten until lightly foamy**
½ **teaspoon celery seed**
1 **teaspoon sage**
1 **teaspoon basil**
1 **tablespoon reduced-salt tamari or soy sauce**
1 **teaspoon grated fresh ginger**

Bake eggplant for 1 hour at 350°F. Peel, place in a large bowl, and mash. Add all the remaining ingredients and mix thoroughly. Moisten your hands with cold water, take 2 table-spoons of this mixture, and form into a ball. Repeat until all the mixture is used. Place the eggplant balls on a nonstick baking sheet, cover with aluminum foil, and bake 10 minutes at 350°F. Uncover and bake 10 minutes more at the same temperature. Great to serve with whole-wheat or semolina-flour spaghetti and Italian Sauce (page 251).

◄§ ZUCCHINI BALLS

Makes 24–30 balls

5–6 **medium zucchini (unpeeled)**
3 **slices whole-wheat or sourdough bread, crumbled**
4 **cloves garlic, peeled and chopped fine**
1 **carrot, scraped and grated**
2 **tablespoons chopped parsley**
1 **onion, peeled and chopped fine**
½ **cup diced mushrooms**
2 **egg whites, beaten until lightly foamy**
½ **teaspoon celery seed**
1 **teaspoon sage**
1 **teaspoon basil**
1 **tablespoon reduced-salt tamari or soy sauce**
1 **teaspoon grated fresh ginger**

Steam the zucchini for 12 minutes, place in a bowl, and mash. Add all the remaining ingredients and mix thoroughly. Moisten your hands with cold water, take 2 tablespoons of this mixture, and form into a ball. Repeat until all the mixture is used. Place the zucchini balls on a nonstick baking sheet, cover with aluminum foil, and bake 10 minutes at 350°F. Uncover and bake 10 minutes more at same temperature. Like Eggplant Balls (page 150), these are great with whole-wheat or semolina-flour spaghetti and Italian Sauce (page 251) or Spicy Spaghetti Sauce (page 252). Try Onion Garlic Rolls (page 304) as an accompaniment.

✒️ LASAGNE

A few years ago I met a beautiful young woman who came from an Italian family. Our first problem was not the difference in our backgrounds, but the difference in our diets. She was Italian food all the way; I was one hundred percent vegetarian. For a while things looked grim. Then I came up with a recipe that both solved the problem and sealed our relationship: an absolutely fat-free version of one of her favorite foods—lasagne.

Serves 4–6

SAUCE

- ½ onion, peeled and chopped fine
- 4 cloves garlic, peeled and chopped fine
- 2 teaspoons oregano
- 1 teaspoon basil
- ½ teaspoon fennel seed (whole or ground)
- ½ teaspoon rosemary
- 1 tablespoon reduced-salt tamari or soy sauce

1 28- or 29-ounce can crushed tomatoes in heavy puree (no salt added)
a dash of Tabasco

Simmer the onion, garlic, herbs, and tamari in 2 tablespoons water for 10 minutes over a low flame. Add the crushed tomatoes and Tabasco and simmer for 15 minutes.

CHEESE MIXTURE

- **1 pound dry cottage cheese**
- **1 tablespoon frozen apple-juice concentrate**
- **1 teaspoon basil**
- **1 tablespoon reduced-salt tamari or soy sauce**
- **1 cup sliced mushrooms**
- **1 tablespoon arrowroot**

Place the cheese-mixture ingredients in a blender or food processor and blend until smooth.

NOODLES

9 whole-wheat or semolina-flour lasagne noodles

Fill a 2½–3-quart pot with water to within 1 inch of the top and bring to a boil. Boil the noodles for 10 minutes, or until soft but not falling apart. Drain the noodles and add ice or cold water to keep them from cooking further.

Now the sauce, noodles, and cheese mixture are ready to "construct" the lasagne. Coat the bottom of an 8-inch-square baking dish with ½ cup of the sauce. Place 3 noodles side by side on top of the sauce, covering it completely. Spoon about ⅓ of the cheese mixture evenly over the noodles. Repeat this procedure 2 more times, ending with a layer of tomato sauce on top. Cover the dish with aluminum foil, carefully crimping the edges to seal. Place in a 350°F. oven for 1 hour.

◄§ EGGPLANT-MILLET LASAGNE

Serves 4–6

1 28–29-ounce can crushed tomatoes in heavy puree
2 fresh chili peppers, chopped fine
2 tablespoons fine-chopped bell pepper
2 cloves garlic, chopped fine
½ cup fine-chopped onions
1 tablespoon chopped parsley
½ teaspoon fennel seed (optional)
2 teaspoons oregano
½ teaspoon rosemary
2 teaspoons basil
1 tablespoon reduced-salt tamari or soy sauce
2 tablespoons Marsala wine (optional)
1 eggplant, peeled and sliced ¼ inch thick
1 cup nonfat milk
1 cup raw millet
2 cups dry cottage cheese *or* 1 cup ricotta cheese

Combine the tomatoes, both the peppers, and the garlic, onion, and herbs with the tamari. Bring to a boil, then reduce heat and simmer for 20 minutes. Remove from the heat and add the Marsala. Line the bottom of a baking dish with some of this sauce. Dip the eggplant slices in the milk, then in the raw millet. Lay the coated slices in an 8½×13-inch baking dish. Sprinkle some of the cottage cheese on top of the eggplant slices to form a layer.

Starting with the sauce, repeat the layering process, reserving 1 cup of sauce for the top. Cover and bake 1 hour at 325°F.

Note: For variety, this dish may be made with 6 zucchini, sliced, or 1 pound fresh mushrooms, sliced, instead of eggplant.

❧ ZUCCHINI LASAGNE

Serves 4–6

8–10 medium zucchini, cut lengthwise into ¼-inch-thick slabs

SAUCE

½ onion, peeled and chopped fine
4 cloves garlic, peeled and chopped fine
2 teaspoons oregano
1 teaspoon basil
½ teaspoon fennel seed (whole or ground)
½ teaspoon rosemary
1 tablespoon reduced-salt tamari or soy sauce
1 28- or 29-ounce can crushed tomatoes in heavy puree (no salt added)
a dash of Tabasco

Sauté the onions, garlic, herbs, and tamari for 10 minutes over a low flame. Add the tomato puree and Tabasco and simmer for 15 minutes.

CHEESE MIXTURE

1 pound dry cottage cheese
1 tablespoon frozen apple-juice concentrate, partially thawed
1 teaspoon basil
1 tablespoon tamari or soy sauce
1 cup sliced mushrooms
1 tablespoon arrowroot powder

Place the cheese-mixture ingredients in a blender or food processor and blend until smooth.

Steam zucchini in 1 cup water for 10 minutes or until soft

but not falling apart. Drain in order to keep the zucchini from cooking further.

To "construct" the lasagne, coat an 8-inch-square baking dish with ½ cup of sauce. Place zucchini side by side on top to cover the sauce completely. Spoon about ⅓ of the cheese mixture evenly over the zucchini. Repeat this layering 2 more times, ending with tomato sauce on top. Cover the dish with aluminum foil, carefully crimping the edges to seal. Place in a 350°F. oven for 1 hour.

⋖§ VEGETABLE FOO YUNG

This is one of the most versatile recipes in this book. It's good either hot or cold, and makes fabulous next-day leftovers (or it can be frozen for storage for as long as three months). These patties are especially delicious served cold with yogurt, or hot with the Chinese sauces on pages 128–29.

Serves 4–6

½ head red or green cabbage, shredded thin
1 large carrot, scraped and sliced very thin
½ onion, peeled and sliced thin
3 cloves garlic, peeled and chopped fine
2 stalks celery, chopped fine
1 cup bean sprouts
1 cup sliced fresh mushrooms
1 tablespoon grated fresh ginger
2 tablespoons frozen apple-juice concentrate
1 tablespoon reduced-salt tamari or soy sauce
1 teaspoon Dijon mustard
1 cup defatted chicken stock (page 86), vegetable stock (page 90), or water
1 small can deveined shrimp, drained *or* ½ chicken breast, diced *or* ¼ pound white fish in small chunks (optional)
3 egg whites

Place all the ingredients except the egg whites in a large nonstick frying pan or wok. Sauté for 5 to 6 minutes until the vegetables have turned bright in color. Turn off the heat and drain by placing the mixture in a strainer over a large bowl. When *all* the liquid has drained into the bowl, pour it into a saucepan and set it aside for the sauce. Pour the vegetables from the strainer into the bowl and mix in the egg whites thoroughly. Form the mixture into patties, using about 1 cup for each. Place the patties in a nonstick frypan over a medium flame, and brown them on both sides. As the patties are done, keep them warm in foil in an oven.

SAUCE

   reserved vegetable liquid
   2 cups defatted beef stock (page 88)
   1 tablespoon cornstarch dissolved in ¼ cup beef stock or
   water

Add the beef stock to the reserved liquid in the saucepan and bring to a boil. Add the cornstarch solution and continue to cook until the sauce thickens. Pour the sauce over the patties and serve.

✎§ VEGETABLE MEDALLIONS

Can't live without burgers? Well, these medallions are made to order for burger-lovers: they can be served on buns or in whole-wheat pita pockets, taken on picnics, even stored for use the next day if you wish. And for condiments, instead of ketchup (which is made with lots of sugar) you can use the sauce on the following page, plus the traditional lettuce, fresh tomato, and so on. Just to make that quintessential American meal complete, serve the medallion-burgers with my fat-free French fries (page 225).

Makes 6–8 patties

1 cup fresh or frozen green beans, cut into ¼-inch lengths
1 cup fresh or frozen asparagus, cut into ¼-inch lengths
1 cup celery, cut in ¼-inch chunks
1 cup frozen cut corn
1 cup scraped and shredded carrots
1 cup frozen peas
1 small can water chestnuts, drained and chopped into medium pieces
4 cloves garlic, peeled and chopped fine
1 onion, peeled and chopped into small chunks
1 tablespoon grated fresh ginger
1 teaspoon basil
¼ teaspoon celery seed
1 tablespoon Dijon mustard
1 tablespoon reduced-salt tamari or soy sauce
1 cup defatted chicken stock (page 86), beef stock (page 88), or water
3 egg whites
2 cups toasted and crumbled sourdough or whole-wheat bread

Place all the ingredients except the egg whites and bread crumbs in a 1½–2-quart pot, and steam for 10 minutes. Put the steamed blend in a strainer over a bowl, and allow it to cool and drain completely. Reserve the liquid for the sauce. Mix the cooled vegetable mixture with the egg whites and bread crumbs in a large bowl. Form into patties, using approximately 1 cup of the mixture at a time, and place the patties on a nonstick baking sheet. Bake for 20 minutes at 350°F.

SAUCE

reserved juice from cooking the vegetables
1 35-ounce can crushed tomatoes in heavy puree
1 tablespoon Dijon mustard
1 tablespoon frozen apple-juice concentrate, partially thawed
1 onion, peeled and chopped fine
½ teaspoon celery seed
2 cloves garlic, peeled and chopped fine
1 tablespoon fine-chopped fresh parsley
1 tablespoon reduced-salt tamari or soy sauce

Combine all the ingredients and simmer over low heat for 15 to 20 minutes. Serve hot with Vegetable Medallions.

◄§ SWEET-AND-SOUR STUFFED CABBAGE

This is my version of my mother's favorite recipe—in fact, I practically grew up on stuffed cabbage. At any rate, this one's got all the flavor of Mom's original, but none of the fat or cholesterol.

Serves 4–6

- 1 **head green cabbage**
- ½ **cup brown rice**
- ½ **cup wild rice**
- ½ **cup millet**
- ½ **cup lentils**
- 5 **cups defatted chicken stock (page 86) or water**
- 1 **carrot, scraped and chopped**
- 2 **celery stalks, chopped fine**
- 1 **onion, sliced thin**
- 1 **bell pepper, chopped**
- 1 **tomato, quartered and diced**
- 4 **cloves garlic, chopped fine**
- a **pinch of cinnamon**
- 1 **teaspoon vanilla**
- 1 **teaspoon Dijon mustard**
- 1 **tablespoon reduced-salt tamari or soy sauce**

Place cabbage in a 1½–2-quart pot with 2 inches of water, and steam, covered, for 15 minutes or until the cabbage is slightly tender. Put the grains and the lentils in a pot, add 4½ cups chicken stock or water, cover, and cook for 45 minutes, steaming lightly. Stir-fry the vegetables, garlic, and seasonings in ½ cup chicken stock and tamari over a low flame for about 8 to 10 minutes, or until the liquid is gone. Combine the vegetable mixture, mustard, and cooked grain-and-lentil mixture in a bowl. Place ½ to ¾ cup of this mixture on a cabbage leaf (with the stem pointed toward you), fold the stem portion over the filling, tuck in the sides, and roll the packet forward until the mixture is enclosed. (Use a toothpick to secure the ends of the leaf.) Place the rolls in a baking dish. Pour ½ the sauce (See below) over the rolls. Cover and bake 45 minutes at 325°F. Pour the remaining sauce over the rolls before serving.

SAUCE

> 8 fresh tomatoes, cored and quartered *or* 1 16-ounce can crushed tomatoes in heavy puree
> 4 cloves garlic, peeled and chopped fine
> 2 teaspoons sweet basil
> ½ teaspoon celery seed
> 2 tablespoons lemon juice
> 1 tablespoon rice or apple-cider vinegar
> 2 tablespoons frozen apple-juice concentrate, partially thawed
> 1 tablespoon reduced-salt tamari or soy sauce
> ½ teaspoon ground cardamom

Combine all ingredients in a saucepan. Cover and cook over a low flame for 15 minutes.

❧ STUFFED BELL PEPPERS

Serves 4–6

  6 **bell peppers**
  2 **cups kasha (buckwheat groats)**
  ½ **cup lentils**
  4½ **cups defatted chicken stock (page 86), vegetable stock (page 90), or water**
  ½ **onion, chopped fine**
  4 **cloves garlic, peeled and chopped fine**
  ½ **cup chopped water chestnuts**
  ¼ **cup fine-chopped parsley**
  1 **tablespoon reduced-salt tamari or soy sauce**
  a dash of **Tabasco**
  1 **tablespoon dry sherry**
  1 **teaspoon Dijon mustard**
  2 **egg whites**
  1 **tomato, cut in ½-inch slices**
  1 **cup whole-wheat or sourdough bread crumbs**

Cut the tops off the peppers and carefully scoop out the seeds and core. Cook the kasha and lentils in 4 cups stock or water for 20 minutes. Sauté the onion, garlic, and water chestnuts in ½ cup stock for 15 minutes or until the liquid is gone. Allow to cool. Combine the vegetables, grains, parsley, tamari, Tabasco, sherry, and mustard with the egg whites in a bowl. Stuff the bell peppers with this mixture, filling the pepper cavities completely. Place the stuffed peppers in a baking pan, garnish the top of each with a tomato slice, and sprinkle with bread crumbs. Add ¼ inch water to the bottom of the baking pan. Cover with aluminum foil and bake 40 minutes at 325°F. Serve alone or with Spanish Sauce (page 257) or Italian Sauce (page 251).

Seafood and Poultry Entrées

Dinner can be the most disheartening time of day for newcomers to a fat-free diet. Most novices feel themselves limited to a no-frills plate of steamed vegetables. But there's no reason to put up with the bare-plate syndrome, or with anemic-looking entrées that are as tasteless as they are uninspiring. Leaf through the following chapter—you'll find recipes for dishes you never thought you'd be able to eat on your diet: things like Chicken Kiev, Cioppino . . . even Lobster Bahamian Cream! You'll be able to do Italian dishes like fettuccine and cannelloni; and for the holidays, a sumptuous roast turkey with sweet potato pie. Serve these with stir-fried vegetables and you'll have evening meals that will be not only superbly healthful, but rich enough in flavor to be applauded even by the most discriminating gourmet.

Because of their high fat and cholesterol content, red meats such as beef, pork, and lamb are not used in this book (the exception is defatted beef stock, from which all fats have been removed). For those whose diets allow animal protein, "white" meats such as poultry, fish, and lobster are more healthful substitutes, in that they contain half or less as much fat and cholesterol as red meats. Followers of stricter diets should eat dishes from this chapter only once a week (Remember that I've already calculated the amounts of protein per serving, so if you stick to one serving a week you don't have to worry about exceeding a 1½-ounce-per-week allowance). Followers of other diets based on similar principles should consult the charts in those diets to determine permissible amounts of animal protein.

Fish

Fish is one of the world's most healthful and efficient sources of vital protein. Of all sources of animal protein, white fishes are among the lowest in fats and cholesterol, while such darker fishes as salmon and swordfish still have less than half the fat and cholesterol content of red meat. You should, however, check your diet for the amount of animal protein allowed in order to decide how frequently to eat these dishes.

One thing should be clear: there's nothing wrong with frozen fish. If you can get your fish fresh, so much the better, because it does tend to be more flavorful. But if the only fish available is frozen, that's fine: the only thing freezing does to a fish is dry it out; there's no change whatsoever in its nutritional value.

By the way, don't worry about substituting one white fish for another in these recipes. If the recipe calls for halibut and all that's available is flounder, then go right ahead: use the flounder. Any white fish will substitute for any other white fish. (This is not true, however, for the darker fishes. Swordfish, for example, is not an acceptable substitute for salmon.)

A final word about cooking fish: how to tell when it's done. I prefer the color method: when a fish, no matter what variety, changes from its original color to a lighter shade of the same color, it's ready. When it starts to dry out, it's over-cooked.

✍§ BAKED FISH

This recipe gives you a simple, basic, and flavorful way to prepare fish without fat, oil, or butter.

Serves 4–6

6 3-ounce fillets of red snapper, sea bass, cod, haddock, swordfish, or any lean fish
3 lemons, cut in ¼-inch slices

Take a large piece of aluminum foil approximately 18 inches long and place a layer of lemon slices on half of it, making a bed large enough for the fish. Lay the fish on top of the lemon slices and then put more slices on top. Fold the foil over the fish carefully and seal the edges completely. Bake in a 350°F. oven for 20 minutes.

✍§ TOASTED FISH FILLETS

Here's a low-fat version of good old fried fish, but done without greasy oils. Serve it with my fat-free French fries (page 225), and you've got fish and chips!

Serves 4–6

2 egg whites
1 teaspoon reduced-salt tamari or soy sauce
a dash of paprika
1 pound white fish fillets, cut into strips
½ cup nonfat milk
½ cup whole-wheat flour
1 cup bread crumbs

Beat the egg whites lightly with the tamari, and sprinkle with paprika. Dip the fish fillets in the nonfat milk, then in the whole-wheat flour, next in the egg-white mixture, and finally in the bread crumbs, being sure to coat the fillets thoroughly. Lay the fish out flat on a nonstick cookie sheet. Bake 20 minutes at 350°F.

Serve with Italian Sauce (page 251).

❧ RED SNAPPER À LA MEUNIÈRE

Serves 4–6

- ¼ bell pepper, chopped
- ¼ onion, chopped
- 4 medium tomatoes, peeled and chopped
- 1 jalapeño pepper, seeded and chopped fine
- 2 cloves garlic, minced fine
- 3 tablespoons chopped fresh cilantro or parsley
- ½ teaspoon oregano
- ¼ teaspoon cinnamon
- 1 cup defatted chicken stock (page 86), fish stock (page 89), or water
- 1 tablespoon lemon juice
- 1 whole red snapper or ocean trout, head removed, cleaned and scaled *or* 1–1½ pounds snapper or ocean trout fillets

In a large frying pan, sauté the vegetables, herbs, and cinnamon in the stock and lemon juice until the onions and peppers are tender. Very carefully, lay the fish in the sauce and reduce the heat to a low simmer. Simmer for 6 minutes on each side. Do not overcook. Serve hot.

✎§ BAKED HADDOCK AND VEGETABLES

Serves 6–8

1 pound haddock fillets
1 chili pepper, seeded and chopped
½ onion, sliced thin
½ bell pepper, chopped
1 1-pound can crushed tomatoes in heavy puree
1 teaspoon basil
1 carrot, scraped and chopped
1 tablespoon lemon juice

Mix all the ingredients except the fish together in a bowl. This will make a saucy mixture. Pour ½ the mixture into a 2-quart covered baking dish and place the fish on top. Pour the remainder of the sauce on top of the fish and bake in a 350°F. oven for 25 minutes or until the fish changes to a lighter color.

✑§ FISH CHOWDER

Serves 6–8

4 cups defatted chicken stock (page 86) or fish stock (page 89)
2 teaspoons basil
1 teaspoon oregano
2 bay leaves, crumbled
¼ bunch fresh parsley or cilantro, chopped
2 cloves garlic, minced fine
2 carrots, scraped and chopped
1 chili pepper, seeds removed, chopped
½ onion, chopped
½ bell pepper, chopped
3 stalks celery, chopped
1 16-ounce can crushed tomatoes in heavy puree (no salt)
1 whole fish (sea bass, red snapper, halibut) weighing about 2 pounds, with head, backbone, and tail removed and set aside for broth, *or* 2 pounds fish fillets, cut into ½-inch chunks
¼ cup dry sherry
juice of 1 lemon

Bring the stock to a boil in a 2½–3-quart pot. Add the herbs and vegetables, except the tomatoes, and simmer for 30 minutes. Add the tomatoes and fish and simmer again for 20 minutes. Add the dry sherry and simmer another 5 minutes. Add lemon juice. Do not overcook this chowder. Serve steaming hot with brown rice or boiled potatoes.

✑§ CIOPPINO

As I searched for new dishes that could be modified for a low-fat diet, I remembered the cioppino I had eaten when I lived in an Italian-American fishing community on the Northern California coast. It delighted me no end that this traditional fisherman's dinner could now be easily converted to a low-fat version.

Serves 8–10

½ onion, chopped
2 cloves garlic, minced fine
½ green pepper, chopped
1 chili pepper, seeded and chopped
6 tomatoes, cored and chopped
2 teaspoons oregano
1 teaspoon thyme
½ teaspoon rosemary
1 tablespoon sweet basil
4 cups defatted chicken stock (page 86) or fish stock (page 89)
¼ cup Marsala wine
1 pound halibut, cut into chunks (any solid-meat fish may be used)
½ small can deveined cocktail shrimp, drained
½ small lobster tail, cut into chunks *or* 1 small can lobster tail

Using a large pan, sauté the onion, garlic, peppers, tomatoes, and herbs in ½ cup of the stock until the vegetables are tender. Add the Marsala, cover, and simmer for 10 minutes. Add the fish, shrimp, and remaining stock. Cook, covered, for an additional 15 minutes. Uncover, add the lobster, and simmer 5 minutes longer. Serve with garlic bread.

◀ξ FISH-BALL-AND-NOODLE STEW

Serves 4–6

4 cups defatted chicken stock (page 86) or fish stock (page 89)

1 tablespoon lemon juice

1 pound raw fish fillets (cod, haddock, or pike), cut into chunks

¼ onion, chopped

¼ bell pepper, chopped

1 stalk celery, chopped

2 cloves garlic, minced fine

¼ pound bean sprouts

¼ cup frozen peas

½ can bamboo shoots

2 egg whites

¼ bunch cilantro

2 scallions, sliced

2 slices whole-wheat or sourdough bread, toasted and crumbled

Bring the stock and lemon juice to a boil in a large pot. Meanwhile, place the fish in a food processor or blender and turn into a medium paste. Add the onion, pepper, celery, and garlic and blend once again. Turn into a bowl and mix in the bread crumbs. Wet your hands with cold water, take 1 tablespoon fish mixture, roll into a small ball, and drop into the boiling stock. Repeat until all the fish paste is used. Five minutes before serving, drop the bean sprouts, peas, and bamboo shoots into the boiling stock with the fish balls. Put the stew in a serving bowl. Simmer for 5 minutes. Stir the egg whites in a bowl. DO NOT BEAT! Drop 1 tablespoon egg white at a time on top of the fish-stock soup to make egg flowers. Sprinkle with the scallions and cilantro. Serve with whole-wheat or semolina-flour cooked noodles. For a delightful variation, chill the fish balls (without the broth) and serve with horse-radish. Presto! Gefiltefish!

❦ HALIBUT CREOLE

Serves 6–8

½ onion, chopped
½ bell pepper, chopped
2 stalks celery, chopped
2 cloves garlic, minced fine
2 tomatoes, diced
1 15-ounce can crushed tomatoes in heavy puree (no salt added)
2 tablespoons dry sherry
1 tablespoon chopped parsley
½ teaspoon thyme
1 chili pepper, seeded and chopped
1 pound halibut or whitefish, cut into bite-size pieces

Combine the onion, pepper, celery, garlic, tomatoes (fresh and canned), and sherry in a saucepan. Simmer until the onion becomes clear. Add the parsley, thyme, and chili pepper and cook the sauce for 2 minutes. Add the fish and allow to simmer for 10 minutes, turning after 5 minutes. Serve about 1 cupful per person over steamed rice.

❦ FLOUNDER ROLLS FLORENTINE

At a time when I was working in a fine dinner house, I was asked to come up with a light but unusual dinner. Well, the fresh flounder was in, so I decided to complement it with florentine stuffing—low-fat, of course—and give the dish a special eye appeal by rolling the fish. The customers, by the way, had no idea that they were eating a low-fat dish, and they loved it!

Serves 6–8

6–8 flounder fillets, weighing 3 ounces each
1 cup dry cottage cheese
1 tablespoon arrowroot powder or cornstarch
1 bunch fresh spinach, washed thoroughly and chopped
3 scallions, sliced thin
2 cloves garlic, minced fine
1 tablespoon capers (optional)
1 tablespoon tamari
¼ teaspoon thyme
2 slices whole-wheat or sourdough bread, toasted and crumbled

In a blender, blend the cheese with the arrowroot or cornstarch until smooth. Turn into a bowl and mix with the rest of the ingredients, except for the fish. Divide the mixture among the flounder fillets, putting an equal amount in the center of each. Roll up the fillets and secure each with a toothpick. Dip the rolled flounder in the bread crumbs and bake for 20 minutes in a 350°F. oven.

✎ SALMON CRÊPES WITH LIGHT HOLLANDAISE SAUCE

If you go to a fine restaurant in Stockholm or Copenhagen, you may well find this dish served as an appetizer.

Serves 4–6

1 7–8-ounce can red salmon
1 pound dry cottage cheese
1 small jar pimento, rinsed in cold water and chopped

¼ cup whole-wheat flour
½ cup nonfat milk
½ cup nonfat dry milk
a dash of cayenne
½ tablespoon reduced-salt tamari or soy sauce
6 egg whites, beaten stiff
1 recipe crêpes (page 294)

Place all the ingredients except the egg whites and crêpes in a blender. Blend until smooth. Fold in the egg whites. Place ¾ cup of this mixture in each crêpe. Roll the crêpes and put them in a nonstick baking dish. Cover and bake 25 minutes at 325°F.

Light Hollandaise Sauce

2 cups defatted chicken stock (page 86) cooked down to ½ cup liquid
2 cups nonfat yogurt (page 72)
⅛ teaspoon turmeric
dash Dijon mustard
1 tablespoon lemon juice

Warm stock and yogurt slowly, stirring in spices and lemon juice. DO NOT BOIL. Pour ½ cup over each crêpe and serve immediately.

✎§ SALMON-RICE PATTIES

- 1 16-ounce can red salmon, bones and skin removed
- 2 egg whites
- ½ onion, chopped
- 2 cloves garlic, minced fine
- 1 tablespoon lemon juice
- ½ teaspoon celery seed
- 1 tablespoon tamari
- 1 tablespoon frozen apple-juice concentrate
- 1 teaspoon sweet basil
- 1 cup frozen peas, thawed
- 1 small can water chestnuts, drained and chopped
- 2 carrots, scraped and sliced
- 2 cups cooked brown rice (for a slight variation in flavor, whole-wheat bread crumbs may be substituted)

Mix all the above ingredients together in a bowl; this should be a moist and sticky mixture. With an ice cream scoop or small open teacup dipped in cold water, press scoopfuls of the mixture and release them on a nonstick baking sheet. Bake in a 350°F. oven for 20 minutes.

SAUCE

- 2 tablespoons dry sherry
- 2 cups defatted chicken stock (page 86)
- 1 tablespoon tamari
- 2 tablespoons nonfat dry milk
- ½ onion, chopped
- ½ cup frozen green peas
- ½ jar pimento, chopped
- 2 cloves garlic, minced fine
- 2 tablespoons capers (optional)
- 1 teaspoon curry powder
- 2 teaspoons arrowroot powder or cornstarch dissolved in 2 tablespoons of water

Bring the sherry, stock, tamari, and dry milk to a boil and add the vegetables and seasonings. Simmer for 10 minutes or until the onions are clear. Then add the arrowroot or cornstarch solution to the sauce and stir until thickened. Serve this hot over the salmon-rice patties.

✌§ TUNA-RICE SALAD

Serves 4–6

- 1 8–10-ounce can water-packed tuna
- 1 stalk celery, chopped
- 3 scallions, sliced fine
- 1 chili pepper, seeded and chopped
- 1 clove garlic, minced fine
- 1 tablespoon lemon juice
- ½ teaspoon celery seed
- 1 tablespoon reduced-salt tamari or soy sauce
- 1 tablespoon frozen apple-juice concentrate, partially thawed
- 1 teaspoon sweet basil
- 1 cup frozen peas, thawed
- 1 small can water chestnuts, chopped
- 2 carrots, scraped and sliced
- 2 cups cooked brown rice

Mix all the ingredients together in a mixing bowl. Press into an ice cream dipper or cup, dipped in cold water, and release on a lettuce leaf. For added color, garnish with tomato slices dipped in fine-chopped parsley.

❧ TUNA-POTATO SALAD

Serves 4–6

2 medium red or white baking potatoes, cut into ½-inch cubes
1 onion, cut into 1-inch cubes
¼ bell pepper, chopped
2 stalks celery, diced
½ cup frozen green peas, thawed *or* ½ cup fresh peas, steamed 8 minutes
1 6½-ounce can water-packed tuna, drained
1 teaspoon paprika
2 cloves garlic, minced fine
1 chili pepper, seeded and chopped
2 tablespoons diced pimento
1 tablespoon frozen apple-juice concentrate
1 cup nonfat yogurt (page 72)
romaine lettuce

Boil the potato cubes in 2 cups of water for 30 minutes. Set aside. In a separate bowl, mix all the other ingredients until they are creamy. Spoon this mixture over the potatoes. Chill and serve on a bed of romaine lettuce leaves.

Shellfish

Like fish, shellfish is one of the world's most efficient sources of protein. In terms of cholesterol content, shrimp is the highest (almost as high as red meat, in fact), and should be eaten only in due moderation. That's why the recommended serving in the following recipes is only 2 per person. Crabmeat has a lower cholesterol content, and lobster's is lower still—about half that of shrimp. Mollusks such as mussels, clams, and oysters don't appear here at all—they are much too high in cholesterol. In any case, follow the guidelines of your particular diet very closely in determining how often and in what amounts you can eat any shellfish.

✑ LOBSTER VERONA

Serves 4–6

½ onion, sliced thin
½ bell pepper, sliced thin
2 cloves garlic, minced fine
½ cup defatted chicken stock (page 86) or water
6 fresh tomatoes, peeled and seeded
1 tablespoon reduced-salt tamari or soy sauce
1 teaspoon sweet basil
½ teaspoon oregano
½ teaspoon thyme
1 tablespoon dry sherry
¼ cup whole-wheat flour
2 lobster tails, removed from shell

Sauté the onion, pepper, and garlic in the stock until the onions are clear. Add the tomatoes, tamari, and herbs. Simmer for 10 minutes. Then add the sherry. Cut the lobster into 1-inch chunks, dust with whole-wheat flour, and place in the sauce. Slowly simmer for 5 minutes. DO NOT OVERCOOK. Serve with brown rice or whole-wheat noodles.

✑ LOBSTER DIJON

Because of the lobster, the sherry, and the brandy, this dish sounds almost too rich to be true for someone on a low-fat diet. Well, it's rich, all right, but the richness is all in the flavor. Actually, the whole recipe has less fat and cholesterol than one bite of a hot dog! (By the way, it's okay to use the sherry and brandy because the sugar in them cooks out with the alcohol.)

Serves 4–6

2 cups defatted chicken stock (page 86) *or* lobster shell and
   body, cooked in 1 quart water for 30 minutes and strained
   for 1 pint of clear broth
1 clove garlic, minced fine
½ chili pepper, seeds removed and minced fine
1 tablespoon Dijon mustard (salt-free)
½ small onion, minced fine
¼ bell pepper, sliced very thin (optional)
1 tablespoon frozen apple-juice concentrate
2 lobster tails (shell removed), cut into 1-inch chunks
2 tablespoons dry sherry
1 teaspoon brandy
1 tablespoon arrowroot powder dissolved in 2 tablespoons
   cold water

Bring the stock to a boil in a 1½–2-quart pot and add the garlic, chili pepper, mustard, onions, bell pepper, and apple-juice concentrate. Simmer for 15 minutes or until the onion is clear. Drop in the lobster meat. Stir occasionally, add sherry, brandy, and arrowroot, and simmer for 6 minutes. DO NOT OVERCOOK. Serve over brown rice or semolina noodles.

◄§ LOBSTER BAHAMIAN CREAM

Of all the recipes in this book, I'd have to call this one the *pièce de résistance.* I cooked it for a group of executives who were cruising the Caribbean on a private yacht, and after the meal, they actually called me into the dining room and applauded!

Serves 6

2 lobster tails (¾ pound each), removed from shells and cut into 1-inch chunks

2 cups defatted chicken stock (page 86) *or* lobster shell and body, cooked in 1 quart water for 30 minutes and strained for 1 pint of clear broth

1 cup frozen peas

1 carrot, scraped and sliced thin

½ onion, sliced thin

1 chili pepper, seeded and chopped

1 clove garlic, minced fine

1 tablespoon arrowroot powder dissolved in 2 tablespoons cold water

3 tablespoons nonfat dry milk dissolved in ½ cup water

1 tablespoon dry sherry

1 tablespoon reduced-salt tamari or soy sauce

Bring the stock to a boil in a large pot and add the peas, carrot, onion, chili pepper, and garlic. Cook for 20 minutes over a medium flame. Add the arrowroot solution, reduce the heat, and add the nonfat milk. Add the lobster chunks, sherry, and tamari and simmer for 5 to 6 minutes. DO NOT OVER-COOK. Serve over Rice Pilaf (page 239) or Wild and Brown Rice (page 243).

✥§ SHRIMP SCAMPI

Serves 6–8

>   1 16-ounce can crushed tomatoes in heavy puree *or* 4 fresh
>   tomatoes, skinned, seeded, and chopped fine
>   12 large or 16 medium uncooked shrimp
>   3 cloves garlic, peeled and minced fine
>   ½ onion, chopped
>   1 bell pepper, chopped
>   1 tablespoon sweet basil
>   2 teaspoons oregano
>   1 teaspoon thyme
>   1 jalapeño pepper, seeded and chopped
>   1 teaspoon paprika
>   1 tablespoon reduced-salt tamari or soy sauce (optional)

Shell and devein the shrimp. Place the shells in a pot with 1 quart of water and boil for 30 minutes; then strain. You should have 2 cups of clear broth. Combine the vegetables, spices, and stock in a saucepan and simmer for 20 minutes. Butterfly the shrimp by slicing halfway through the shrimp along the vein line and opening them out. Set the shrimp in the sauce and cook for 4 to 5 minutes. Serve immediately with slices of sourdough toast.

VARIATION: You can make a lower-cholesterol version of this dish by substituting 1½–2 pounds of crab legs for the shrimp. Remove the meat from the shells, cut into 1-inch lengths, and proceed as above.

✥§ CRISPY SHRIMP

If you're a lover of deep-fried shrimp and thought you'd have to give them up when you went on a low-fat diet, don't fret. This recipe will give you back your old favorite, but in a form in which the fats and cholesterol have been greatly reduced.

Serves 6–8

12 large or 16 medium shrimp, shelled, deveined, and butter-flied

in one small bowl: 1 cup nonfat milk, combined with 1 clove garlic, minced fine

on one large plate: ½ cup rice flour or whole-wheat flour

in another small bowl: 2 egg whites, stirred (do not beat), mixed well with 1 chili pepper, seeded and mashed

on another large plate: 2 slices whole-wheat or sourdough bread, toasted and crumbled

Hold each shrimp by the tail and dip into the milk mixture; shake; dip into the flour; shake off the excess; then dip into the egg whites; and finally dip into the bread crumbs. Place on a nonstick baking sheet and bake for 12 minutes in a 350°F. oven.

Serve with the Chinese sauces found on pages 128–29.

VARIATION: You can substitute 1½–2 pounds of crab legs, removed from the shells and cut into 1-inch lengths, for the shrimp.

✒ SHRIMP DIJON

Serves 6–8

12 large or 16 medium shrimp, shelled, deveined, and cut in half lengthwise
 2 cups defatted chicken stock (page 86) *or* the shrimp shells cooked in 1 quart water and boiled for 30 minutes, then strained for 1 pint of clear broth
 1 clove garlic, minced fine
 ½ small onion, minced fine
 ¼ bell pepper, sliced very thin (optional)
 ½ chili pepper, seeded and chopped
 1 tablespoon frozen apple-juice concentrate
 1 tablespoon Dijon mustard (salt-free)
 2 tablespoons dry sherry
 1 teaspoon brandy
 1 tablespoon arrowroot powder dissolved in 2 tablespoons water

Bring the stock to a boil in a 1½–2-quart pot, and add the garlic, onion, bell pepper, and chili pepper. Simmer for 15 minutes; then add the apple-juice concentrate, mustard, sherry, and brandy. Drop in the shrimp and simmer for 6 minutes. Stir in the arrowroot solution to thicken the sauce. Serve with brown rice or semolina-flour noodles.

Variation: 1½–2 pounds of crab legs can be substituted for the shrimp, providing a dish with lower cholesterol. Remove the shells, cut the meat in 1-inch lengths, and slice these pieces in half lengthwise. Then proceed as above.

Poultry Entrées

In general, most poultry is lower in fat and cholesterol than red meat; thus its health benefits. A breast of turkey, for example, has less than half the fat and cholesterol of an equal volume of red meat. A word of caution, though: dark poultry meats, such as chicken or turkey legs, and especially "gamy" poultry like duck and goose, can be even *higher* in cholesterol and fat than an equal volume of T-bone steak. So almost all the recipes in this section call for chicken or turkey white meat only. Again, if you're on an exceptionally strict low-fat diet, these dishes should be eaten no more than once a week. That way you'll be taking in no more than 1½ ounces of animal protein on a weekly basis. More lenient low-fat diets may allow more frequent use of poultry, or larger servings.

Actually, although I call this the "poultry section," the truth is that the meat is used more as a flavoring agent than as the main component of the dish. Instead of being the whole orchestra, in other words, the animal protein is reduced to the position where it belongs in terms of good health: somewhere right around second fiddle.

Preparing poultry for cooking is simply a matter of removing the skin. You can do this easily by laying the poultry on its back and making a cut along the full length of the breast with scissors or a knife. Then simply pull the skin back on each side—it's just like taking a sweater off a small child—and the meat will be exposed and ready for cooking. A hint: since the skin tends to be slippery and hard to pull, it helps to grasp it with a dry cloth or paper towel.

❧ CANTONESE-STYLE STIR-FRY WITH CHICKEN

Serves 4

1 cup defatted chicken stock (page 86) or water
6 cloves garlic, peeled and minced fine
1 onion, peeled and slivered lengthwise
4 scallions, slivered lengthwise
2 tablespoons finely grated fresh ginger (about 2 1-inch cubes)
½ teaspoon celery seed
1 head bok choy, with the green leaves quartered and the stalks sliced in ½-inch lengths
1 bell pepper, seeded and sliced thin
½ small can water chestnuts, drained and sliced
½ small can bamboo shoots, drained and sliced
½ pound mushrooms, sliced thin
1 pound fresh or 1 package frozen snow peas
1 whole chicken breast (all skin and fat removed), boned and cut into ½-inch strips
1 pound bean sprouts, rinsed in cold water
1 tablespoon reduced-salt tamari or soy sauce
1 tablespoon frozen apple-juice concentrate, partially thawed
1 tablespoon arrowroot powder or cornstarch dissolved in ½ cup chicken stock or water

Put the chicken stock or water, garlic, onion, ginger, and celery seed in a 2½–3-quart pot or wok. Heat until the liquid begins to boil; then add the bok choy, bell pepper, water chestnuts, and bamboo shoots. Stir thoroughly and simmer for 3 minutes; then add the mushrooms, snow peas, chicken, and bean sprouts. Cook and stir until the vegetables are bright in color and fragrant (about 4 minutes).

Finally, add the tamari, apple-juice concentrate, and arrowroot solution and continue to stir until the sauce thickens.

Serve over brown rice or whole-wheat or semolina-flour noodles. Like many Chinese foods, this recipe is good cold or reheated the next day.

⇜§ CHICKEN RATATOUILLE

Serves 4–6

- 1 cup defatted chicken stock (page 86) or water
- 2 whole chicken breasts, skinned, boned, and cut into 1-inch pieces
- 2 small unpeeled zucchini, sliced thin
- 1 small eggplant, peeled and cut into 1-inch cubes
- 1 large onion, sliced thin
- 1 medium bell pepper, seeded and cut into 1-inch pieces
- ½ pound mushrooms, sliced
- 3 whole tomatoes, cut into wedges
- 4 cloves garlic, minced fine
- 2 teaspoons basil
- 1 teaspoon oregano
- 1 tablespoon reduced-salt tamari or soy sauce
- ¼ teaspoon cayenne pepper

Heat the chicken stock or water in a large skillet and add the chicken. Sauté for about 1 minute on each side. Add the zucchini, eggplant, onion, bell pepper, and mushrooms and cook for 15 minutes or until tender, stirring occasionally. Add the tomato wedges, garlic, basil, oregano, tamari, and cayenne. Simmer for 5 minutes. Serve with hot rice.

❧ CHICKEN-AND-CHEESE ENCHILADAS

Makes 8-12 enchiladas, to serve 4-6

8 corn tortillas

SAUCE

1 small onion, chopped
1 clove garlic, minced fine
2 tablespoons minced fresh jalapeño pepper
1 teaspoon basil
1 teaspoon oregano
1 teaspoon coriander
1 teaspoon paprika
2 teaspoons cumin
2 teaspoons chili pepper
⅛ teaspoon cayenne pepper
½ cup defatted chicken stock (page 86)
½ cup tomato juice (no salt)
1 1-pound can tomatoes (no salt)
2 tablespoons tomato paste

Sauté the onion, garlic, jalapeño pepper, herbs, and spices in the stock until the vegetables are tender. Add the tomato juice and simmer an additional 10 minutes. In a blender, puree the tomatoes and tomato paste. Add to the sauce and continue to simmer for 10 minutes at low temperature.

FILLING

1 pound dry cottage cheese
½ cup grated zucchini (optional)
½ cup chopped tomato
½ pound chicken breast (1 whole breast), skinned, boned, and
    cut into chunks

In a blender, puree the cheese and zucchini until smooth. Then mix in the tomato and chicken.

Dip each tortilla into the warm sauce, put about ½ cup cheese mixture in the middle of each, then roll them up. Place side by side in a baking dish and pour the remaining sauce over the top. Cover securely with aluminum foil. Bake for 30 minutes at 350°F. Serve with fat-free "Refried" Beans (page 234).

✍️ CHICKEN TACOS

Serves 6–8

   2 **cups diced chicken breast (2 whole chicken breasts, bones, skin, and fat removed)**
   2 **fresh tomatoes, cut into cubes**
   ½ **small onion, diced**
   1 **bell pepper, diced**
   1 **tablespoon lemon juice**
   2 **tablespoons chopped cilantro**
   ¼ **teaspoon cumin**
   ¼ **teaspoon Tabasco**
   12 **corn tortillas**
   ¼ **head iceberg lettuce, shredded**
   1 **recipe Salsa Picante (page 258)**

Combine the chicken, vegetables, lemon juice, cilantro, cumin, and Tabasco in a large bowl and marinate in the refrigerator for 1 hour. Take each tortilla and gently bend it so that it is hanging centered on one bar of the oven rack. Toast 6 at a time for 9 minutes in a 350°F. oven. While the tortillas are still warm, place ½ cup chicken-vegetable mixture in each toasted shell. Top with shredded lettuce and Salsa Picante.

ᵥᵇ CHICKEN-VEGETABLE CURRY

Serves 4–6

2 small carrots, scraped and cut into chunks
2 turnips, cut into chunks
½ onion, peeled and diced
1 stalk celery, sliced
2 cups defatted chicken stock (page 86)
1 apple, peeled and grated
1 tablespoon tomato sauce
1 tablespoon frozen apple-juice concentrate, partially thawed
1 tablespoon apple cider vinegar
2 tablespoons curry powder
1 tablespoon chopped fresh ginger
¼ teaspoon thyme
¼ cup currants or raisins (optional)
2 whole chicken breasts
2 tablespoons arrowroot or cornstarch
3 cloves garlic, peeled and minced fine

Using an uncovered skillet, simmer the carrots and turnips in about 3 cups water until they are partially cooked. Add the onion and celery and cook until all the vegetables are tender. Drain and reserve the vegetable broth. Set the vegetables aside. Bring the chicken stock and 1 cup of the reserved vegetable broth to a boil in a large skillet. Add the apple, tomato sauce, apple juice, vinegar, seasonings, and currants or raisins (if used). Cook together over moderate heat for 10 minutes. Slice the chicken breasts across the grain, cut the slices into small chunks, and add to the sauce. Mix the arrowroot or cornstarch with ¼ cup cold water and add to the simmering sauce, stirring constantly until the sauce has thickened. Add the cooked carrots, turnips, onion, and celery and simmer until the vegetables are heated through. By this time, the chicken will be cooked. Serve with brown rice.

ᴥ§ CHICKEN NO-FRIED RICE

Here's a low-fat edition of that old favorite: fried rice. For an unusual taste treat, try serving it with lemon wedges.

Serves 4–6

meat of 1 whole chicken breast (skin and fat removed), cut into ½-inch chunks
½ small onion, chopped
2 cloves garlic, minced fine
1 carrot, scraped and diced
1 cup fresh or frozen peas
2 green onions, chopped
1 stalk celery, chopped
½ teaspoon celery seed
1 teaspoon poultry seasoning
1 tablespoon reduced-salt tamari or soy sauce
1 cup defatted chicken stock (page 86) or water
4 cups cooked brown rice

Sauté all the vegetables and seasonings in the water or stock over moderate heat until the vegetables are about half done. Add the chicken and cook until tender. Add the rice and mix gently. Turn off the heat and let stand to blend the flavors. Serve hot.

⋖§ CHICKEN-SPAGHETTI CASSEROLE

Serves 4–6

> 1 onion, chopped
> 4 cloves garlic, minced
> 1 bell pepper, chopped
> 1 chili pepper without seeds, chopped fine
> 2 teaspoons oregano
> 1 teaspoon basil
> ½ cup defatted chicken stock (page 86)
> 1 12-ounce can tomato puree
> 2 tablespoons tomato paste, diluted in 2 cups water
> 1 whole chicken breast, skin, fat, and bones removed, cut into small pieces
> ½ package whole-wheat spaghetti or semolina-flour noodles
> 1 pound dry cottage cheese

Place the onion, garlic, bell pepper, chili pepper, herbs, and stock in a saucepan and cook over medium heat, stirring until browned. Add the tomato puree and diluted tomato paste. Cook 20 minutes; then add the chicken. Cook over a low flame for 5 minutes longer.

Cook the spaghetti until *al dente.* Drain. Turn the spaghetti into a bowl and mix it with the cheese. Put half the sauce in the bottom of a 2-quart baking dish. Add the spaghetti and cheese, and top with the remaining sauce. Cover and bake 20 minutes at 350°F. Serve with garlic toast (page 304).

✌§ CHICKEN RAMEN

Serves 4–6

5–6 cups defatted chicken stock (page 86) or water
  ½ package whole-wheat or semolina-flour noodles
  1 medium onion, cut into chunks
  1 celery stalk, sliced
  1 cup chopped leeks
 10 mushrooms, sliced
  2 bell peppers, cut into chunks
  1 9-ounce package frozen artichoke hearts, centers and fiber removed
  1 cup chopped bok choy or cabbage, cut into ½-inch strips
  1 cup fresh *or* 1 6-ounce package frozen snow peas
  1 can water chestnuts, drained and sliced
  1 can bamboo shoots, drained and sliced
  2 cloves garlic, minced fine
  1 cup diced chicken (1 whole chicken breast, skin, bones, and fat removed)
 ¼ cup chopped cilantro (optional)
  1 tablespoon reduced-salt tamari or soy sauce
  1 tablespoon chopped fresh ginger
 ¼ teaspoon chili powder

Bring the broth or water to a boil and add the noodles, onion, celery, leeks, and mushrooms. Cook, uncovered, over high heat for 10 minutes. When vegetables are almost tender, add the bell pepper, artichoke hearts, bok choy, snow peas, water chestnuts, bamboo shoots, garlic, and chicken. Stirring frequently, allow the vegetables to cook until tender. Season with the rest of the spices and serve hot.

◄§ CHICKEN GUMBO

I was once invited to a party in Baton Rouge, Louisiana—the heart of Cajun country. Since the hostess knew that I was a specialist in low-fat cooking, she challenged me to come up with a Louisiana-style gumbo that would measure up to Creole tastes. This recipe is the outcome of that challenge. (P.S.: It was a great hit at the party!)

Serves 4–6

½ cup whole-wheat flour
2 quarts defatted chicken stock (page 86) or water
1 onion, chopped fine
6 cloves garlic, minced fine
1 teaspoon sweet basil
2 carrots, cut into ½-inch chunks
1 cup okra (fresh, frozen, or canned)
1 bell pepper with seeds removed, cut into small pieces
1 chili pepper with seeds removed and chopped fine (optional)
1 cup lentils (optional)
1 whole chicken breast with skin removed and all fat trimmed off
3 tablespoons gumbo filé
2 tablespoons reduced-salt tamari or soy sauce

Toast the flour in a saucepan over a low flame, stirring constantly, for 3 minutes. Slowly add 1 cup chicken stock or water to make roux. Put the onion and garlic in a 2½–3-quart pot and cook until clarified. Add the remaining stock or water, along with the roux, the basil, and all the vegetables. If you are using lentils, add them now. Cook over a low flame for 1 hour. Bone the chicken, cut it into small pieces, and add them to the pot. Add the gumbo filé and tamari. Simmer 15 minutes longer. Serve with ½ cup cooked long-grain brown rice in each bowl.

◆§ CHICKEN CRÊPES WITH MUSHROOM SAUCE

Serves 4–6

1 whole chicken breast with skin, fat, and bones removed
1 pound dry cottage cheese
½ cup nonfat milk
½ cup nonfat dry milk
1 tablespoon arrowroot powder or cornstarch
½ teaspoon basil
⅛ teaspoon sage
1 tablespoon reduced-salt tamari or soy sauce
1 recipe crêpes (page 294)

Place all ingredients except the crêpes in a blender or food processor. Puree until smooth and thick. Place ¾ cup of this mixture in each crêpe. Roll the crêpes and place in a nonstick baking dish. Cover with aluminum foil and bake for 20 minutes at 350°F. Serve with Mushroom Sauce (page 252).

~§ CHICKEN SOUFFLÉ

Serves 4–6

½ **pound dry cottage cheese or 1 cup nonfat yogurt (page 72)**
1 **whole 6–8-ounce chicken breast, skin, bones and fat removed, cut in chunks**
4 **ounces nonfat evaporated milk**
1 **tablespoon oat flour or whole-wheat flour**
1 **tablespoon frozen apple-juice concentrate, partially thawed**
1 **tablespoon reduced-salt tamari or soy sauce**
1 **teaspoon basil**
¼ **teaspoon sage**
¼ **teaspoon dillweed**
a **dash of Tabasco or cayenne pepper**
6 **egg whites**
½ **cup whole-wheat or sourdough bread crumbs**

Place the cottage cheese or yogurt in a blender or food processor. Add the chicken and evaporated milk. Blend until smooth. Slowly stir in the flour, frozen apple-juice concentrate, tamari, herbs, and Tabasco or cayenne. In a separate bowl beat the egg whites until stiff. Fold the egg whites gently into the blended mixture. Pour into a 2-quart baking dish, sprinkle bread crumbs over the top, and bake at 350°F. for 20 minutes. Serve with Mushroom Sauce (page 252).

⋙ CHICKEN-RICE CASSEROLE

Serves 4–6

- **1 onion, chopped**
- **1 cup chopped celery**
- **1 can water chestnuts, drained and sliced**
- **1 cup defatted chicken stock (page 86) or water**
- **½ teaspoon sage**
- **a dash of rosemary**
- **1 package frozen peas (no salt)**
- **1 12-ounce can tomato puree**
- **1 whole chicken breast with skin, fat, and bones removed, cut into small pieces**
- **3–4 cups cooked brown rice (page 237)**
- **6 egg whites, beaten stiff**

Sauté the onion, celery, and water chestnuts with stock in a saucepan until thoroughly cooked. Stir in the sage, rosemary, and peas, cooking over a low flame for 5 minutes. Add the tomato puree and the chicken. Put the cooked rice in a large bowl, mix in tomato-chicken sauce and fold in the egg whites. Place in a 1½-quart baking dish, cover, and bake for 30 minutes at 350°F.

~§ CHICKEN-MILLET SUPREME

Although it is a basic staple food in many parts of the world, the use of millet is very limited in this country. Actually, it's one of my favorites in the grain family. It's got about half the fat of oats, is very high in protein, and has a delicious, nutty flavor that can be enhanced still further by toasting.

Serves 4–6

1 whole chicken breast, skin, fat, and bones removed, cut into 1-inch cubes
1 bunch broccoli, cut into florets
1 pound fresh mushrooms, sliced
1 onion, chopped
4 cups cooked millet (page 245)
2 carrots, scraped and sliced thin
4 cloves garlic, minced
1 pound dry cottage cheese
1 tablespoon reduced-salt tamari or soy sauce
a dash of cayenne
2 tomatoes, sliced
½ cup whole-wheat or sourdough bread crumbs
1 6-ounce (¾ cup) can dietetic V-8 or dietetic tomato juice

Mix the chicken, broccoli, mushrooms, onion, millet, carrots, garlic, cottage cheese, tamari, and cayenne thoroughly and place in a 2-quart casserole. Lay slices of tomato on top and sprinkle on bread crumbs. Pour V-8 or tomato juice over the entire surface and cover. Bake 20 minutes at 350°F. Uncover and bake 5 minutes longer.

⋍§ CHICKEN IN THE POT

Serves 6–8

1 3-pound broiler chicken (skin and fat removed), dusted with whole-wheat flour
½ onion, sliced thin
1 teaspoon chopped fresh dill
1 sprig fresh parsley
1 tomato, peeled and diced
2 carrots, scraped and cut into chunks
2 celery stalks, cut into chunks
2 new potatoes, cut into chunks
½ cup dry white wine
3 cups defatted chicken stock (page 86) or water
1 tablespoon lemon juice
1 bay leaf
1 jalapeño pepper, seeded and chopped

Place the chicken in a Dutch oven and add the onion, dill, and parsley. Arrange the tomato, carrots, celery, and potatoes around the chicken. Then add the wine and stock, lemon juice, bay leaf, and jalapeño pepper. Cover tightly and bake for 1 hour at 350°F. or until chicken is tender. Serve with matzoh balls (See below).

MATZOH BALLS

1 cup matzoh meal
2 egg whites
¼ teaspoon reduced-salt tamari or soy sauce
¼ teaspoon baking powder

Mix all the ingredients together in a mixing bowl. Refrigerate for 1 hour. Wet your hands with cold water and form the dough into balls, using about 1 tablespoon of dough for each matzoh ball. Bring a 3-quart pot of water to a boil. Drop in the matzoh balls, cover, and cook for 3 minutes. DON'T PEEK. Remove the matzoh balls with a slotted spoon and arrange around the chicken.

⊸§ ARROZ CON POLLO

Arroz con pollo (chicken with rice) is a standard favorite throughout Latin America, where it is usually made with achiote, a herbal paste that gives the white rice a pleasant yellow color. Well, here's my version, using brown rice instead of white, and therefore no achiote.

Serves 6–8

> 2 **whole chicken breasts, skinned, boned, and cut into 1-inch strips**
> 1 **large bell pepper, chopped**
> 1 **jalapeño pepper, chopped**
> 2 **cloves garlic, minced fine**
> 2 **onions, chopped**
> 4½ **cups defatted chicken stock (page 86)**
> 4 **fresh tomatoes, crushed and pureed**
> ½ **small jar pimentos, sliced**
> 1 **tablespoon capers, drained**
> ½ **teaspoon cumin**
> 1 **teaspoon chili powder**
> 2 **cups uncooked brown rice**

Broil the strips of chicken until they lose their pinkness (about 3–4 minutes each side). Set aside and keep warm.

Place both peppers and the garlic, onions, chicken stock, tomatoes, pimentos, capers, and spices in a skillet and bring to a boil. Cover and simmer for 45 to 50 minutes or until the rice has absorbed the liquid. Stir the rice, arrange the chicken on top, and serve in the skillet.

✌§ HERB NO-FRIED CHICKEN

Eat your heart out, Colonel. Here's a "no-fried" chicken recipe that's low in fat and cholesterol, but mighty high in flavor.

Serves 8

4 large chicken cutlets, skin removed, cut in half

Herb Marinade

½ **cup rice vinegar**
½ **cup frozen apple-juice concentrate**
¼ **cup lemon juice**
¼ **cup reduced-salt tamari or soy sauce**
1 **clove garlic, minced fine**
½ **teaspoon thyme**
a dash of sage
½ **teaspoon oregano**
1 **teaspoon curry powder**

In a large bowl, combine all ingredients. Set aside.

Breading

½ **cup toasted and crumbled whole-wheat or sourdough bread**
½ **cup cornmeal**
4 **teaspoons whole-wheat flour**
1 **teaspoon paprika**
1 **teaspoon poultry seasoning**
¼ **teaspoon Tabasco**

Marinate the chicken overnight or for several hours in the refrigerator. Remove it from the marinade and roll it in the breading mixture. Place the chicken on a nonstick baking sheet, cover with foil, and bake in a 350°F. oven for 10 minutes. Remove the foil and continue baking for 10 more minutes, or until the chicken is tender.

⤳ SPICY NO-FRIED CHICKEN

Serves 8

½ teaspoon oregano
½ teaspoon ginger
¼ cup cornmeal
1 teaspoon basil
2 cloves garlic, minced fine
4 chicken cutlets, skin removed, cut in half and rubbed with a little lemon juice
1 egg white, stirred but not beaten
¼ teaspoon Tabasco
¼ cup bran flakes

Combine oregano, ginger, cornmeal, basil, and garlic and sprinkle over both sides of the chicken. Mix the egg white and the Tabasco. Dip each piece of chicken in this mixture and then roll in the bran flakes. Place the "breaded" chicken on a nonstick baking sheet and bake in a preheated 350°F. oven for 20 minutes or until crisp.

⤳ TOASTED CHICKEN

Serves 8

4 chicken cutlets, skin and fat removed, cut in half
2 egg whites
a dash of sage
1 tablespoon reduced-salt tamari or soy sauce
2 cloves garlic, peeled and minced fine

½ **cup nonfat milk**
½ **cup whole-wheat flour**
2 **cups whole-wheat or sourdough bread crumbs**

Pound the pieces of chicken breast flat. Mix the egg whites lightly with the sage, tamari, and garlic. Dip the pounded chicken in the nonfat milk, then in the whole-wheat flour, then in the egg-white mixture, and finally roll in the bread crumbs. Lay the chicken flat on a nonstick cookie sheet. Bake 20 minutes at 325°F. Serve with Mushroom Sauce (page 252).

⊷§ CHICKEN AUX CHAMPIGNONS

I first made this dish on a Caribbean cruise, where the guests demanded the sort of rich French cooking usually found in cruise-ship dining rooms. This one seemed to satisfy everyone's palate, yet it is exceptionally low in fat and cholesterol.

Serves 2–4

2 **boneless and skinless half chicken breasts (chicken cutlets), cut in half**
1 **pound fresh mushrooms, sliced**
¼ **cup white wine**
½ **teaspoon lemon juice**
⅛ **teaspoon dillweed**
½ **cup canned evaporated skim milk**
¼ **cup whole-wheat or sourdough bread crumbs**

Pound the chicken breasts flat between two sheets of waxed paper. Set aside. Simmer the mushrooms in the white wine, lemon juice, and dillweed; cook until the wine is almost evaporated. Put a portion of the mushroom mixture in the center of each flattened chicken breast and roll it up. Dip the roll in milk and roll it in bread crumbs. Place the breaded chicken breast rolls on a nonstick baking sheet and bake at 350°F. for 35 minutes or until the chicken is tender. Serve with whole-wheat or buckwheat noodles.

⋽ CHICKEN KIEV

Serves 6–8

> 6 half chicken breasts, skin, fat, and bones removed (chicken cutlets)
> 1 clove garlic, minced fine
> 2 tablespoons chopped parsley
> 1 teaspoon tarragon
> 1 tablespoon reduced-salt tamari or soy sauce
> a dash of cayenne pepper (optional)
> 1 recipe cooked Wild and Brown Rice with Mushrooms (page 243)
> ½ cup whole-wheat flour
> 3 egg whites, stirred until slightly foamy
> 1 cup whole-wheat or sourdough bread crumbs

Wash the chicken and dry well with a towel. Flatten the chicken by placing the cutlets on a board between 2 sheets of waxed paper and pounding with a small mallet or the bottom of a glass or small skillet until the chicken is about ¼ inch thick. Avoid breaking the chicken into pieces. Mix the garlic, parsley, tarragon, tamari, and cayenne together in a small bowl and pat the pounded chicken with this mixture. Place 1 tablespoon of the Rice with Mushrooms in the center of each chicken cutlet and fold the corners to the center, overlapping them. Pin with a toothpick. Roll each piece in whole-wheat flour, then dip in egg white and immediately roll in bread crumbs, coating evenly. Shape the chicken into ovals with your hands and place it in the refrigerator, covered, for 30

minutes until firm. Put the chicken on a baking sheet, cover
with aluminum foil, and cook in a preheated 350°F. oven for
30 minutes. Turn the oven up to 400°F., remove the foil, and
continue baking for an additional 5 minutes, until the rolls are
toasty. Serve atop the rest of the Rice with Mushrooms mixture.

₰ CHICKEN (OR TURKEY) À LA KING

Serves 4–6

1 small onion, chopped
1 stalk celery, chopped
½ pound mushrooms, washed and sliced
1½ cups defatted chicken stock (page 86)
1 cup evaporated skim milk (fresh nonfat milk can be sub-
    stituted, but the resulting dish will not be as rich)
2 tablespoons arrowroot powder or cornstarch
¼ cup dry sherry
1 cup frozen green peas, thawed
¼ cup diced pimento
1 tablespoon chopped parsley
½ teaspoon tarragon
2 cloves garlic, minced fine
1 small chili pepper, seeded and chopped *or* ½ teaspoon Ta-
    basco
2 cups cooked chicken or turkey breast, cut into chunks

In a skillet, sauté the onion, celery, and mushrooms in ½
cup stock or water until soft and lightly browned. Set aside.
In a double boiler, heat the milk and ¾ cup chicken stock until
it simmers. Meanwhile, blend the arrowroot or cornstarch
with the sherry and remaining stock to a smooth paste. Pour
this slowly into the chicken-broth liquid, stirring constantly
until the sauce is thick. Add the green peas, sautéed vegeta-

bles, pimento, seasonings, and chicken or turkey and stir gently. Simmer 5–10 minutes. Serve over hot brown rice (page 237).

✎§ TURKEY POT PIE

Serves 4–6

1½ cups toasted whole-wheat or sourdough bread crumbs
½ bell pepper, chopped
½ stalk celery, chopped
½ small onion, chopped fine
¼ cup thin-sliced mushrooms
¾ cup breast of turkey, skin removed and cubed
1½ cups defatted chicken stock (page 86)
1½ boiled new potatoes, cut in ½-inch cubes
½ cup nonfat dry milk
1 teaspoon arrowroot powder mixed with 2 tablespoons water
½ teaspoon curry powder
½ teaspoon celery seed
2 cloves garlic, minced fine
1 tablespoon tamari
1 small can water chestnuts, sliced and drained
1 package frozen carrots and peas, thawed

Moisten the toasted bread crumbs with water and press half of them into the bottom of a 9-inch pie pan. In a skillet, sauté the bell pepper, celery, onion, and mushrooms in a small amount of water. Add the turkey, chicken stock, cooked potatoes, nonfat dry milk, arrowroot mixture, curry powder, celery seed, garlic, tamari, sliced chestnuts, and carrots and peas. Stir well. Heat and stir until the gravy thickens. Pour the turkey-and-vegetable mixture into the piecrust and top with the remaining bread crumbs. Bake for 20 minutes at 350°F.

✒ GLAZED TURKEY BREAST WITH VEGETABLES AND STUFFING

Here's your holiday turkey, all dressed up for the occasion and served with a choice of delicious stuffings. The great thing about it is that it's so low in fat and cholesterol that you won't feel like a sinner the next day.

Serves 16–18

1 whole turkey breast (about 4 pounds), skin and any fat removed

1 6-ounce can (¾ cup) frozen orange-juice concentrate, thawed

1 cup defatted chicken stock (page 86) or water

½ teaspoon thyme

½ teaspoon sage

1 tablespoon reduced-salt tamari or soy sauce

1 teaspoon cornstarch

Place the turkey breast in a roasting pan. Combine the orange-juice concentrate, stock, thyme, sage, tamari, and cornstarch in a small saucepan. Bring this mixture to a boil and stir constantly until the mixture thickens and clears. Spoon part of the sauce over the turkey breast. Roast the turkey in a 350°F. oven for 1½ to 2 hours, or until tender. Baste frequently with the remaining sauce.

✑ TURKEY GRAVY

Serves 6–8

- 4 cups defatted chicken stock (page 86) and defatted turkey drippings if available
- 1 clove garlic, peeled and minced fine
- ¼ small onion, peeled and minced fine
- ½ carrot, scraped and grated
- ½ teaspoon celery seed
- ½ teaspoon sage
- ¼ teaspoon thyme
- 1 tablespoon reduced-salt tamari or soy sauce
- 2 tablespoons arrowroot powder or cornstarch dissolved in ½ cup chicken stock or water
- 1 tablespoon dry sherry

Put all of the ingredients except the arrowroot and sherry in a 1½–2-quart pot. Bring to a boil, reduce the heat, and simmer for 30 minutes. Stir in the arrowroot mixture and sherry and continue to simmer and stir until the gravy thickens. Serve hot over Glazed Turkey Breast (page 205).

✑ CORN-BREAD STUFFING

Serves 6–8

- 5 cups finely crumbled corn bread (page 307) (The corn bread can be up to a week old.)
- 2 cups finely crumbled whole-wheat or sourdough bread
- 1 onion, chopped fine
- 1 stalk celery (without leaves), chopped fine
- 3 carrots, scraped and chopped fine
- 4 cups defatted chicken stock (page 86)
- 2 cloves garlic, minced fine
- 1 teaspoon poultry seasoning
- 1 tablespoon crushed sage
- 1 tablespoon reduced-salt tamari or soy sauce

Combine the bread crumbs in a mixing bowl and set aside. Sauté the onion, celery, and carrots in ½ cup stock until soft and tender. Add to the bread crumbs and mix thoroughly. Add the garlic, poultry seasoning, sage, and tamari and mix thoroughly again. Add the rest of the chicken stock and mix once again. Bake in a casserole dish for 20 minutes at 375°F. Leave the casserole uncovered if you want a crust to form, covered if you do not. Serve hot.

✺§ CHESTNUT STUFFING

Serves 6–8

2 stalks celery, chopped fine
1 bell pepper, seeds removed, chopped fine
1 onion, peeled and chopped fine
½ cup defatted chicken stock (page 86) or water
1 cup fresh chestnuts (If fresh chestnuts are not in season, use canned chestnuts and add 2 tablespoons frozen apple-juice concentrate)
3 egg whites
1 tablespoon tamari or soy sauce
7 cups crumbled bread (any combination of corn bread, whole-wheat bread, and sourdough bread)

Sauté the celery, bell pepper, and onion in the stock for about 5 minutes. Prepare the chestnuts by cutting a gash in the hard outer coating and roasting in a hot oven (about 450°F.) for 25 to 30 minutes in a pan covered tightly with foil. Shake the pan occasionally. Cool and peel the chestnuts, then chop them. Add the egg whites, chestnuts, and tamari to the vegetable mixture. Combine the vegetables and bread crumbs and mix together. Place in a nonstick baking dish and bake for 20 minutes at 350°F.

✑§ CORNISH HENS WITH MANDARIN GLAZE

This recipe was developed while I was working as a chef at a beautiful health resort in Hawaii. I wanted to use Cornish hens, but to give them a uniquely tropical touch—thus the Mandarin glaze, the ginger, and the mustard.

Serves 4

  2 1-pound Cornish hens
  ½ cup frozen apple-juice concentrate, partially thawed
  ½ cup frozen orange-juice concentrate, partially thawed
  1 teaspoon cinnamon
  1 tablespoon arrowroot powder or cornstarch
  1 teaspoon Dijon mustard
  3 lemon slices
  1 teaspoon chopped fresh ginger
  2 teaspoons tamari

Wash the hens and arrange them in a small roasting pan. In a saucepan, combine the apple juice, orange juice, cinnamon, and arrowroot and mix until smooth. Add the lemon slices, ginger, and tamari and cook over medium heat, stirring until the glaze thickens. Brush the hens with glaze, reserving some of it. Roast the glazed hens in a 375°F. oven for 1 hour or until tender. Baste several times during the cooking for additional flavor. Cut the hens in half and serve hot with the remaining glaze.

Vegetable Side Dishes

One of the great challenges of dinner preparation is how to make the vegetables interesting. For many people, the answer to this challenge is to bypass fresh vegetables altogether and buy frozen "pouch-type" concoctions in which the vegetables, spices, and condiments have already been combined.

The problem with these packaged dishes is that they're often high in fats because of their butter content, and they're loaded with salt. So my thought was to reintroduce people to the fresh-produce section of the market, to give them exciting, flavorful side-dish recipes for just about every vegetable that can be found there. Once again, it's a question of flavor without fat.

One of the best ways to prepare vegetables is stir-frying. Since this is an unfamiliar cooking method for many Americans, a few hints may be in order. First of all, you don't necessarily need a wok—a plain old frying pan will do the job just fine. Heat the pan over a medium flame until the surface is hot. Then add a stock (chicken, vegetable, beef, or fish, depending on the recipe) just as you would use butter, oil, or margarine, and heat it until it boils. Then *quickly* place the vegetables and seasoning ingredients in the stock, stirring to make sure all the vegetables are coated with the hot liquid. Cover and cook for about 2 minutes. Then remove the cover and repeat the process: stir, cover, cook. Repeat the procedure until the vegetables have a slightly crisp (*al dente*) texture— usually 8 to 10 minutes, depending on the vegetable.

✒ ASPARAGUS WITH DILL SAUCE

Serves 4

>   2   cloves garlic, chopped fine
>   1   teaspoon dill
>   2   scallions, sliced thin
>   1½   cups defatted chicken stock (page 86) or water
>   2   carrots, scraped and sliced thin
>   1   pound fresh or frozen asparagus, cut into 2-inch lengths
>   1   tablespoon arrowroot or cornstarch dissolved in ½ cup chicken stock or water
>   1   tablespoon lemon juice
> lemon wedges and parsley for garnish

In a large frying pan or wok, sauté the garlic, dill, and scallions in ½ cup chicken stock or water for 5 minutes over low heat. Add the carrots and stir thoroughly; continue to cook for 5 minutes. Add the rest of the chicken stock or water and the asparagus, cover, and simmer for 5 minutes. Stir the arrowroot mixture into the vegetables and mix gently and thoroughly until the sauce has thickened. Add the lemon juice. Serve with lemon-wedge and parsley garnish.

⋖§ BASIC ARTICHOKES

Although I enter this here as a vegetable side dish, it makes a great appetizer.

Serves 6

3 medium-size artichokes
1 clove garlic, crushed
½ teaspoon whole cloves
½ lemon

Remove the stem up to 1 inch of the base of each artichoke. Remove the prickly barbs on the outside leaves by cutting ½ inch off the leaf tips with scissors. Cut the artichokes in half lengthwise. Place the 6 half artichokes in a large pot along with 1 quart of water and the garlic, cloves, and lemon. Bring to a boil, cover, and reduce the heat until only a light steam escapes from under the lid. Continue cooking for 20 to 25 minutes. Test by pulling out one large leaf; if it removes easily, the artichokes are ready. Pour off the water and chill the artichokes in the refrigerator for 30 to 45 minutes. Remove the fuzzy purple-and-white artichoke centers by placing a spoon on the line at the top of the heart and scooping out this inedible fiber. The base of each leaf and the center, or heart, are edible.

Serving suggestion: The leaves and heart may be dipped in any of the cheese spreads in the Lunch and Sandwich Spreads section (pages 48–55) or in Slender Mayonnaise (page 70).

✑ STEAMED GREEN BEANS

Serves 4

1 pound fresh green beans, stems broken or cut off
1 tablespoon fresh lemon juice
1 clove garlic, minced fine (optional)
a dash of Tabasco or a pinch of cayenne
1 cup vegetable stock (page 90) or water

Put the green beans, lemon juice, garlic, Tabasco, and vegetable stock or water in a saucepan. Cover and simmer for 10 to 12 minutes or until the green beans are *al dente* (slightly crunchy). DO NOT OVERCOOK.

✑ STEAMED WAX BEANS

Serves 4

1 pound fresh wax beans, stems broken or cut off
1 tablespoon fresh lemon juice
1 clove garlic, minced fine (optional)
a dash Tabasco or a pinch of cayenne
1 tablespoon frozen apple-juice concentrate
1 cup vegetable stock (page 90) or water

Combine the wax beans, lemon juice, garlic, Tabasco, apple-juice concentrate, and vegetable stock in a saucepan. Cover and simmer for 10 to 12 minutes or until the wax beans are *al dente* (slightly crunchy). DO NOT OVERCOOK. Spoon the cooking liquid over the beans.

◆§ GLAZED FRESH BEETS

Serves 4

1 bunch fresh beets (retaining the greens if possible), soaked
   for 15 minutes and washed thoroughly
2 cups vegetable stock (page 90) or water
1 tablespoon frozen apple-juice concentrate
½ teaspoon cinnamon
1 teaspoon grated lemon rind
1 teaspoon arrowroot or cornstarch dissolved in 2 tablespoons cold water

If the beet greens are still on the beets, cut them off and set
them aside. Place the beets and 1 cup vegetable stock in a
saucepan. Cover the pan and simmer for 15 to 20 minutes or
until the liquid is almost gone. Peel the beets and cut them
into ¼-inch slices. Put the slices in a saucepan with the remaining stock or water, apple juice, cinnamon, and lemon
rind. The greens may be added at this time. Simmer, covered,
for 10 minutes. Slowly stir the arrowroot or cornstarch solution into the sauce until it thickens.

◆§ ZESTY BEETS

Serves 4

1 bunch fresh beets (if possible, with greens), soaked for 15
   minutes and washed thoroughly
2 cups vegetable stock (page 90) or water
2 tablespoons frozen apple-juice concentrate
1 clove garlic, minced fine
1 teaspoon sweet basil
2 ounces rice vinegar

If you are lucky enough to have the beet greens, cut them off the beets and set them aside. In a saucepan place 1 cup vegetable stock or water and the beets. Cover the pan and allow the beets to simmer for 15 to 20 minutes or until the liquid is almost gone. Peel the skins off the beets and cut them into ¼-inch slices. Put the slices in a saucepan with the remaining vegetable stock or water, apple juice, garlic, sweet basil, and rice vinegar. The greens may be added at this time. Simmer, covered, for 10 minutes. Place the contents of the saucepan in a covered crock or bowl and refrigerate for 1 hour. The beets are now ready to serve.

✌§ SIMPLE BROCCOLI

Serves 4

    1 medium bunch broccoli
    1 tablespoon lemon juice
    1 clove garlic, minced fine
    ¼ onion, sliced thin
    ½ teaspoon celery seed
    2 cups vegetable stock (page 90) or water
    1 teaspoon arrowroot powder or cornstarch

Take whole broccoli and slice ½ inch off the bottom of each stem. With a peeler, peel from the flowers down, removing the heavy outside of the stalk. Slice the stem into ¼-inch pieces all the way to the base of the flowers. Divide the broccoli top into florets. Place all the broccoli, lemon juice, garlic, onion, and celery seed in a saucepan along with the vegetable stock or water. Cover and simmer for 12 to 15 minutes or until the broccoli is tender and still bright green. In a separate cup, dissolve the arrowroot or cornstarch in 2 tablespoons of cold water. Slowly stir this solution into the sauce until it thickens.

⤳ SAUTÉED BRUSSELS SPROUTS

Serves 4

1 pound brussels sprouts
1 clove garlic, minced fine
1 tablespoon chopped parsley
½ teaspoon dillweed
1 teaspoon arrowroot or cornstarch
2 cups vegetable stock (page 90) or water

Cut ¼ inch off the stem of each brussels sprout. Put them in a saucepan with the garlic, parsley, dillweed, and vegetable stock or water. Simmer for 15 to 20 minutes or until the brussels sprout stems are tender and can be pierced with a fork. Dissolve the arrowroot or cornstarch in 2 tablespoons of water in a cup. Slowly stir this solution into the sauce until it thickens.

⤳ STEAMED CABBAGE

Serves 4

1 head cabbage (stem removed), cut into quarters
½ onion, sliced thin
½ teaspoon paprika
½ teaspoon thyme
2 cups vegetable stock (page 90) or water
1 teaspoon arrowroot or cornstarch dissolved in 2 tablespoons cold water

Place the cabbage, onion, paprika, thyme, and vegetable stock or water in a saucepan. Cover and steam for 15 to 20 minutes or until the cabbage is tender. Uncover and allow to simmer for an additional 5 minutes. Slowly stir the arrowroot or cornstarch solution into the sauce until it thickens.

❧ GLAZED CARROTS

Serves 4

6–8 medium carrots, scraped
  2 tablespoons frozen apple-juice concentrate
  ½ teaspoon cinnamon
  1 teaspoon grated lemon rind
  2 cups vegetable stock (page 90) or water
  1 teaspoon arrowroot powder or cornstarch dissolved in 2 tablespoons cold water

Holding your knife at about a 45° angle to the carrots, slice them into oval disks about ½ inch thick. Put the carrots, apple-juice concentrate, cinnamon, and lemon rind in a saucepan with the vegetable stock or water. Cover and simmer for 15 to 20 minutes until the carrots are tender. Uncover and continue to simmer for 5 minutes. Slowly stir the arrowroot or cornstarch solution into the sauce until it thickens.

❧ ROSEMARY CARROTS (A TSIMMES)

Serves 4

  8 medium carrots, scraped
  6 stalks celery, sliced thin (crosswise)
  1 cup defatted chicken stock (page 86) or water
  ½ small can dietetic crushed pineapple
  2 cloves fresh garlic, peeled and chopped
  1 tablespoon frozen apple-juice concentrate
  1 teaspoon rosemary
  2 teaspoons cornstarch dissolved in 2 tablespoons cold water

Slice the carrots at an angle instead of straight across, making little ovals about ¼–½ inch thick. Place the carrots and the celery in a 1½- or 2-quart pot with 1½ inches boiling water for 6 minutes. Drain the carrots and celery and set aside.

Meanwhile, bring the stock or water, pineapple, garlic, apple-juice concentrate, and rosemary to a boil in a saucepan and simmer for 10 minutes. Mix in the cornstarch solution and simmer until the sauce thickens. Remove from heat and pour over the carrots.

~§ SIMPLE CAULIFLOWER

Serves 4

1 head cauliflower
½ teaspoon sweet basil
1 tablespoon sherry
2 scallions, sliced thin
1 teaspoon tamari
a dash of Tabasco or cayenne
2 cups vegetable stock (page 90) or water
1 teaspoon arrowroot powder or cornstarch

Break the cauliflower crown into florets. Then slice the remaining core and green leaves into ¼-inch pieces. Put all the cauliflower in a saucepan with the sweet basil, sherry, scallions, tamari, Tabasco, and vegetable stock or water. Cover and simmer for 15 to 20 minutes or until the cauliflower is tender and the pieces of stems can be pierced by a fork. Dissolve the arrowroot or cornstarch in 2 tablespoons of water in a separate cup. Slowly stir into the sauce until it thickens.

✑ CELERY SUPREME

Serves 4

1 medium bunch celery (heel removed), including the leaves, cut diagonally into 1-inch slices
¼ onion, sliced thin
1 teaspoon rosemary
1 clove garlic, minced fine
1 tablespoon frozen apple-juice concentrate
2 cups vegetable stock (page 90) or water
1 tablespoon dry sherry (optional)
1 teaspoon arrowroot or cornstarch

Put the celery, onion, rosemary, garlic, apple-juice concentrate, vegetable stock or water, and sherry in a saucepan. Cover and simmer for 12 to 15 minutes, or until the celery is tender. Uncover and continue to simmer for 5 minutes. Dissolve the arrowroot or cornstarch in 2 tablespoons of water in a separate cup. Slowly stir it into the sauce until it thickens.

✑ CORN ON THE COB

Serves 4–6

2 cups vegetable stock (page 90) or water
6 ears of fresh or frozen sweet corn
1 cup nonfat milk

Bring the stock or water to a boil in a 1½- or 2-quart pot. Slide in the corn, cover, and simmer for 3 minutes or until the corncob can be pierced with a fork. Add the nonfat milk. Cover and continue to simmer for 3 minutes. The corn is now ready. Try serving it with lemon wedges.

CREAMY CUCUMBER STIR-FRY

Serves 4–6

6 cucumbers, peeled and sliced thin
4 cloves garlic, peeled and chopped fine
1 teaspoon chervil or parsley
2 tablespoons chopped pimento
1 tablespoon capers
a dash of cayenne pepper
2 carrots, scraped and chopped fine
1 8–10-ounce can water-packed artichoke hearts (Frozen, quartered artichoke hearts may be used instead.)
1 cup defatted chicken stock (page 86) or water
1 cup nonfat yogurt (page 72)
fresh parsley for garnish

Heat a wok or 12-inch frying pan and stir-fry all the vegetables and seasonings. (See the description of this cooking technique on pages 209–210.) When the vegetables are done, add the yogurt, turn off the heat, and stir gently. Serve with a parsley garnish.

EGGPLANT MARSALA

Serves 4–6

1 medium eggplant (peeled or unpeeled, as you prefer), cut into 1-inch cubes
½ onion, sliced thin
2 cloves garlic, minced fine
1 teaspoon sweet basil
1 teaspoon oregano
1 tablespoon Marsala wine
1 tablespoon tomato paste *or* 1 fresh tomato cut into small chunks
2 cups vegetable stock (page 90) or water

Put the eggplant, onion, garlic, sweet basil, oregano, Marsala wine, and tomato paste in a saucepan with the vegetable stock or water. Cover and simmer for 15 to 20 minutes or until the eggplant is tender. Uncover and continue to simmer for 5 minutes or until the sauce has thickened. The finished dish should have a thick and creamy consistency.

⊷§ MUSHROOMS WITH DILL SAUCE

Serves 4

>   2 cloves garlic, chopped fine
>   1 teaspoon dill
>   2 green onions, sliced thin
> 1½ cups defatted chicken stock (page 86) or water
>   2 carrots, scraped, sliced thin
>   1 pound mushrooms, quartered
>   1 tablespoon arrowroot powder or cornstarch dissolved in ½
>   cup chicken stock or water
>   1 tablespoon lemon juice
> lemon wedges and parsley for garnish

Using a large frying pan or wok, sauté the garlic, dill, and green onions in ½ cup chicken stock for 5 minutes over low heat. Add the carrots and stir thoroughly. Continue to cook for 5 minutes. Add 1 cup chicken stock or water and the mushrooms, cover, and simmer for 5 minutes. Add the arrowroot or cornstarch mixture and mix it gently and thoroughly into the vegetables until the sauce has thickened. Add the lemon juice. Serve with lemon-wedge and parsley garnish.

❧ ONION RINGS

Serves 4

1 large onion, cut crosswise into ½-inch slices and separated
  into rings
2 cups nonfat milk
1 slice toasted whole-wheat or sourdough bread, crushed into
  crumbs
2 cloves garlic, minced fine
1 cup rice flour or whole-wheat flour
4 egg whites, stirred until slightly foamy (Do not beat)
1 teaspoon reduced-salt tamari or soy sauce

Soak the onion rings in the nonfat milk for 15 minutes.
Mix the toasted bread crumbs and the garlic. Remove the
rings from the milk and dust with flour, then dip in egg white.
Roll the onion rings in the bread-crumb/garlic mixture. Place
on a nonstick baking sheet and bake 15 minutes at 350°F. or
until toasty.

❧ PARSLEYED ONIONS

Serves 4–6

4–6 medium onions, peeled and cut into ⅛-inch wedges
  2 tablespoons chopped fresh parsley
  2 cloves garlic, minced fine
  1 tablespoon dry sherry
  ½ teaspoon celery seed
a dash of Tabasco or a pinch of cayenne
  2 teaspoons tamari (optional)
  2 cups vegetable stock (page 90) or water
  1 teaspoon arrowroot or cornstarch

Put the onions, parsley, garlic, sherry, celery seed, Tabasco, tamari, and vegetable stock or water in a saucepan. Cover and simmer for 15 minutes. Uncover and continue to simmer for 5 minutes. Dissolve the arrowroot or cornstarch in 2 tablespoons of water in separate cup. Slowly stir into the cooking onions until the sauce thickens.

⊷§ SPICY BELL PEPPERS

Serves 6

6 bell peppers (red, green, or mixed), seeded and cut into 1-inch chunks
1 jalapeño pepper, seeded and chopped fine
½ onion, chopped fine
2 cloves garlic, minced fine
2 teaspoons tamari
1 tablespoon Marsala wine (optional)
2 cups vegetable stock (page 90) or water
1 teaspoon arrowroot or cornstarch, dissolved in 2 tablespoons cold water

Combine the peppers, onion, garlic, tamari, Marsala wine, and vegetable stock or water in a saucepan. Simmer, covered, for 10 to 12 minutes. Uncover and continue to simmer 5 minutes. Slowly stir the arrowroot or cornstarch solution into the sauce until it thickens.

⊷§ KOSHER-STYLE DILLS

Makes ½ gallon pickles

5 pounds pickling cucumbers
1 bunch fresh dill
2 heads garlic, broken in half

¼ cup tamari or soy sauce
1 2-ounce package of pickling spice mix
1 cup rice vinegar or distilled white vinegar

Place all the ingredients in a ½-gallon container. Cover with water. Store in a cool place. If you want a crunchy pickle, store 3–5 days. For a tender pickle, store 7–9 days. Remove from brine, chill, and serve.

⌘ CASEROLE POTATOES

Serves 6

6 medium potatoes
1½ cups vegetable stock (page 90) or water
1 clove garlic, minced fine
1 tablespoon tamari
1 teaspoon arrowroot or cornstarch

Soak the potatoes for 10 minutes and wash them thoroughly. Carefully remove all the eyes and any skin that has a greenish cast. The balance of the skin may remain. Cut them into 1-inch slices. Place the vegetable stock, tamari, arrowroot, and garlic in a 2-quart baking dish with a lid. Stir until the ingredients are well mixed. Place the potatoes in the liquid, turning them so they are completely coated. Cover and bake in a 400°F. oven for 45 to 55 minutes or until the potatoes can be easily pierced by a fork. Baste with the sauce before serving.

✎§ MASHED POTATOES

Serves 4

3 medium russet potatoes, peeled and cut into 1-inch-thick
  slices
1 cup nonfat yogurt (page 72)
1 tablespoon reduced-salt tamari or soy sauce
a dash of Tabasco or red pepper
1 tablespoon frozen apple-juice concentrate

Boil the potatoes in 3 cups of water in a 1½–2-quart pot for
30 minutes, or until tender. Drain off the liquid. Mash, adding
the yogurt, tamari, Tabasco and apple juice. Combine
thoroughly until the potatoes are smooth and without lumps.
Heat and serve.

✎§ BAKED POTATO SUPREME

Serves 8

4 extra-large baking potatoes
1 medium bell pepper, chopped fine
1 medium onion, chopped fine
2 cloves garlic, peeled and minced fine
1 carrot, grated
1 cup nonfat yogurt (page 72)
8 tomato slices
½ cup defatted chicken stock (page 86) or water
pinch of dill (optional)
1 tablespoon reduced-salt tamari or soy sauce

Wash the potatoes and wrap them in aluminum foil. Bake
them for 45 minutes at 400°F. Cool to room temperature and
cut into halves lengthwise. Spoon out the insides. Sauté the
vegetables until brown in ½ cup chicken stock or water, ap-

proximately 10 minutes. Mix the pepper, onion, garlic, carrot, and dill with the potato insides and yogurt. Refill the empty potato skins with this mixture, mounding it high. Place the potatoes on a nonstick baking tray and top each with a tomato slice. Bake 20 minutes at 375°F.

⋲§ NO-FAT FRENCH FRIES

Serves 4

    2 potatoes, peeled and cut into ½-inch-wide sticks
    1 tablespoon cornstarch
    1 tablespoon reduced-salt tamari or soy sauce

Soak the potato sticks in 2 cups of water with the cornstarch and soy sauce for 30 minutes. Drain. Place on a nonstick cookie sheet and bake for 20 minutes at 375–400°F., turning after 10 minutes.

⋲§ OLD-FASHIONED RUTABAGAS

Serves 6

    6 medium rutabagas, peeled and cut into ¼-inch slices
    1 teaspoon rosemary
    ½ teaspoon celery seed
    1 tablespoon frozen apple-juice concentrate
    1 tablespoon reduced-salt tamari or soy sauce
    2 cups vegetable stock (page 90) or water
    1 teaspoon arrowroot or cornstarch

Put the rutabagas, rosemary, celery seed, apple juice, tamari, and vegetable stock in a saucepan. Cover and simmer for 20 minutes. Uncover and continue to simmer for 5 minutes. Dissolve the arrowroot or cornstarch in 2 tablespoons of water in a separate cup. Slowly stir into the rutabagas until the sauce thickens.

~§ BAKED ACORN SQUASH

Serves 4–6

2–3 acorn squash, cut in half lengthwise and seeded
¼ cup frozen apple-juice concentrate
½ teaspoon cinnamon (optional)

Using a pastry brush, paint the surface of each squash half with the apple juice. Sprinkle lightly with cinnamon and wrap each half in aluminum foil. Place in a 400°F. oven and bake for 35 to 40 minutes or until tender. Test by piercing with a fork.

~§ BAKED BANANA SQUASH À L'ORANGE

Serves 4–6

1½–2 pounds banana squash, seeds discarded, cut into 4- to
    6-inch squares
¼ cup frozen orange-juice concentrate
½ teaspoon cinnamon
a dash of ground cloves (optional)

With a pastry brush, paint each squash square with the orange juice. Sprinkle the cinnamon lightly over the squash. Seal each square in aluminum foil, or place in a covered baking dish. Bake in a 400°F. oven for 35 to 40 minutes or until tender. Test by piercing with a fork.

❧ BAKED BUTTERNUT SQUASH

Serves 4–6

1½–2 **pounds butternut squash, cut into 4- to 6-inch squares**
¼ **cup frozen apple-juice concentrate**
½ **teaspoon cinnamon**
1 **teaspoon pure vanilla extract**

Using a pastry brush, paint all the pieces of squash with the apple juice. Sprinkle lightly with cinnamon and vanilla extract and seal each square in aluminum foil. Place in a 400°F. oven and bake for 40 to 50 minutes or until tender. Test by piercing with a fork.

❧ SPAGHETTI SQUASH

This very unusual squash takes its name from the fact that when cooked, it turns out looking exactly like strands of spaghetti! But the flavor is pure squash—light and sweet, almost like that of sweet potatoes. For dedicated weight-losers, it makes a great substitute for pasta.

Serves 4–6

1 **medium spaghetti squash, approximately 1½–2 pounds, cut in half lengthwise and seeded**
2 **cups vegetable stock (page 90) or water**

Pare away about a ¼-inch thickness of the squash's hard outer rind. Put the squash halves open side down in a large baking dish with vegetable stock or water. Cover and bake 35 to 45 minutes or until the squash is tender. Test by scraping a fork across the inside of the squash: when done, the squash will come up in strings of "spaghetti." Set the spaghetti squash on a plate and flatten. When turned over, the squash will be in strings. Separate them with a fork and serve with Basic Italian Sauce (page 251) or Spicy Spaghetti Sauce (page 252).

◄§ SHERRIED YELLOW SQUASH

Serves 4–6

6–8 medium yellow (crookneck) squash, stems removed, cut into ½-inch slices
1 small red bell pepper, stem and seeds removed, sliced thin *or* 1 tablespoon chopped pimento
¼ onion, sliced thin
1 tablespoon frozen apple-juice concentrate
¼ teaspoon celery seed
1 clove garlic, minced fine
1 tablespoon dry sherry
1½ cups vegetable stock (page 90) or water
1 teaspoon arrowroot or cornstarch

Put the squash, pepper or pimento, onion, apple-juice concentrate, celery seed, garlic, sherry, and vegetable stock or water in a saucepan. Cover and simmer for 10 to 12 minutes. Uncover and continue to simmer for 5 minutes. Dissolve the arrowroot in 2 tablespoons of water in a separate cup. Slowly stir into the squash until the sauce thickens.

◄§ ZUCCHINI ITALIAN STYLE

Serves 4–6

6–8 medium zucchini, stems removed, cut into 1-inch slices
½ medium onion, sliced thin
2 cloves garlic, minced fine
1 teaspoon sweet basil

> 1 teaspoon oregano
> 1 tomato *or* 1 tablespoon tomato paste
> ½ teaspoon thyme
> 1 tablespoon tamari (optional)
> 1 tablespoon Marsala wine
> 1½ cups vegetable stock (page 90) or water
> 1 teaspoon arrowroot or cornstarch

Place the zucchini, onion, garlic, sweet basil, oregano, tomato, thyme, tamari, wine, and vegetable stock or water in a saucepan. Cover and simmer for 10 to 12 minutes. Uncover and continue to simmer 5 minutes more. Dissolve the arrowroot or cornstarch in 2 tablespoons water in a separate cup. Slowly stir this solution into the zucchini until the sauce thickens.

✥ STEWED TOMATOES

Serves 4

> 6–8 medium tomatoes, cut into quarters
> 2 stalks celery, sliced thin
> ½ bell pepper, sliced thin
> ¼ onion, sliced thin
> ½ teaspoon thyme
> ½ teaspoon sweet basil
> 2 cloves garlic, minced fine
> 1 tablespoon burgundy (optional)

Put all the ingredients in a saucepan. Cover and simmer 8 to 10 minutes. Uncover and continue to simmer for 5 minutes, stirring occasionally. The stewed tomatoes are now ready to serve.

✒ OLD-FASHIONED TURNIPS

Serves 4–6

8–10 turnips, peeled and sliced into 1-inch cubes
1 tablespoon dry sherry
1 teaspoon rosemary
½ teaspoon celery seed
1 tablespoon frozen apple-juice concentrate
1 tablespoon tamari
2 cups vegetable stock (page 90) or water
1 teaspoon arrowroot powder or cornstarch

Put the turnips in a saucepan with the dry sherry, rosemary, celery seed, apple juice, tamari, and vegetable stock. Cover and simmer for 20 minutes. Uncover and continue to simmer for 5 minutes. Dissolve the arrowroot or cornstarch in 2 tablespoons of water in a separate cup. Slowly stir into the turnips until the sauce thickens.

✒ BAKED YAMS

Serves 6–8

6–8 medium yams

Soak the yams for 10 minutes. Cut away any blackened portions of the skin. Wrap the yams individually in foil and bake in a 400°F. oven for 45 to 55 minutes or until tender. Test by piercing with a fork. Serve with Leona's Sour Cream (page 71).

ᴇᔔ ORANGE-GLAZED YAMS

Serves 4–6

4–6 yams, peeled and cut into 1-inch slices
2 cups vegetable stock (page 90) or water
2 tablespoons frozen apple-juice concentrate
½ teaspoon cinnamon
1 teaspoon orange rind
1 teaspoon arrowroot powder or cornstarch
1 teaspoon brandy (optional)

Put the vegetable stock, apple juice, cinnamon, orange rind, arrowroot, and brandy in a baking dish with a lid. Stir until the ingredients are well mixed. Place the yam slices in the liquid, turning them so they are well coated. Cover and bake in a 400°F. oven for 45 to 55 minutes or until the yams can be easily pierced with a fork. Spoon the glaze over them before serving.

ᴇᔔ STIR-FRY ITALIANA

Serves 4–6

3 tomatoes, cut into cubes *or* 1 16-ounce can crushed tomatoes (no salt added)
1 tablespoon tamari or soy sauce
4 cloves garlic, peeled and minced fine
1 teaspoon sweet basil
1 teaspoon oregano
4 zucchini, cut at an angle into large slices
1 bell pepper, sliced thin
1 onion, chopped fine
1 pound mushrooms, quartered
1 can water-packed artichoke hearts *or* ½ package frozen artichoke hearts, sliced

Heat a wok or 12-inch frying pan and pour in the tomatoes and tamari. Cover and cook for 3 minutes. Add the remaining ingredients and stir-fry in the liquid from the tomatoes and tamari. (See method pages 209–210.) Serve over whole-wheat or semolina-flour noodles.

✎§ VEGETABLE STIR-FRY SPANISH STYLE

Serves 4–6

  6 summer or crookneck squash, cut into ½-inch slices
  1 onion, peeled and sliced thin
  ½ 35-ounce can crushed tomatoes in heavy puree
  1 bell pepper, seeded and sliced thin
  2 jalapeño peppers, seeded and chopped fine
  ½ package frozen peas
  3 carrots, scraped and sliced thin
  1 tablespoon chili powder
  1 teaspoon ground cumin or coriander
  6 cloves garlic, peeled and chopped fine
  1 tablespoon reduced-salt tamari or soy sauce
  ½ cup defatted chicken stock (page 86), beef stock (page 88),
    or vegetable stock (page 90)
parsley or cilantro for garnish

Heat a wok or 12-inch frying pan, add the stock, and stir-fry the vegetables according to the instructions on pages 209–10. Serve garnished with cilantro (Spanish parsley) or fresh parsley over brown rice or whole-wheat or semolina-flour noodles.

Dried Beans

For most of the world, beans are the number one source of protein. In fact, there's more protein in a cup of beans than in a pound of steak. Kept clean and dry, they store indefinitely; once cooked, they can be frozen. What's more, they contain only 4 percent fat, and no cholesterol at all!

To save cooking time and fuel, beans can be soaked overnight in a pot of cold water; this will cut the cooking time by half.

⋽ RED BEANS

Serves 4–6

>1 pound red beans, soaked overnight in water to cover
>1½ quarts defatted chicken stock (page 86), beef stock (page 88), or water
>2 onions, peeled and chopped fine
>6 cloves garlic, peeled and minced fine
>¼ cup tomato paste
>1 bell pepper, seeds removed, chopped fine
>¼ teaspoon chili powder
>1 bay leaf
>1 tablespoon tamari or soy sauce
>¼ cup chopped pimento

Place the beans in a 2½–3-quart pot. Add the stock or water and all the other ingredients. Bring to a boil, reduce the heat, and simmer for 2 hours. The finished dish should have a thick, creamy consistency.

⟞§ "REFRIED" BEANS

Serves 4–6

1 pound pinto beans
1 onion, peeled and chopped
6 cloves garlic, peeled and chopped fine
2 jalapeño peppers, seeded and chopped
1 bell pepper, seeded and chopped
1 teaspoon coriander
1 tablespoon paprika
1 tablespoon dark chili powder
1 tablespoon reduced-salt tamari or soy sauce
1 teaspoon cumin
1 teaspoon basil
1 teaspoon gumbo filé
1 teaspoon oregano
2 quarts defatted beef stock (page 88), chicken stock (page 86), or water

Place all the ingredients in a 2½–3-quart pot and bring to a boil. Reduce the heat and simmer for 2 hours or until the beans are tender and the liquid has thickened with the broken beans. The finished dish should have a dry, pasty consistency.

⟞§ REBECCA'S COUNTRY LIMAS

This is a Louisiana dish, based on an old Creole favorite, and inspired—as are so many good things—by a beautiful woman.

Serves 4–6

2 cups large dried lima beans
7 cups defatted beef stock (page 88) or water
6 cloves garlic, peeled and chopped fine
1 jalapeño pepper, seeded and chopped

1 teaspoon chervil
1 teaspoon rosemary
1 tablespoon reduced-salt tamari or soy sauce
1 onion, peeled and chopped fine
1 bell pepper, seeded and chopped
1 tablespoon oregano
1 tablespoon basil
1 teaspoon thyme

Place all the ingredients in a 2½–3-quart pot and bring to a boil. Reduce the heat and simmer for 2 hours. The beans are done when they are tender and beginning to break up.

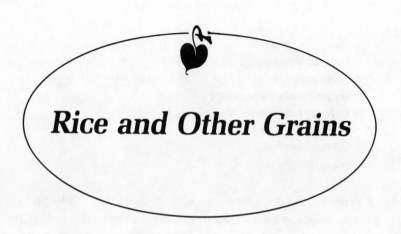

Rice and Other Grains

Rice and other grains are probably the world's most important food crops. In many cultures, rice and such grains as wheat, barley, and millet are not only the main dietary staple, but also the chief source of protein, amino acids, vitamins, minerals, and fiber. And although most people think of these foods—rice in particular—as being "fattening," or high in calories, the truth is that rice has about the same caloric content as beans, which is only about one-third that of turkey, the lowest-calorie of all the meats.

Because of their nutritional value, these foods are now playing a vital role in today's low-fat, high-fiber diets. Cook them in defatted chicken stock (page 86) or defatted beef stock (page 88), add a sweet-and-sour or mushroom sauce, and you'll have a meal supplement—or even a major entrée—that will boost your energy supply without breaking your diet.

A cooking hint: For soft, tender rice and grains, add two to three tablespoons of water to the amount called for in these recipes. For a drier texture, cook a few minutes longer.

Brown Rice

Brown rice is used throughout this book instead of white rice because it constitutes a true whole grain: the fiber-rich hull has not been removed, as it has in white rice, nor has it been bleached. For most of the recipes that call for rice, I recommend using the long-grain variety, since it has a somewhat lighter texture than short-grained rice, as well as a noticeably more elegant look.

A cooking hint: To give the rice a fluffier texture, gently toast it on a baking sheet in a 350-degree oven for 10 minutes, turning occasionally to toast evenly. Then simply follow the recipe for Long-Grain Brown Rice below, but shorten the cooking time by 5 to 10 minutes.

✑ LONG-GRAIN BROWN RICE

Makes 3–3½ cups of rice

1 cup brown rice
2 cups water

Put the rice and water in a 1½–2-quart pot. Cover and bring to a boil, then reduce the heat until only light steam escapes from under the lid. Cook for 30–45 minutes. Don't stir—and don't peek. When the steaming stops, the rice should be cooked. A defatted stock may be used instead of water for added flavor.

◅§ SPANISH RICE

Serves 2–4

  2½ cups tomato juice (no salt)
   1 cup brown rice (long- or short-grain)
   1 cup frozen peas
  ½ onion, chopped fine
   2 cloves garlic, minced fine
   1 bell pepper, seeded and chopped
   1 teaspoon chili powder
  ½ teaspoon cumin
   1 teaspoon basil
  ½ teaspoon oregano
  ¼ teaspoon celery seed
   1 tablespoon reduced-salt tamari or soy sauce
  ¼ teaspoon Tabasco
  ½ cup defatted chicken stock (page 86) or water

Bring the juice to a boil in a 1½–2-quart pot, and add the rice. Cover and reduce the heat. Simmer for 45 minutes to an hour until no more steam escapes from under the lid. Sauté the rest of the ingredients in the stock or water, stirring occasionally, for about 15 minutes. When the rice is done, it should be tender. Combine the sautéed vegetables and herbs with the rice, folding them together gently, and serve hot. Try serving this dish with Spanish Sauce (page 257).

◅§ ORIENTAL RICE

Serves 2–4

  3 cups defatted chicken stock (page 86) or water
  1 cup brown rice
  2 scallions, sliced fine
  2 cloves garlic, minced fine

    1 **tablespoon fresh ginger, chopped fine**
    ½ **small can water chestnuts, chopped**
    1 **cup frozen peas**
    ½ **onion, chopped**
    1 **tablespoon reduced-salt tamari or soy sauce**
    1 **egg white**

Bring 2½ cups chicken stock or water to a boil in a 1½–2-quart cooking pot and add the rice. Cover and reduce the heat until only a light steam escapes from under the lid. Simmer until the liquid is absorbed (45 minutes to 1 hour). Place all the remaining ingredients except the egg white in a frying pan and sauté in ½ cup of stock or water, stirring occasionally, for about 15 minutes. Mix the egg white in a cup or small bowl and trail it over the steaming sauté. As it becomes opaque, break it up and stir it in. Combine the sautéed vegetables and herbs with the rice, folding them together gently. Serve hot with Cantonese Stir-Fry with Chicken (page 184).

◄§ RICE PILAF

Serves 2–4

    1 **cup brown rice**
    3 **cups defatted chicken stock (page 86) or water**
    1 **cup frozen peas**
    ½ **onion, chopped fine**
    2 **cloves garlic, minced fine**
    1 **teaspoon paprika**

Bring 2½ cups chicken stock to a boil in a 1½–2-quart cooking pot and stir in the rice. Cover and reduce the heat until the liquid simmers gently. Simmer for about 45 minutes to 1 hour. Put all the rest of the ingredients in a frying pan with ½ cup stock or water and sauté, stirring occasionally, for about 15 minutes or until the ingredients are tender. Fold the sautéed vegetables and spices gently into the rice and serve hot.

⊷§ INDIAN CURRIED RICE

This dish has all the richness and flavor of traditional East Indian cooking. One caution, though: it's hot, and I don't mean temperature! For the brave only.

Serves 4–6

1½ cups brown rice
½ cup defatted chicken stock (page 86)
2 fresh green chili peppers (jalapeño or serrano), seeded and chopped fine
1 onion, chopped fine
3 cloves garlic, minced fine
1 tablespoon reduced-salt tamari or soy sauce
1 tablespoon curry powder

In a pot bring 3½ cups of water to a boil and add the rice. Cover and reduce the heat until only light steam escapes from under the lid. Simmer for 45 minutes to 1 hour. Sauté the remaining ingredients in the chicken stock for about 15 minutes, stirring occasionally. A half cup of stock may be added if the mixture seems too dry. Continue to cook these ingredients until they are tender. Combine the spices with the rice, folding them in gently. Serve hot.

⊷§ DIRTY RICE

"Dirty" rice, of course, is not dirty at all—it's simply a Southern term for rice cooked with dark meats like chicken giblets. Well, I've substituted mushrooms for the chicken giblets and come up with a Dirty Rice that from a health stand-point is just about as clean as a whistle.

Serves 8–10

6½ cups defatted chicken stock (page 86)
3 cups long-grain brown rice
1 half chicken breast, skin, fat, and bone removed, cut into ½-inch chunks (optional)
3 cloves garlic, peeled and minced fine
1 onion, peeled and chopped fine
1 carrot, scraped and shredded
1 cup chopped mushrooms
1 red or green bell pepper, seeded and cut into small chunks
1 tablespoon reduced-salt tamari or soy sauce

Bring 6 cups of stock to a boil, stir in the rice, lower the heat, cover, and simmer for 45 minutes. Sauté the chicken breast (if used), garlic, onion, carrot, mushrooms, and bell pepper in ½ cup chicken stock and the tamari. Combine with the rice. Serve.

◄§ STUFFING MEDITERRANEAN

Stuffing can make a great change from the potato or rice routine. Use it for a holiday stuffing, or to give a heartier flavor and texture to baked fish. Or serve it by itself, with or without sauces. Any way you try it, it's great!

Serves 4–6

3 cups defatted chicken stock (page 86), defatted beef stock (page 88), or water
½ cup brown rice
½ cup wild rice
1 stalk celery, chopped
½ onion, chopped
½ bell pepper, chopped
½ can water chestnuts, chopped
3 cloves garlic, minced fine
2 tablespoons chopped pimento
1 tablespoon reduced-salt tamari or soy sauce
2 teaspoons dry sherry
1 cup crumbled corn bread (page 307) (may be stale or dry)
1 cup crumbled whole-wheat or sourdough bread (may be stale or dry)

Bring 2½ cups stock or water to a boil in a 2-quart pot and add the rice. Cover and reduce the heat until only light steam escapes from under the lid. Simmer for 45 minutes to 1 hour until steaming stops. Place all the remaining ingredients except the bread crumbs in a frying pan with ½ cup stock or water, and sauté, stirring occasionally, for about 15 minutes or until the ingredients are tender. Combine the sautéed vegetables and spices with the rice and gently fold in the bread crumbs. Put the stuffing in a 2-quart covered baking dish and bake for 20 minutes at 350°F. Serve as a side dish with any of the chicken or fish recipes.

≤§ WILD AND BROWN RICE WITH MUSHROOMS

Serves 4–6

1 cup brown rice
½ cup wild rice
½ pound mushrooms, sliced thin
3 cups defatted chicken stock (page 86) or water

In a small pot (1–1½ quarts), bring the stock or water to a boil and stir the brown rice, wild rice, and mushrooms into the boiling liquid. Cover and reduce the heat. Simmer without stirring for 35 to 45 minutes, or until the rice is tender.

≤§ WILD RICE BANQUET

Wild rice has long been considered the most aristocratic of all the rices. Actually, it's a completely natural product—unadulterated in any way. This recipe has a deliciously solid, almost meaty flavor, yet except for the stock, it's entirely meat-free. It makes a wonderful dish for special occasions.

Serves 4–6

½ cup wild rice
½ cup brown rice
½ cup dried lentils
½ onion, chopped
2 cloves garlic, minced fine
1 small carrot, scraped and sliced fine
½ bell pepper, chopped fine
¼ teaspoon Tabasco
1 teaspoon rice vinegar
1 tablespoon frozen apple-juice concentrate
1 tablespoon reduced-salt tamari or soy sauce
4 cups defatted chicken stock (page 86) or water

Bring 3½ cups chicken stock or water to a boil in a 1½-2-quart cooking pot and add the wild rice, brown rice, and lentils. Cover and reduce the heat until only light steam escapes from under the lid. Simmer for 45 minutes to an hour until all the liquid is absorbed. Place the rest of the ingredients in a frying pan and sauté in ½ cup stock or water, stirring occasionally, for about 15 minutes. Combine the sautéed vegetables and spices with the rice, folding them in gently, and serve hot.

Variety Grains

Some of the grains in this section will be unfamiliar to many Americans, to whom the word "grain" usually means rice, wheat, oats, or rye. I've already told you a bit about millet (See page 236). Bulgur is actually a wheat, but it's left as a whole grain rather than ground into a flour; so it has the flavor of wheat, but the consistency of rice. It's usually found in the Middle East, in such dishes as Tabuli (See page 247). Kasha is a grain grown in Eastern Europe, from where it was exported to America and eventually translated into "buckwheat," or "buckwheat groats." Kasha has a light, delicate flavor that makes it a perfect complement to almost any entrée, and invites experimentation with just about any spice in your cabinet.

By the way, the same toasting trick that gives rice that nutty flavor (See page 237) will work for these variety grains.

ঌ MILLET

For information about millet, see page 236.

Makes 3½–4 cups

> **1 cup millet**
> **2½–3 cups water**

Put the millet and water in a 1½–2-quart pot. Cover and bring to a boil. Reduce the heat until only light steam escapes from under the lid. Cook for 45–60 minutes. When the steaming stops, the millet is done. A defatted stock may be used instead of water to add flavor.

ঌ MILLET TAMPICO

Serves 2–4

> **1 cup millet**
> **3 cups water**
> **1 bell pepper, chopped**
> **1 long green chili pepper *or* 1 jalapeño pepper, chopped fine**
> **½ onion, chopped fine**
> **2 cloves garlic, minced fine**
> **1 tomato, cut into small chunks**
> **1 teaspoon chili powder**
> **½ teaspoon cumin**
> **1 cup frozen peas**
> **1 tablespoon reduced-salt tamari or soy sauce**

Bring 2½ cups of water to a boil in a pot and add the millet. Cover and reduce the heat. Simmer for 45 minutes to 1 hour. Put all the other ingredients in a frying pan and sauté in ½ cup water, stirring occasionally, for about 15 minutes, or until tender. When the millet is done, it should be tender and similar to rice in consistency. (If it's still too hard, cook it longer.) Combine the sautéed vegetables and spices with the millet, folding gently, and serve hot. May be served with Spanish Sauce (See page 257).

◆§ SIMPLE KASHA (BUCKWHEAT GROATS)

Serves 2

 1 cup buckwheat groats
1½ cups boiling water or defatted chicken stock (page 86)

Spread the buckwheat groats on a cookie sheet and place in the oven for 15 minutes at 350°F. Then put them in a 1½–2-quart pot with the boiling water or chicken stock, reduce heat, and simmer for 20–25 minutes over a low flame.

◆§ MUSHROOM KASHA (BUCKWHEAT GROATS)

Serves 4–6

 2 cups whole or medium-ground toasted buckwheat groats
 1 cup defatted chicken stock (page 86)
10 mushrooms, chopped
 ½ onion, chopped
 4 cloves garlic, minced fine
 1 tablespoon tamari

Bring the stock to a boil in a 2-quart pot and carefully and gently stir in the buckwheat kasha. Bring the liquid to a boil again and turn heat down very low. Cover and cook over a low flame for about 13 to 15 minutes. Turn off the heat, and let stand covered for 10 minutes. Gently fold in the balance of the ingredients and put the lid back on. Leave covered for an additional 10 minutes to steam awhile longer.

◅ TABULI (BULGUR SALAD)

Serves 4–6

> 1 cup bulgur
> 2 cups boiling water
> ½ cup fine-chopped scallions
> ½ cup fine-chopped parsley
> ½ cup fine-chopped fresh mint
> 1 pound tomatoes, chopped coarsely
> ¼ teaspoon Tabasco
> ⅓ cup lemon juice (more if desired)
> 1 teaspoon frozen apple-juice concentrate, partially thawed
> 1 teaspoon sweet basil
> 1 tablespoon chopped pimento
> 1 tablespoon reduced-salt tamari or soy sauce

Put the bulgur in a bowl. Pour the boiling water over it, cover, and let the bulgur soak for 2 hours. Drain well and then add the remaining ingredients, mixing gently. Chill overnight in the refrigerator.

Sauces

As every cook knows, the *élément de résistance* of any dish is the sauce—in fact, in many cases it is the sauce that imparts most of the flavor to the meal. But many people make the unfortunate assumption that once they embark on a low-fat diet the sauces go out the window. Not true! In this chapter I present a collection of delicious sauces—everything from a spicy Spanish Sauce to a creamy Hollandaise—which are not only mouth-watering, but entirely approved for even the most restrictive diets.

Note: Stocks used in making these sauces can be prepared in advance and frozen in ice-cube trays or Styrofoam cups to make them instantly available (See recipes pages 85–91). Finished sauces can be refrigerated for two to three days, and frozen for up to three months. For people on rigidly salt-free diets, the tamari or soy sauce called for in many of these recipes should be left out.

∽§ NONFAT HOLLANDAISE SAUCE

Makes 1 pint

2 cups defatted chicken stock (page 86)
1 clove garlic, minced fine
2 tablespoons frozen apple-juice concentrate
1 tablespoon fresh lemon juice
1 teaspoon reduced-salt tamari or soy sauce
a dash Tabasco or cayenne pepper
2 cups nonfat yogurt (page 72)

Combine all the ingredients except the yogurt in a saucepan and bring to a boil. Boil until the mixture is reduced to ¼ the original volume. Reduce the heat until the sauce barely simmers and add the yogurt. DO NOT BOIL. Serve immediately. Suggested uses: Serve on Simple Cauliflower (page 217) or Baked Fish (page 165).

◄§ SWEET-AND-SOUR SAUCE

This is another recipe that came out of a Hawaiian sojourn. It has all the flavor of a traditional sweet-and-sour, but with less than ¹⁄₁₀ the sugar.

Makes 1½ pints

    2 cups defatted chicken stock (page 86) or water
    2 tablespoons frozen apple-juice concentrate
    1 tablespoon tomato paste
    1 teaspoon tamari
    1 cup fresh pineapple chunks *or* one small can dietetic pine-
       apple chunks with the juice in which they are packed
    1 small (4- to 6-ounce) can dietetic apricots or plums, pits re-
       moved (reserve packing liquid)
    ½ onion, cut in ¼-inch wedges
    1 medium tomato, cut into 8 wedges
    ½ bell pepper, cut into chunks
    1 tablespoon rice vinegar
    1 tablespoon fresh lemon juice
    2 teaspoons arrowroot powder or cornstarch, dissolved in 2
       tablespoons cold water

Put the stock or water, apple-juice concentrate, tomato paste, tamari, and juice from the canned fruits in a saucepan. Bring to a boil and continue to boil for 5 minutes. Add all the vegetables and the apricots or plums. Reduce the heat and simmer for 15 to 20 minutes until the onions are clarified. Add the pineapple, vinegar, and lemon juice and continue to simmer for 5 minutes. Slowly stir in the arrowroot or cornstarch solution. Cook until the sauce has thickened. The sauce is now ready to serve.

Suggested uses: Pour over Toasted Chicken (page 200) or Chicken No-Fried Rice (page 189).

⋖§ ITALIAN SAUCE

Here's your low-fat spaghetti sauce. But don't confine its uses to pasta—it's great over any steamed vegetables or to liven up rice or millet.

Makes 1½ pints

½ onion, chopped fine
½ bell pepper, sliced thin
4 cloves garlic, minced fine
2 teaspoons sweet basil
1 teaspoon oregano
½ teaspoon thyme
1 grated carrot *or* 1 tablespoon frozen apple-juice concentrate (optional)
6 fresh tomatoes, cut in wedges *or* 1 28–29-ounce can crushed tomatoes in heavy puree
1 tablespoon reduced-salt tamari or soy sauce

Combine the onions, pepper, garlic, spices, and carrot or apple-juice concentrate in a nonstick saucepan or frying pan. Sauté for 10 minutes with 1 tablespoon water until the onions clarify. Add the tomatoes and tamari and simmer over low heat for 20 minutes. The sauce is now ready to serve.

⊷§ SPICY SPAGHETTI SAUCE

A slightly more piquant version of the preceding Italian Sauce. Not *too* spicy, though.

Makes 1½ pints

- 1 onion, chopped fine
- 6 cloves garlic, chopped fine
- 1 tablespoon oregano
- 2 teaspoons sweet basil
- 1 bay leaf, crushed
- ½ teaspoon thyme
- ½ teaspoon rosemary
- ¼ teaspoon cayenne pepper or Tabasco
- 1 28–29-ounce can Italian plum tomatoes
- ½ small can tomato paste
- 1 tablespoon reduced-salt tamari or soy sauce
- 10 medium mushrooms, sliced (optional)

Sauté the onion, garlic, herbs, and spices in ½ cup water until the water has been absorbed or evaporated. Add the tomatoes and tomato paste. Continue to simmer for 30 to 40 minutes. Add tamari and the mushrooms, if used, and continue to simmer over low heat for an additional 5 minutes. The sauce is now ready to serve. Suggested uses: As a topping for Zucchini Balls (page 151) or Millet (page 245).

⊷§ MUSHROOM SAUCE

Makes 1½ pints

- ½ small onion, chopped fine
- 2 cloves garlic, minced
- 1 teaspoon sweet basil
- ½ teaspoon dillweed

½ teaspoon tarragon (optional)
½ teaspoon celery seed
2 cups defatted chicken stock (page 86) or water
1 pound fresh mushrooms, sliced
1 tablespoon reduced-salt tamari or soy sauce
1 tablespoon dry sherry
1 teaspoon brandy
2 teaspoons arrowroot powder or cornstarch dissolved in 2 tablespoons water or stock

Sauté the onion, garlic, and herbs in ½ cup defatted chicken stock or water until the liquid has cooked out. Add the remainder of the stock and bring to a boil. Add the mushrooms, tamari, sherry, and brandy and continue to simmer for 10 minutes. Slowly stir the arrowroot or cornstarch solution into the liquid. Continue to cook over low heat until the sauce has thickened. The sauce is now ready to serve. This sauce may be made creamy by addition of 1 cup nonfat yogurt and 1 tablespoon frozen apple-juice concentrate at the very end of the cooking process. Warm the sauce after the yogurt is added, but DO NOT BOIL. Serve immediately.

Suggested uses: Serve on Mashed Potatoes (page 224) or Basic Crêpes (page 294).

⇥ CLASSIC CHICKEN SAUCE

This is a rich, flavorful sauce with a French flair. Try it with any of the chicken dishes in this book, or use it as a medium for poaching sliced chicken strips (white meat, of course).

Makes 1 pint

¼ onion, minced fine
1 clove garlic, minced fine
1 teaspoon sweet basil
½ teaspoon thyme
½ teaspoon sage
a dash of Tabasco or red pepper
2 cups defatted chicken stock (page 86) or water
1 tablespoon reduced-salt tamari or soy sauce
2 tablespoons dry sherry or white Sauterne
2 teaspoons arrowroot or cornstarch

Sauté the onion, garlic, herbs, and spices in ½ cup stock or water until the onion is clarified. Add the remaining stock or water, the tamari, and the sherry. Cook for approximately 10 minutes over moderate heat. Dissolve the arrowroot or cornstarch in 2 tablespoons water, slowly stir into the sauce, and cook until thickened. The sauce is now ready to serve.

✑§ CLASSIC BEEF SAUCE

If you're addicted to the flavor of beef, this sauce is a good way to get that flavor without any of the fat or cholesterol that usually go along with it.

Makes 1 pint

¼ onion, chopped fine
3 cloves garlic, minced fine
1 teaspoon sweet basil
½ teaspoon oregano
½ teaspoon tarragon
½ teaspoon celery seed
1 teaspoon paprika
2 cups defatted beef stock (page 88)
2 tablespoons red wine
½ bell pepper, chopped fine
1 jalapeño pepper, seeded and chopped fine (optional)
1 tablespoon tamari (optional)
2 teaspoons arrowroot or cornstarch

Sauté the onion, garlic, herbs, and spices in ½ cup stock until the onion is clarified. Add the remaining stock, the wine, and both the peppers and simmer for approximately 20 minutes. Then add the tamari. Dissolve the arrowroot or cornstarch in 2 tablespoons water, slowly stir it into the sauce, and cook until the sauce has thickened. Try serving this sauce with Simple Broccoli (page 214) or Steamed Green Beans (page 212).

⌁§ CLASSIC SAUCE JARDINIÈRE (VEGETABLE)

Makes 1 pint

- 1 medium carrot, sliced
- 1 stalk celery, sliced
- ½ onion, sliced
- 2 cups defacloves garlic, chopped
- ¼ cup chopped fresh parsley *or* 2 tablespoons dry parsley
- 1 teaspoon sweet basil
- ½ teaspoon celery seed
- ½ teaspoon thyme
- ½ teaspoon marjoram
- 2 cups defatted chicken stock (page 86), vegetable stock (page 90), or water
- 2 tablespoons dry sherry
- 2 teaspoons arrowroot or cornstarch

Simmer all the vegetables and herbs in 4 tablespoons water over very low heat until the vegetables are tender (approximately 10 minutes). Place this sautéed mixture in a blender and blend until smooth. Put the resulting puree in a saucepan, add the stock or water, and bring to a boil. Reduce the heat to a simmer and add the sherry. In a separate cup dissolve the arrowroot or cornstarch in 2 tablespoons of water and slowly stir into the sauce. Cook until thickened. The sauce is now ready to serve.

Suggested uses: Serve on Steamed Cabbage (page 215) or Baked Fish (page 165).

◄§ WHITE SAUCE FOR QUICHE

The idea of putting a sauce on quiche may sound strange to quiche-lovers. Well, when quiche is made with dry cottage cheese instead of the usual Muensters, Jacks, and so on (all of which, by the way, are about ⅓ fat), it will have a drier texture than you are used to. Hence this sauce, which should be served over the quiche on page 137.

Makes 1 pint

2 cups defatted chicken stock (page 86) or water
1 teaspoon rosemary
1 tablespoon reduced-salt tamari or soy sauce
1 tablespoon cornstarch dissolved in ½ cup cold water
1 cup nonfat yogurt (page 72)

Bring the stock to a boil in a 1-quart pot. Add the rosemary, tamari, and cornstarch solution. Continue to cook until the liquid has thickened. Turn off the heat, add the nonfat yogurt, stir, and serve.

◄§ SPANISH SAUCE

Makes 1½ pints

½ onion, chopped fine
2 cloves garlic, minced fine
½ bell pepper, chopped fine
1 teaspoon ground cumin
1 teaspoon coriander
½ teaspoon oregano
1 tablespoon chili powder
1 teaspoon paprika
6 fresh tomatoes cut into quarters or 1 28–29-ounce can crushed tomatoes in heavy puree
1 tablespoon reduced-salt tamari or soy sauce

Place the onion, garlic, bell pepper, spices, and herbs in a frying pan with ½ cup water. Sauté until the liquid is gone. Add the tomatoes and continue to simmer over low temperature for 20 minutes. A few minutes before the sauce is done, stir in the tamari. This sauce is delicious over Enchiladas (page 132), Steamed Cabbage (page 215), or Dirty Rice (page 240).

◄§ SALSA PICANTE

Makes 1 pint

  4 fresh tomatoes, cut into ½-inch cubes
  1 onion, peeled and chopped fine
  1 fresh or canned jalapeño pepper, seeded and chopped fine
  1 clove garlic, peeled and minced fine
  a dash of cayenne (optional)
  juice of 1 lemon or lime
  ½ cup chopped fresh cilantro or 2 tablespoons dry (optional)
  1 tablespoon reduced-salt tamari or soy sauce

Mix all ingredients thoroughly in a large bowl. Chill and serve with toasted corn tortilla chips.

◄§ CURRY SAUCE

This sauce can be made either sweet or spicy. Use apple-juice concentrate if you prefer a sweet sauce; use the cayenne or Tabasco if you want a spicy one.

Makes 1 pint

  ½ onion, chopped fine
  2 cloves garlic, minced fine
  ½ bell pepper, seeds removed, chopped fine

　　1　small jalapeño pepper, seeds removed, chopped fine
　　2　tablespoons frozen apple-juice concentrate *or* ¼ teaspoon
　　　　cayenne or Tabasco
　1½　teaspoons curry powder
　　2　cups defatted chicken stock (page 86) or water
　　1　tablespoon reduced-salt tamari or soy sauce
　　2　teaspoons arrowroot or cornstarch

Sauté the onion, garlic, bell pepper, jalapeño, apple-juice concentrate (if used), and spices in ½ cup stock or water until the onion is clarified. Then add the remaining stock or water and the tamari and simmer over low heat for 20 minutes. In a separate cup dissolve the arrowroot or cornstarch in 2 table-spoons cold water and slowly stir it into the sauce. Simmer an additional 2 to 3 minutes until the sauce is thickened.

Suggested uses: Spoon over Toasted Fish Fillets (page 165) or Steamed Green Beans (page 212).

✒§ TANGY LEMON SAUCE

Makes 1 pint

　　2　cups nonfat yogurt (page 72)
　　2　tablespoons frozen apple-juice concentrate
　　1　tablespoon fresh lemon juice
　　1　teaspoon grated lemon rind
　　1　teaspoon dillweed
　½　teaspoon tarragon
　　1　tablespoon arrowroot or cornstarch

Place all the ingredients in a double boiler. Stir until the ingredients are thoroughly mixed and heat for approximately 15 minutes. DO NOT BOIL. Serve immediately.

Suggested uses: Serve on Baked Fish (page 165) or Simple Broccoli (page 214).

❧ DILL SAUCE

Makes 1 cup

1 cup nonfat yogurt (page 72)
1 tablespoon frozen apple-juice concentrate
1 tablespoon dillweed
½ teaspoon Dijon mustard
1 teaspoon salt-reduced tamari

Mix all the ingredients together thoroughly, heat but DO NOT BOIL, and serve immediately. Note: a double boiler is recommended but not required.

Suggested uses: Spoon over Baked Haddock and Vegetables (page 167) or Country Baked Tomatoes (page 144).

❧ MUSTARD-DILL SAUCE

Makes 1 pint

½ onion, minced fine
2 cloves garlic, minced fine
1 jalapeño pepper, seeds removed, minced fine
1 teaspoon dillweed
½ teaspoon coriander
2   cups defatted chicken stock (page 86) or water
2 tablespoons Dijon mustard (salt-free if possible)
2 tablespoons frozen apple-juice concentrate
1 tablespoon reduced-salt tamari or soy sauce (optional)

Sauté the onion, garlic, jalapeño, dill, and coriander in ½ cup defatted chicken stock or water until the liquid has cooked out. Add the remainder of the ingredients and simmer over low heat for 10 to 15 minutes. The sauce is now ready to serve.

Suggested uses: Serve with Squash Soufflé (page 141) or Kasha (page 246).

⊷§ PEPPER-BEEF SAUCE

Makes 1 pint

½ onion, minced fine
2 cloves garlic, minced fine
1 teaspoon sweet basil
1 teaspoon paprika
½ teaspoon celery seed
2 cups defatted beef stock (page 88)
2 tablespoons Marsala wine
1 bell pepper, sliced thin
1 jalapeño pepper, seeds removed, chopped fine
2 tablespoons fine-chopped pimento
1 tablespoon reduced-salt tamari or soy sauce (optional)
2 teaspoons arrowroot or cornstarch

Sauté the onion, garlic, basil, paprika, and celery seed in ½ cup stock until the onion is cooked. Add the remaining stock and the wine, both peppers, and the pimento and simmer for approximately 20 minutes. Stir in the tamari. Dissolve the arrowroot or cornstarch in 2 tablespoons water, slowly stir it into the sauce, and cook until the sauce has thickened.

Suggested uses: Pour over Stuffing Mediterranean (page 242) or Steamed Cabbage (page 215).

✑ CREAMY PARSLEY SAUCE

Makes 1 pint

2 cups nonfat yogurt (page 72)
1 tablespoon grated lemon rind
1 tablespoon chopped pimento
1 tablespoon dried sweet basil *or* 2 teaspoons chopped fresh basil
¼ cup chopped fresh parsley *or* 2 tablespoons dry parsley
½ teaspoon celery seed
1 tablespoon reduced-salt tamari or soy sauce
2 teaspoons arrowroot or cornstarch

In a double boiler or a saucepan, heat the yogurt until it is steaming. DO NOT BOIL. Slowly stir in the lemon rind, pimento, herbs, and tamari. In a separate cup dissolve the arrowroot or cornstarch in 2 tablespoons of water, and slowly stir into the heated sauce. Continue to cook over low heat until the sauce is thickened. The sauce is now ready to serve.

Suggested uses: Serve over Toasted Fish (page 165) or Simple Cauliflower (page 217).

✑ CREAMY CAULIFLOWER SAUCE

Makes 1½ pints

½ medium cauliflower, cut into 1-inch cubes
2 cups defatted chicken stock (page 86) or water
1 potato, baked in foil for 1 hour at 400°F.
1 cup nonfat yogurt (page 72)
2 tablespoons frozen apple-juice concentrate
½ onion, chopped fine
2 cloves garlic, minced fine
1 tablespoon Dijon mustard (salt-free if possible)
1 teaspoon dillweed

1 teaspoon sweet basil
½ teaspoon curry powder
¼ teaspoon cayenne or Tabasco (optional)

Place the cauliflower and 1 cup stock or water in a saucepan. Steam for 12 minutes or until the cauliflower is tender. Put the cauliflower with its cooking liquid in a blender. Remove the skin from the baked potato and add the potato to the blender along with the yogurt and apple juice. Blend until smooth. Sauté the onion, garlic, mustard, and spices in the remaining stock or water until the onion is cooked. Slowly stir in the blended puree and heat until the sauce is steaming. DO NOT BOIL. The sauce is now ready to serve.

Suggested uses: Spoon over Baked Haddock and Vegetables (page 167) or Mashed Potatoes (page 224).

◄§ RATATOUILLE SAUCE

Makes 1½ pints

½ onion, sliced thin
6 cloves garlic, minced fine
2 teaspoons dried basil
1 teaspoon oregano
1 teaspoon paprika
1 cup defatted chicken stock (page 86) or water
1 eggplant, peeled and cut into 1-inch chunks
2 fresh tomatoes, cut into 1-inch chunks
½ pound fresh mushrooms, quartered
1 tablespoon Marsala wine or Burgundy

Sauté the onion, garlic, herbs, and paprika in the stock until the onions clarify. Add the eggplant and tomatoes and continue to cook until the eggplant is very tender and soft.

Add the mushrooms and wine and simmer an additional 7 to 10 minutes. The sauce is now ready to serve. If desired, the sauce may be blended until smooth.

Suggested uses: Pour over Zucchini Balls (page 151) or brown rice (page 237).

Desserts

To most people the word "diet" is synonymous with the word "sacrifice," and what usually gets sacrificed first is the dessert. Well, I have good news: you're about to learn how to make delicious, wholesome, and satisfying desserts that are not only almost entirely fat-free, but guilt-free as well.

Here the basic secret lies in replacing refined sugar and honey (which has the same metabolic effect as sugar) with fruits and frozen fruit concentrates. The natural sugars in fruits will impart a tantalizing sweetness to your desserts without ravaging your body at the same time. You'll be amazed at what you can do: cookies, pies, cakes of all sorts, cheesecakes ... almost anything in the realm of desserts can be yours!

Puddings, Pies, and Cookies

One of the best ways to take advantage of the food value of grains and fruits—yet still satisfy the old sweet tooth—is to use them in puddings, pies, or cookies. And perhaps the best

265

thing about these recipes is that the amount of fat and cholesterol is just about zero. (By the way, the caloric level of these
recipes is about ⅓ that of their sugar-and-butter counterparts.)

I'll never forget an architect I once cooked for who thought
when he'd gone on his low-fat diet that he'd given up his
mom's cherished apple-raisin pie forever. Well, I made one
for him. Two or three bites later, he offered to build a guest-
house for me in his backyard!

✑ OLD-FASHIONED BREAD PUDDING

Serves 4–6

> 3 cups nonfat milk
> 1 6-ounce can (¾ cup) frozen apple-juice concentrate
> 1 teaspoon pure vanilla extract
> 1 teaspoon cinnamon
> ½ cup raisins
> 6 egg whites
> 5–6 slices whole-wheat bread, crust removed, cut into 1-inch
> squares

Preheat your oven to 350°F. Warm the milk in a saucepan,
remove it from the heat, and add the apple-juice concentrate,
vanilla, cinnamon, and raisins. In a large bowl, beat the egg
whites until stiff. Place the bread in an 8-inch-square Pyrex
dish. Pour the milk mixture slowly into the egg whites, folding
them together gently. Pour the milk-and-egg mixture over the
bread and set the baking dish in a roasting pan with ½ inch of
water in the bottom. Place in the preheated oven for 40 to 50
minutes or until a fork inserted in the center comes out clean.
Serve hot or cold, topped with Yogurt Cream (page 319).

✎§ OLD-FASHIONED RICE PUDDING

Serves 4–6

2 cups cooked long-grain brown rice
2 bananas, mashed
1 cup nonfat milk
½ teaspoon cinnamon
½ cup frozen apple-juice concentrate
¼ cup raisins
3 egg whites, lightly beaten until foamy

Preheat the oven to 350°F. Mix together all the ingredients except the egg whites. When the mixture is smooth, fold in the egg whites, pour the pudding into an 8-inch-square Pyrex baking dish, and place in a 350°F. oven for 40 minutes or until completely set. Serve hot or cold with "Whipped Cream" Topping (page 318).

✎§ RICE CUSTARD

Serves 4–6

1 tablespoon raisin-juice concentrate *or* 2 tablespoons frozen apple-juice concentrate
1 cup cooked long-grain brown rice
1 tablespoon pure vanilla extract
3 cups nonfat dry milk
1 tablespoon grated lemon rind
½ cup tapioca flour
¼ cup raisins

Bring 2 cups of water and the raisin- or apple-juice concentrate to a boil in a 1½–2-quart pot and add the rice, vanilla, nonfat milk, and lemon rind. Mix the tapioca flour with 1 cup of cold water and stir into the boiling liquid. Remove from the heat, stir in the raisins, and pour into 4–6 individual bowls. Cover the bowls with waxed paper to prevent a "skin" from forming on top, and refrigerate for 1 hour. Serve chilled with "Whipped Cream" Topping (page 318).

⊷§ TAPIOCA SUPREME

Serves 4–6

1 cup old-fashioned dry pearl tapioca
1 tablespoon arrowroot or cornstarch
1 teaspoon grated orange rind
1 tablespoon pure vanilla extract
1 6-ounce can (¾ cup) frozen apple-juice concentrate
½ teaspoon cinnamon
6 egg whites, beaten until stiff

Soak the tapioca in 2 cups of water until it is softened (approximately 30 minutes); then drain. Place all the ingredients except the egg whites in the top of a double boiler. Heat until steam starts to rise from the surface of the hot liquid. Whip in the eggs until the pudding is light and fluffy. Pour into 4 to 6 serving cups and chill.

⊷§ CAROB MOUSSE

Serves 4–6

2½ cups nonfat milk
4 tablespoons carob powder (unsweetened)
2 tablespoons cornstarch
1 teaspoon pure vanilla extract
6 egg whites

Preheat your oven to 350°F. Warm the milk, carob, and cornstarch in a saucepan until the mixture is steamy and thickening. Remove from the heat and stir in the vanilla extract. In a large bowl beat the egg whites until stiff and peaking; then fold in the milk-and-carob mixture. Pour into a nonstick baking dish or piecrust (recipe page 271) and bake in the preheated oven for 25 minutes. Chill and serve with "Whipped Cream" Topping (page 318).

◆§ PEACH FRUIT CREAM

Although I call this "Peach Fruit Cream," it can actually be made with just about any fresh or frozen fruit—the varieties are endless. Try it with strawberries over apples, for example, or raspberries over pears. For an exotic touch, it's delicious using pineapples over melons. Or . . . well, you get the idea.

Serves 4–6

1 cup fresh or frozen blueberries (no sugar added)
1 tablespoon pure vanilla extract
1 tablespoon frozen apple-juice concentrate
2 cups nonfat yogurt (page 72)
3 fresh or frozen peaches, sliced

Puree the berries, vanilla, apple juice, and yogurt in a blender. Pour over the peaches, chill, and serve.

◆§ FRUIT ICE CREAM

Here's a delicious ice cream with a rich, old-fashioned flavor, yet it requires no elaborate machinery. And by the way, you can make it in any fruit flavor that appeals to you, including coconut and, yes, even piña colada! (See the recipes below.)

Keep a plastic bag of peeled bananas in the freezer so you can whip some up anytime.

Serves 4

4 frozen peeled bananas, broken into chunks
½ cup frozen apple-juice concentrate
2 cups frozen mixed berries (blueberries, cherries, strawberries, and so on) or 2 cups whatever fruit you prefer, cut into small pieces and frozen
½ cup nonfat dry milk

Put the bananas and apple-juice concentrate in a blender. Blend until smooth. Add the frozen berries and blend again. Sprinkle in the dry milk and blend. Eat immediately as a soft ice cream, or freeze in a covered container if you prefer hard ice cream.

For an elegant dessert, hollow out orange halves, fill them with ice cream, and top with Grape-Nuts or fresh fruit.

◄§ COCONUT ICE CREAM

Serves 4

4 frozen peeled bananas, broken into chunks
2 teaspoons coconut extract
½ cup frozen apple-juice concentrate
½ cup nonfat dry milk

Blend the bananas, coconut extract, and apple-juice concentrate in a blender or food processor until smooth. Sprinkle in the dry milk and blend again. See Fruit Ice Cream above for serving suggestions.

✌§ PIÑA COLADA ICE CREAM

Serves 4

4 frozen peeled bananas, broken into chunks
1 teaspoon coconut extract
1 tablespoon frozen orange-juice concentrate
½ cup frozen apple-juice concentrate
1 cup pineapple chunks
½ cup nonfat dry milk

Put the bananas, coconut extract, and orange- and apple-juice concentrates in a blender. Blend until smooth. Add the pineapple and blend again. Finally, sprinkle in the dry milk, blend, and serve. See Fruit Ice Cream above for serving suggestions.

✌§ BASIC PIECRUST

1 cup Date Granola (page 37) *or* 1 cup rolled oats *or* 1 cup Grape-Nuts
¼ cup frozen apple-juice concentrate

Moisten the grain you select with the apple-juice concentrate and pat onto the bottom and sides of a 9-inch nonstick pie pan or an 8-inch-square baking dish. Toast for 15 minutes in a 350°F. oven.

Note: If you use rolled oats, 2 tablespoons of such whole-grain flakes as rye, wheat, or bran can be added to vary the flavor of the crust.

✥ APPLE-PUDDING PIE

This "pie" is rich enough to serve without a crust, but use one if you wish.

Serves 6–8

- 1 cup whole-wheat flour
- 2 cups nonfat milk or nonfat yogurt (page 72)
- ½ cup frozen apple-juice concentrate
- 1 tablespoon pure vanilla extract
- 2 egg whites
- 1 teaspoon cinnamon
- 1 tablespoon grated orange rind
- ¼ cup raisins
- 3–4 apples, peeled, cored, and sliced
- 1 piecrust (optional)

Combine the flour, nonfat milk, apple-juice concentrate, vanilla, egg whites, cinnamon, orange rind, and raisins in a bowl. Mix thoroughly, but DO NOT BEAT. Add the apple slices and fold gently, being careful not to break the apples. Place this mixture in a nonstick pie pan or in a prepared crust and bake at 400°F. for 30 to 40 minutes or until lightly browned.

Note: Grape-Nuts or bran flakes can be sprinkled over the pie before baking.

₰§ PUMPKIN PIE

Great news! Pumpkin pie is back! Now your holiday dinners can be just as lavish as they were before you went on your low-fat diet.

Serves 6–8

> 1 16-ounce can pumpkin, or meat from 1 fresh medium pumpkin
> 1 6-ounce can (¾ cup) frozen apple-juice concentrate
> 1 teaspoon cinnamon
> 1 13-ounce can evaporated skim milk
> ½ teaspoon grated fresh ginger or powdered dry ginger
> ¼ teaspoon ground cloves (optional)
> 2 egg whites, stirred but not beaten
> 1 piecrust (page 271)

Put all the ingredients except the crust in a bowl and mix thoroughly. Pour the pumpkin mixture into the piecrust and bake in a 375°F. oven for 50 minutes to 1 hour until the top is firm and slightly cracking.

₰§ SWEET POTATO PIE

For that Soul Food touch!

Serves 6–8

> 1 large or 2 medium yams, wrapped in foil and baked in a 400°F. oven for 1 hour
> 1 6-ounce can (¾ cup) frozen apple-juice concentrate
> 1 teaspoon cinnamon
> 1 13-ounce can evaporated skim milk
> ½ teaspoon grated fresh ginger or powdered dry ginger
> ¼ teaspoon ground cloves (optional)
> 2 egg whites, stirred but not beaten
> 1 piecrust (page 271)

Cool and peel the yams, mash, and measure 2 cups. Place in a bowl with all the other ingredients except the crust and mix thoroughly. Pour the sweet potato filling into the piecrust and bake in a 375°F. oven for 50 minutes to 1 hour until the top is firm and slightly cracking.

✒︎§ STRAWBERRY PIE

Serves 6–8

2 pint baskets fresh strawberries, washed, hulled, and cut into small chunks *or* 2 packages frozen strawberries, thawed and drained
1 6-ounce can (¾ cup) frozen apple-juice concentrate
1 tablespoon pure vanilla extract
1 tablespoon arrowroot powder or cornstarch
1 piecrust (page 271)

Heat the apple juice, vanilla, arrowroot powder or cornstarch, and ½ cup water in a saucepan until the mixture thickens. Pour over the fruit and mix. Pour into the prepared piecrust and refrigerate for 30 minutes.

✒︎§ APPLE-PINEAPPLE PIE

Serves 6–8

2 apples, peeled, cored, and cut into small chunks
1 tablespoon lemon juice
1 fresh pineapple, peeled, cored, and cut into small chunks
1 6-ounce can (¾ cup) frozen apple-juice concentrate
1 tablespoon pure coconut extract
1 tablespoon arrowroot powder or cornstarch
1 piecrust (page 271)

Preheat your oven to 400°F. Soak the apples in a large bowl with 6 cups of water and the lemon juice for several hours. Pour off the liquid and add the pineapple chunks, apple-juice concentrate, and coconut extract. Mix well. Dissolve the arrowroot or cornstarch in ½ cup water and add to the mixture to thicken. Pour into prepared piecrust, cover with foil, and bake for 1 hour.

Note: Grape-Nuts or bran flakes may be sprinkled over the pie before baking.

✦§ PEAR-APPLE-PEACH PIE

Serves 6–8

2 apples, peeled, cored, and cut into small chunks
4 pears, peeled, cored, and cut into small chunks
1 tablespoon lemon juice
2 peaches, peeled and pitted *or* 1 small can water-packed peaches, drained, cut into small chunks
1 6-ounce can (¾ cup) frozen apple-juice concentrate
1 tablespoon pure vanilla extract
1 tablespoon arrowroot powder or cornstarch, dissolved in ½ cup cold water
1 piecrust (page 271)

Preheat your oven to 400°F. Soak the apples and pears in 8 cups of water and the lemon juice for several hours. Pour off the liquid and add the peaches, apple-juice concentrate, and vanilla extract. Mix well. Stir in the arrowroot or cornstarch solution. Pour into the prepared piecrust. Bake, covered with foil, for 1 hour.

Note: Grape-Nuts or bran flakes may be sprinkled over the pie before baking.

⇜§ APPLE-RAISIN PIE

Serves 6–8

8 medium apples, peeled, cored, and cut into chunks
1 tablespoon lemon juice
1 6-ounce can (¾ cup) frozen apple-juice concentrate
¼ cup raisins
¼ cup Grape-Nuts (optional)
1 teaspoon cinnamon
a dash of nutmeg
1 tablespoon dry sherry
1 tablespoon arrowroot powder or cornstarch
1 piecrust (page 271)

Preheat your oven to 400°F. Soak the apples in a bowl with 6 cups of water and the lemon juice for several hours. Pour off the liquid and add the apple-juice concentrate, raisins, Grape-Nuts (if used), cinnamon, nutmeg, and sherry and mix well. Dissolve the arrowroot or cornstarch in ½ cup of water and stir into the filling to thicken it. Pour the filling into the piecrust and bake, covered with foil, for 1 hour.

Note: Omit the raisins if you prefer apple pie only.

⇜§ FRENCH APPLE TART I

Serves 6–8

¼ cup Grape-Nuts
½ cup frozen apple-juice concentrate
4 medium apples, peeled, cored, and sliced thin
1 tablespoon lemon juice
½ teaspoon cinnamon

GLAZE

1 tablespoon arrowroot powder or cornstarch
½ cup frozen apple-juice concentrate

Moisten the Grape-Nuts with ¼ cup frozen apple-juice concentrate and pat into a thin layer in a nonstick tart pan. Use more apple-juice concentrate if the mixture is too dry. Sprinkle the crust with ¼ teaspoon cinnamon. Arrange the apples in overlapping circles, starting at the outside rim and ending in the center. Sprinkle with lemon juice and ¼ teaspoon cinnamon. Cover with foil and bake in a 350°F. oven for 45 minutes or until the apples are tender. Remove from the oven and cool to room temperature.

In a saucepan, combine ½ cup apple-juice concentrate, the arrowroot powder or cornstarch, and 2 tablespoons water and cook and stir until the mixture thickens and clears. Spoon this mixture over the apples and chill.

✒ FRENCH APPLE TART II

Serves 4–6

1 cup uncooked rolled oats
4 cups thin-sliced apples
½ teaspoon cinnamon
½ cup raisins
⅔ cup unsweetened pineapple juice
¼ cup Grape-Nuts

Spread a layer of rolled oats in the bottom of an 8-inch-square baking dish. Toast lightly in a 350°F. oven. Arrange the sliced apples on top of the oats. Sprinkle the cinnamon and raisins on the apples. Pour the pineapple juice over the top of the tart, cover with foil, and bake for 1 hour at 350°F. Remove the cover, sprinkle with Grape-Nuts, and continue to bake for 15 minutes.

✺§ NOUVELLE PIE

This recipe was inspired by the Nouvelle Cuisine of
France, which has a lighter, more delicate texture and relies
more on fruits and less on creams and heavy sauces.

Serves 6–8

2 **apples, peeled, cored, and cut into small chunks**
2 **pears, peeled and cored** *or* 1 **small (6–8 ounces) can water-
packed pears, drained, cut into small chunks**
1 **peach, peeled and pitted,** *or* 1 **small (6–8 ounces) can water-
packed peaches, drained, cut into small chunks**
1 **cup blueberries (if frozen, thawed and drained)**
1 **tablespoon arrowroot powder**
1 **tablespoon brandy**
2 **tablespoons dry sherry**
1 **tablespoon pure vanilla extract**
1 **piecrust (page 271)**
2 **kiwi fruit**
¼ **cup blueberries for topping**

Combine all the fruit, except the kiwi fruit and the blueberries for topping, in a large mixing bowl. Dissolve the arrowroot powder in ½ cup water and pour over the fruit. Add
the brandy, sherry, and vanilla and mix thoroughly. Pour this
mixture into the prepared piecrust. Peel the kiwis and slice
them thin; arrange the slices on top of the pie in a circle, leav-
ing the center open. Pour the reserved blueberries in the center of the kiwi fruit. Cover and bake at 400°F. for 1 hour.

❧ ALL-GRAIN SUPERCOOKIES

Makes 16 3-inch cookies

½ cup whole-wheat flour
2 teaspoons low-sodium baking powder
1 teaspoon baking soda
½ teaspoon cinnamon
½ cup cooked brown rice
½ cup wheat flakes
½ cup rolled oats
1 6-ounce can (¾ cup) frozen apple-juice concentrate
¾ cup nonfat milk
¼ cup raisins
1 tablespoon pure vanilla extract

Preheat your oven to 375°F. Mix the flour, baking powder, baking soda, and cinnamon together in a large bowl. Add all the remaining ingredients and mix thoroughly. DO NOT BEAT. Spoon 2 tablespoons of cookie mixture at a time onto a nonstick baking sheet, keeping the cookies 2 inches apart, and bake for 15 minutes, or until toasty.

ISLAND SPICE COOKIES

Makes 16 3-inch cookies

2 cups whole-wheat flour
2 teaspoons low-sodium baking powder
1 teaspoon baking soda
1 cup crushed pineapple, fresh or dietetic canned, drained
1 apple, peeled, cored, and chopped fine
1 banana, peeled and mashed
1 tablespoon grated orange peel
1 6-ounce can (¾ cup) frozen apple-juice concentrate
1 tablespoon coconut extract
½ teaspoon cinnamon
1 teaspoon fine-minced fresh ginger (optional)
¾ cup nonfat milk or evaporated skim milk

Preheat your oven to 375°F. Mix the flour, baking powder, and baking soda in a large bowl. Add all the remaining ingredients and mix thoroughly. Spoon the cookie batter onto a nonstick baking sheet in 1-tablespoon drops approximately 2 inches apart. Bake for 15 to 20 minutes, until golden brown.

BANANA-BRAN COOKIES

Makes 18–24 2-inch cookies

1 cup whole-wheat flour
2 teaspoons low-sodium baking powder
1 teaspoon baking soda
2 bananas, peeled and mashed until smooth
1 cup bran flakes
½ teaspoon cinnamon
½ cup raisins (optional)
1 6-ounce can (¾ cup) frozen apple-juice concentrate

¼ cup Grape-Nuts (optional)
¾ cup nonfat milk or evaporated skim milk
1 tablespoon pure vanilla extract

Preheat your oven to 375°F. Combine the flour, baking powder, and baking soda in a large bowl. Add all the remaining ingredients and mix thoroughly. Spoon the cookie batter onto a nonstick baking sheet in 1-tablespoon drops approximately 2 inches apart. Bake for 15 to 20 minutes, until the cookies are golden brown.

◄§ SWEET POTATO COOKIES

Makes 18–24 2-inch cookies

1 cup whole-wheat flour
2 teaspoons low-sodium baking powder
1 teaspoon baking soda
1 large yam or sweet potato, baked for 1 hour in aluminum foil
½ cup pitted and chopped dates *or* ½ cup raisins
½ teaspoon cinnamon
1 tablespoon pure vanilla extract
1 6-ounce can (¾ cup) frozen apple-juice concentrate
½ cup nonfat milk or evaporated skim milk
a dash of nutmeg (optional)

Preheat your oven to 375°F. Mix the flour with the baking powder and baking soda in a large bowl. Peel the yam, mash until smooth, and measure 1½ cups. Add, with all the remaining ingredients, to the dry mixture and mix thoroughly. Spoon 1-tablespoon drops of this cookie batter approximately 2 inches apart on a nonstick baking sheet. Bake for 15 to 20 minutes, until the cookies are golden brown.

~§ OATMEAL-RAISIN COOKIES

Makes 16–18 3-inch cookies

1 cup whole-wheat flour
2 teaspoons low-sodium baking powder
1 teaspoon baking soda
1 cup rolled oats
½ cup raisins
1 6-ounce can (¾ cup) frozen apple-juice concentrate
¾ cup nonfat milk or evaporated skim milk
1 tablespoon pure vanilla extract
¼ teaspoon cinnamon

Preheat your oven to 375°F. Combine the flour, baking powder, and baking soda in a mixing bowl. Add the rest of the ingredients and mix together thoroughly. Place 2-tablespoon drops of batter 2 inches apart on a nonstick baking sheet. Bake for 12 to 15 minutes, or until the cookies are golden brown.

~§ APPLE-SPICE COOKIES

Makes 16–18 3-inch cookies

1 cup whole-wheat flour
2 teaspoons low-sodium baking powder
1 teaspoon baking soda
1 teaspoon sesame seed (optional)
½ teaspoon cinnamon
½ cup nonfat milk or evaporated skim milk
½ cup frozen apple-juice concentrate
2 teaspoons pure vanilla extract
1 tablespoon lemon juice
2 apples, peeled, cored, cut into ½-inch wedges and then into little chunks
2 tablespoons chopped raisins

Preheat your oven to 375°F. Put all the dry ingredients in a mixing bowl and mix together thoroughly. Add the liquid ingredients, apples, and raisins and blend together until mixed thoroughly. Place 1-tablespoon drops of this batter 2 inches apart on a nonstick baking sheet. Bake for 12 to 15 minutes, until the cookies are lightly golden.

⊸§ CAROB COOKIES

Makes 18–24 2-inch cookies

- **2 cups whole-wheat flour**
- **6 tablespoons unsweetened carob powder, sifted**
- **2 teaspoons low-sodium baking powder**
- **1 teaspoon baking soda**
- **¼ teaspoon instant Sanka coffee (optional)**
- **¾ cup nonfat milk**
- **¾ cup frozen apple-juice concentrate**
- **1 tablespoon pure vanilla extract**

Preheat your oven to 375°F. Combine all the dry ingredients in a large bowl. Add the milk, apple-juice concentrate, and vanilla extract and mix thoroughly with a whisk or wooden spoon. DO NOT BEAT. Spoon 1–1½ tablespoons of mixture at a time onto a nonstick baking sheet, keeping the cookies 2 inches apart. Bake for 12 to 15 minutes.

Note: For a crunchy texture, the cookies may be sprinkled with raw sesame seed, wheat flakes, or Grape-Nuts before baking. When cooled, each cookie can be topped with 1 teaspoon of Yogurt Cream (page 319), then chilled. Or put 1 teaspoon Yogurt Cream between two cookies.

Cakes and Crêpes

On a low-fat diet, one would think that cakes and crêpes would be the most *verboten* of all the dessert no-no's. Well, these cakes and crêpes are not only fat-free but so nutritious that you can eat them for breakfast! The cakes can be baked as sheet cakes, loaves, or layer cakes, depending on the style you want and the kind of pan you have available. They can be glazed with fruit toppings, with Yogurt Cream (page 319), or with "Whipped Cream" (page 318) or served *au naturel*. These cakes are done when the top cracks in the middle and the cake begins to come away from the sides of the pan. Or stick a toothpick in the center of the cake. If it comes out clean, the cake is done.

The crêpe, of course, is one of the world's most versatile foods. You can stuff it with almost anything, from cheese or salmon, for appetizers or entrées, to fruits with Yogurt Cream toppings for desserts.

❧ STREUSEL COFFEE CAKE

Serves 6–8

TOPPING

- 2 cups Grape-Nuts
- 4 tablespoons frozen apple-juice concentrate
- 1 teaspoon pure vanilla extract
- 1 teaspoon cinnamon
- ¼ teaspoon nutmeg
- ¼ teaspoon ground cardamom

Grind the Grape-Nuts in a blender or food processor long enough to reduce the coarseness; do not grind them too fine. Combine the rest of the topping ingredients in a mixing bowl, fold in the Grape-Nuts, and mix well. Set aside.

CAKE

- 1 **cup raisins**
- 3 **cups whole-wheat flour**
- 1 **tablespoon baking powder**
- 2 **teaspoons baking soda**
- ⅓ **cup carob powder, unsweetened**
- 4 **teaspoons cinnamon**
- ¾ **teaspoon ground cardamom**
- 1 **teaspoon nutmeg**
- 1 **cup frozen apple-juice concentrate**
- 1 **cup evaporated skim milk**
- ⅓ **cup dry sherry**
- 2 **tablespoons pure vanilla extract**
- 2½ **large bananas, mashed**

Soak the raisins in just enough hot water to cover them. In a large mixing bowl, sift together the flour, baking powder, baking soda, carob powder, and spices. Mix the remaining ingredients together in a separate bowl and stir them into the dry ingredients. Drain the raisins, add them to the batter, and stir well. Pour the batter into 2 nonstick 9-inch loaf pans and sprinkle the topping evenly over cakes. Bake, uncovered, for 50 to 60 minutes at 350°F.

✒ BANANA-BRAN LOAF

Serves 6–8

2 cups whole-wheat flour
1 cup bran
2 teaspoons baking powder
2 teaspoons baking soda
1 teaspoon cinnamon
¼ cup raisins, soaked for 15 minutes and drained
6 large bananas
1 tablespoon pure vanilla extract
1 cup frozen apple-juice concentrate
1 13-ounce can evaporated skim milk

Combine the flour, bran, baking powder, baking soda, and cinnamon in a large mixing bowl. Stir in the raisins. Blend the bananas with the vanilla, apple juice, and milk. Mix the banana mixture into the dry ingredients. Bake in a nonstick loaf pan for 45 minutes in a 375°F. oven. Turn the heat up to 400° for the last 10 to 15 minutes to brown the crust. Remove from the oven and let the loaf cool to lukewarm before removing from the pan. Serve warm or cold.

✒ APPLE CAKE

Serves 6–8

5–6 medium apples, peeled, cored, and diced fine
¾ cup (1 6-ounce can) frozen apple-juice concentrate
¼ cup raisins
2 cups whole-wheat flour
1 tablespoon baking powder
2 teaspoons baking soda
2 teaspoons cinnamon
⅛ teaspoon nutmeg

¾ cup evaporated skim milk
1 tablespoon pure vanilla extract
1 cup Grape-Nuts or bran flakes

In a bowl, combine the apples, apple-juice concentrate, and raisins. Cover with plastic wrap and place in the refrigerator for 4 to 6 hours. Mix the flour, baking powder, baking soda, cinnamon, and nutmeg together in a large bowl. Add the apple-raisin mixture, evaporated milk, vanilla, and Grape-Nuts or bran flakes and stir well. Pour into a nonstick bundt pan and bake at 325°F. for 1½ hours.

✌§ BASIC BRAN LOAF

Serves 6–8

1 cup bran flakes
1 cup whole-wheat flour
2 teaspoons baking powder
1 teaspoon baking soda
1 teaspoon cinnamon
a dash of nutmeg
¾ cup (1 6-ounce can) frozen apple-juice concentrate
¾ cup evaporated skim milk

Combine all the dry ingredients in a mixing bowl. Then add the liquids, stirring until the batter is mixed thoroughly. Pour into a nonstick 9-inch loaf pan and bake for 30 minutes at 375°F.

⋖§ APPLE-BRAN CAKE

Serves 6–8

  2 apples, peeled, cored, and diced into small chunks *or* 1½
    cups any other fresh or frozen (thawed) fruit
  ¾ cup (1 6-ounce can) frozen apple-juice concentrate
  1 teaspoon lemon juice
  1 cup bran flakes
1½ cups whole-wheat flour
  2 teaspoons baking powder
  1 teaspoon baking soda
  1 teaspoon cinnamon
a dash of nutmeg
  1 cup evaporated skim milk
  1 tablespoon pure vanilla extract
  ¼ cup black currants or raisins

Soak the apples in the frozen apple-juice concentrate and
lemon juice for 1 hour. Combine the dry ingredients in a mixing bowl, then add the liquids. Mix thoroughly. Fold in the
apples with the liquid in which they have been soaking and
the currants or raisins and bake in a nonstick loaf pan for 30
to 40 minutes at 375°F., until the top of the cake has cracked
and the edges have turned golden brown.

⋖§ CARROT CAKE

Serves 6–8

  2 cups whole-wheat flour
  1 tablespoon baking powder
  2 teaspoons baking soda
  ½ teaspoon cinnamon
  ¾ cup (1 6-ounce can) frozen apple-juice concentrate
  1 tablespoon pure vanilla extract

3 medium carrots, scraped and grated (about 2 cups grated carrot)
1 teaspoon grated orange rind
1 large orange, peeled, seeded, and chopped very fine
¾ cup nonfat milk
¾ cup evaporated skim milk

Combine the flour, baking powder, baking soda, and cinnamon in a large mixing bowl and mix in the apple juice and vanilla. Mix well. Add the grated carrots, orange rind, chopped orange, and all the milk and stir. DO NOT BEAT. Pour the batter into 2 nonstick round 9-inch cake pans and bake in a 350°F. oven for 40 minutes or until done. Cool on a wire rack for 10 minutes and then remove from pans. Ice with Yogurt Cream Topping (page 319) or Blueberry Preserves (page 313).

⋲§ CAROB CAKE

Serves 6-8

1½ cups (2 6-ounce cans) frozen apple-juice concentrate
½ cup decaffeinated coffee, brewed strong
1 cup (8 ounces) evaporated skim milk
1 cup nonfat milk
1 tablespoon dry sherry
2 tablespoons pure vanilla extract
½ cup pastry flour
3 cups whole-wheat flour
¾ cup unsweetened carob powder
1 tablespoon baking powder
2 teaspoons baking soda
¾ cup nonfat dry milk

Combine the liquid ingredients in a small mixing bowl. In a large mixing bowl, mix the dry ingredients and slowly pour in half of the liquids. Stir well, but DO NOT BEAT. Add the remainder of the liquids. Mix thoroughly. Bake for 25 to 35 minutes at 375°F. in two nonstick 9-inch round cake pans, or 35 to 45 minutes in two 9-inch loaf pans. Stick a fork or toothpick in the center of the cake. When it comes out clean, the cake is done. Ice with Yogurt Cream (page 319).

~§ EASY CAROB CAKE

Serves 6–8

- 2 cups whole-wheat flour
- ½ cup unsweetened carob powder
- 1 tablespoon low-sodium baking powder
- 2 teaspoons baking soda
- 1 tablespoon pure vanilla extract
- ¾ cup (1 6-ounce can) frozen apple-juice concentrate
- ¾ cup nonfat milk or evaporated skim milk

In a mixing bowl mix all the dry ingredients together. Combine the liquid ingredients, add them to the dry ingredients, and mix thoroughly. DO NOT BEAT. Pour the batter into a 9×5×4-inch loaf pan and bake for 35 to 45 minutes in a 375°F. oven.

‹§ CHEESECAKE

In my experience in cooking for low-fat diets, this has been the most-requested of all dessert items. Actually, most people find it astounding that it's permitted at all! But this cheesecake manages to be low in sugar and fats, yet exceptionally high in flavor.

Serves 6–8

CRUST

1 cup Grape-Nuts
2 tablespoons frozen apple-juice concentrate

Mix the ingredients together, pat into a nonstick 9-inch pie pan, and bake for 20 minutes at 350°F.

FILLING

1 cup dry cottage cheese
1 cup evaporated skim milk
1 tablespoon arrowroot powder or whole-wheat flour
1 cup nonfat yogurt (page 72)
½ teaspoon lemon juice
⅓ cup frozen apple-juice concentrate
1 tablespoon pure vanilla extract
3 egg whites, beaten lightly

Put the dry cottage cheese in a blender, add the evaporated skim milk, and blend until smooth. Pour the blended cheese mixture into a large mixing bowl. Add the arrowroot powder or whole-wheat flour and nonfat yogurt, mixing thoroughly with a beater or wire whisk until smooth. Then add the lemon juice, apple-juice concentrate, vanilla, and egg whites. Again, mix until smooth. Pour the mixture into the Grape-Nut crust and bake at 350°F. for 20 minutes.

⋖§ YOGURT CHIFFON CHEESECAKE

This is a tangier cheesecake than the buttermilk version which follows.

Serves 6–8

> 3½–4 cups dry cottage cheese
> 1 cup nonfat yogurt (page 72)
> 2 envelopes unflavored gelatin*
> 1 8-ounce can unsweetened crushed pineapple (dietetic)
> ¾ cup (1 6-ounce can) frozen apple-juice concentrate
> 1 tablespoon vanilla extract
> 3 egg whites
> 1½ cups Grape-Nuts or bran flakes
> 2 tablespoons apple-juice concentrate

In a blender place cheese to fill it ¾ full. DO NOT PACK. Add the yogurt and blend to a thick but smooth consistency. In a bowl, moisten the gelatin with the crushed pineapple and mix well. Bring the apple juice and ½ cup water to a boil and pour it over the gelatin-pineapple mixture, stirring to dissolve the gelatin. When this has cooled, add the cheese mixture and vanilla. Beat the egg whites until stiff and fold them in. Pour into two 9-inch pie pans and refrigerate for several hours.

FRUIT TOPPING (OPTIONAL)

> 1 1-pound package frozen strawberries or frozen blueberries, unsweetened
> ½ cup frozen apple-juice concentrate
> 1 teaspoon arrowroot or cornstarch
> 1 teaspoon vanilla extract

Bring the fruit and apple juice to a boil. Thicken with arrowroot dissolved in 2 tablespoons water; then stir in vanilla. Cool. Spread over chilled pie. Refrigerate until topping is set.

* Gelatin is an animal protein, so its use should be restricted. Consult your particular low-fat diet for guidelines.

◄§ AMARETTO BUTTERMILK CHIFFON CHEESECAKE

This is the sweeter of the two chiffon cheesecakes.

Serves 6–8

3½–4 cups dry cottage cheese
   1 cup nonfat buttermilk
   2 envelopes unflavored gelatin*
   1 8-ounce can unsweetened crushed pineapple
   1 6-ounce can (¾ cup) frozen apple-juice concentrate
   1 tablespoon pure vanilla extract
   1 tablespoon Amaretto liqueur
   3 egg whites
1½ cups Grape-Nuts or bran flakes

Crumble enough cheese into a blender to fill it ¾ full. DO NOT PACK. Add the buttermilk (more if necessary) and blend to a thick but smooth consistency. In a bowl, moisten the gelatin with the crushed pineapple and mix well. Bring the apple juice to a boil with ½ cup water, pour it over the gelatin-pineapple mixture, and stir to dissolve. When it has cooled, add the cheese mixture, vanilla, and Amaretto. Beat the egg whites until stiff and fold them in. Pour into two 9-inch pie pans and refrigerate for several hours.

FRUIT TOPPING

   1 bag frozen strawberries *or* 1 box frozen blueberries, unsweetened
  ½ cup frozen apple-juice concentrate
   1 tablespoon arrowroot or cornstarch, dissolved in ½ cup water
   1 teaspoon pure vanilla extract

---

* Gelatin is an animal protein, so its use should be restricted. Consult your particular low-fat diet for guidelines.

Bring the fruit and apple juice to a boil. Thicken with the arrowroot or cornstarch mixture, then stir in the vanilla. Cool, and spread over chilled pies. Refrigerate until topping is set.

✥ BASIC CRÊPES

Makes 6–8 crêpes

1 cup whole-wheat flour
2 teaspoons baking powder
1 teaspoon baking soda
1 cup evaporated skim milk
1 tablespoon frozen apple-juice concentrate
1 teaspoon pure vanilla extract
2 egg whites

Sift and mix the dry ingredients in a mixing bowl. Then add the milk, apple-juice concentrate, and vanilla. Mix thoroughly. Fold the beaten egg whites into the mixture. Season a 6–8-inch pan (See Pancakes, page 42). Pour in about ¼ cup crêpe batter and quickly tilt and turn the pan so that the batter forms a circle filling the bottom of the pan. Cook on both sides until golden brown. Set aside and serve hot.

Note: If you wish to make the crêpes ahead of time and freeze them, place waxed paper between them and wrap them tightly so they are not exposed to the air. Before using the crêpes, bring them to room temperature so that they are soft and pliable; otherwise they will break when you try to fold them.

⋞§ VANILLA-BRAN CRÊPES

Makes 6–8 crêpes

½ cup bran flakes
1½ cups whole-wheat flour
2 teaspoons baking powder
1 teaspoon baking soda
1 tablespoon vanilla extract
1 tablespoon frozen apple-juice concentrate
1 cup evaporated skim milk
1 egg white, beaten stiff

Mix the dry ingredients together in a mixing bowl. Then stir in the liquids. Mix thoroughly until smooth and not lumpy. Fold the beaten egg white into the mixture. To thin the batter, add tablespoons of water, a little at a time. Season a 6–8-inch pan (See Pancakes, page 42). Pour in about ¼ cup of batter to make a 6–8-inch crêpe. After about 2 minutes, bubbles will appear on the crêpe surface. After the bubbling and popping stops, flip the crêpe and cook about 30 seconds on the other side.

Bread, Rolls, and Muffins

The baking of bread is a traditional joy of cooking that is being rediscovered in many homes. The problem with breads in terms of diet and health has to do with the baking process: the yeast used for making the bread rise is usually cultivated ("proofed," in baker's terminology) with sugar. Then, when the rising is done, the activity of the yeast is generally stopped by the addition of salt.

Well, now there's no reason to kick bread out of the house just because you've gone on a diet that restricts sugar and salt. These recipes contain no sugar (except the small amount of natural sugar that occurs in the frozen apple-juice concentrate) and practically microscopic amounts of salt—in fact, some of the recipes contain no salt at all.

Another thing that makes these breads more healthful and nutritious than most commercial breads is the fact that they use whole-grain flours. In the manufacture of commercial flour, the grain is stripped of its hull (bran), which contains most of the fiber and amino acids, then bleached and sprayed with nutrients. The breads in this chapter, on the other hand, are made with flours in which the nutritious bran has been left intact, and which have not been bleached, sprayed, or bromated. (By the way, if you can find a store-bought bread that conforms to all these standards—no sugar, low salt, whole grain, unbleached, unsprayed, unbromated—buy it.) At any rate, the breads in this chapter will keep you in step with the requirements of just about any of the currently popular low-fat, high-fiber diet systems. Also, the whole-grain flours will produce a bread with a more robust flavor and heartier texture than customary white flours and will give a feeling of sustenance and satisfaction that bleached-flour doughs can't hope to match.

Now: about preparation of breads and rolls. Basically, it's a two-bowl process. In the first bowl, put the water heated to about body temperature. (Any hotter or cooler means de yeast die and de bread don' rise. Test it for temperature as you would a baby's formula—by sprinkling a few drops on your wrist.) Add the yeast. Then add the apple-juice concentrate. In the second bowl put all the rest of the ingredients: the flour, baking powder, baking soda, and flavorings as well as any tamari, vegetables, or fruits used in the recipes. Within 30 seconds, the yeast mixture should start to foam. When the entire mixture is foaming, add the dry ingredients a little at a time, mixing thoroughly. At first the dough will be wet and gooey. As the dry ingredients are added (slowly, remember?), the dough will begin to dry out and take on a crumbly texture.

That's when it's time to start kneading. Take the dough out of the bowl and place it on a dry wooden surface that has been lightly dusted with flour. Fold the dough inward from the corners until it forms a ball. Push down on the dough with the heels of your hands, so that the dough squeezes into an elongated, football-like shape. Then fold it in again and repeat the process. Knead the dough in this manner for about 10 minutes, then stop.

At this point, the dough has to rest. Put it back into a bowl and cover it with a dry towel. The dough is now ready for its first rising. Put the covered bowl in a warm place—near the stove, for example. Just be sure not to put it directly on a heat source, like a radiator or a turned-on oven. Allow the dough to rise for 20 to 30 minutes. When it has risen to the point where it's actually pushing the towel off the bowl, remove the towel and punch the dough with your fists until it "collapses" and sinks to the bottom of the bowl.

Now the dough is ready to form into any shape called for in the individual recipe. To form a loaf, take about 1 pound of the dough and place it on a wooden board that has been dusted with flour. Roll it with a rolling pin, working from the center out, until the dough looks like a big pancake about 1 inch thick. Then roll it with your hands into a cylinder and tuck the ends underneath. Put it in a nonstick loaf pan seam side down.

To form rolls, take about ½ cup of dough, roll it into a long, thin cylinder (looks something like a snake), then tie the cylinder into a knot. For breadsticks, make a cylinder but don't tie it. To form pita (pocket) bread, take about 1 tablespoon of dough and roll it into a ball. Then pat it with your hands until you get a thin, flat, round disk—looking like a frisbee. Take two of the "frisbees" and join them by pinching the edges together all the way around. For chapaties, use only one "frisbee"—no joining, no pinching. The dough used for one 9-inch loaf of bread will make about 8 rolls, 8–10 pitas, or 16–20 chapaties.

Now it's time for the second rising. Unless you're making chapaties, for which only one rising is necessary, put your formed dough into the container in which it's going to be baked. Cover it with a dry towel and return it to a warm place for 20 to 30 minutes. In that time, the dough will just about double in size. Uncover, and you're ready to bake!

Note: These instructions will produce a full, hearty bread. If you like a lighter, more delicate texture, withhold ⅓ of the flour and knead the dough a second time, just before you form it into loaves, rolls, or pitas.

⋖§ QUICK WHOLE-WHEAT BREAD

Makes 2 9-inch loaves

- **3 cups lukewarm water**
- **2 packages active dry yeast**
- **2 tablespoons frozen apple-juice concentrate**
- **8 cups whole-wheat flour**
- **2 teaspoons baking powder**
- **1 teaspoon baking soda**

Follow the preparation instructions on pages 297–98. Bake the loaves 40 to 45 minutes at 350°F. Rolls take 20 minutes at 350°F., and chapaties or pita bread take 5 minutes at 450°F. Try dressing up this easy-to-make bread with Dutch Crunch Topping (page 310).

FOR VARIATION: Add ½ teaspoon tamari or ½ teaspoon fresh chopped garlic or 3 tablespoons chopped onion to the dry ingredients.

ᵉᵍ OLD-FASHIONED WHOLE-WHEAT BREAD

Makes 3 9-inch loaves

11 **cups whole-wheat flour**
½ **cup bran**
¾ **cups defatted chicken stock (page 86)**
¼ **teaspoon tamari (optional)**
3 **cups nonfat dry milk, reconstituted in 1½ cups water**
1½ **packages active dry yeast**
3¾ **cups warm water (warm to wrist)**
½ **cup frozen apple-juice concentrate**
1 **tablespoon raisin-juice extract (optional)**
6 **egg whites**

Follow the preparation instructions on pages 297–98. Form the dough into loaves, rolls, pitas, or chapaties. Bake loaves at 350°F. for 40 to 45 minutes or until lightly toasted. If you are making rolls, bake 20 minutes at 350°F. Pitas and chapaties take 5 minutes at 450°F.

ᵉᵍ RYE BREAD

Makes 2 9-inch loaves

3 **cups lukewarm water**
2 **packages active dry yeast**
2 **tablespoons apple-juice concentrate**
5½ **cups whole-wheat flour**
½ **cup cornmeal**
2 **cups rye flour**
2 **teaspoons baking powder**
1 **teaspoon baking soda**
1 **tablespoon caraway seeds**

Follow the preparation instructions on pages 297–98. If you are making loaves, sprinkle a little cornmeal in the bottom of your nonstick loaf pans before putting in the dough. Bake loaves for 40 to 45 minutes in a 350°F. oven. For rolls, bake 20 minutes at 350°F., and for pitas or chapaties bake 5 minutes at 450°F.

✎§ EASY HERB BREAD

Makes 2 9-inch loaves

- 3 cups lukewarm water
- 2 packages active dry yeast
- 2 tablespoons frozen apple-juice concentrate
- 8 cups whole-wheat flour
- 2 teaspoons baking powder
- 1 teaspoon baking soda
- 1 tablespoon basil
- 1 teaspoon oregano
- 1 teaspoon thyme
- ½ teaspoon rosemary
- ½ teaspoon aniseed
- ¼ teaspoon celery seed
- ¼ teaspoon dill
- 1 tablespoon tamari (optional)

Follow the preparation instructions on pages 297–98. Bake loaves for 40 to 45 minutes in a 350°F. oven. Bake rolls for 20 minutes at 350°F., pitas for 5 minutes at 450°F., and breadsticks for 15 minutes at 350°F.

✑ GARLIC BREAD IN A CROCK

Makes 4 loaves

3 cups lukewarm water
2 packages active dry yeast
2 tablespoons frozen apple-juice concentrate
8 cups whole-wheat flour
2 teaspoons baking powder
1 teaspoon baking soda
¼ cup minced garlic
1 teaspoon dill
1 tablespoon caraway seed

Follow the preparation instructions on pages 297–98. Once you have punched down the dough, divide it into 4 equal portions. Take each portion and roll out into a 12-inch circle. Fold in half and roll 3 times from one point to the other, so that it takes on a cone-like appearance. Moisten a paper towel with 1 teaspoon of vegetable oil and wipe the inside of a 1-pound coffee can. Place the cone of dough, point down, inside the coffee can. Repeat this procedure for each of the other 3 pieces of dough. Bake for 50 minutes at 400°F.

✑ RAISIN BREAD

Makes 2 9-inch loaves

3 cups lukewarm water
2 packages active dry yeast
2 tablespoons frozen apple-juice concentrate
8 cups whole-wheat flour
2 teaspoons baking powder
1 teaspoon baking soda
1 tablespoon grated orange rind

1 tablespoon cinnamon
½ cup raisins
1 tablespoon pure vanilla extract

Prepare the dough according to the instructions on pages 297–98. Form into loaves or rolls, cover, and let rise until double in bulk. Bake at 350°F. Loaves will take 40 to 45 minutes; rolls will take about 20 minutes.

✺ ZUCCHINI BREAD

This makes great breadsticks.

Makes 2 9-inch loaves

3 cups lukewarm water
2 packages active dry yeast
2 tablespoons frozen apple-juice concentrate
8 cups whole-wheat flour
2 teaspoons baking powder
1 teaspoon baking soda
1 teaspoon oregano
1 teaspoon thyme
3 cloves garlic, minced fine
1 cup grated zucchini
1 teaspoon sweet basil

Follow the preparation instructions on pages 297–98. Bake loaves in nonstick loaf pans in a 350°F. oven for 40 to 45 minutes. Bake breadsticks on a nonstick cookie sheet for 15 minutes at 400°F.

◄§ GARLIC TOAST

2 cloves garlic, peeled and minced fine
½ cup nonfat milk
8 slices whole-wheat or sourdough bread*

Mix the garlic and milk in a small bowl. Brush this mixture generously over one side of each slice of bread. Place on a nonstick baking sheet and toast in a 350°F. oven for 7 to 10 minutes, or until the surface turns golden brown.

◄§ ONION-GARLIC ROLLS

Makes 24 rolls

3 cups lukewarm water
2 packages active dry yeast
2 tablespoons frozen apple-juice concentrate
8 cups whole-wheat flour
2 teaspoons baking powder
1 teaspoon baking soda
1 tablespoon chopped onion
1 teaspoon minced garlic

TOPPING

1 cup chopped onion
1 tablespoon minced garlic
1 tablespoon apple-juice concentrate

Prepare the dough according to the instructions on pages 297–98.

While the dough is rising, sauté the onion and garlic in the apple-juice concentrate for the topping. Put this mixture in

* Although sourdough breads are made with white flour, the sourdough culture is their nutritional "saving grace."

the bottom of the loaf pan. Shape the dough into a roll and roll out into a ½-inch-thick square. Roll up the sheet of dough and cut into 2-inch slices. Let rise until size has doubled. Place the slices on the onion mixture in the loaf pan. Bake 20 to 30 minutes at 375 °F.

⋖§ SESAME ROLLS

Makes 24–30 rolls

- **3 cups lukewarm water**
- **2 packages active dry yeast**
- **2 tablespoons frozen apple-juice concentrate**
- **8 cups whole-wheat flour**
- **2 teaspoons baking powder**
- **1 teaspoon baking soda**
- **¼ cup sesame seeds**

Prepare the dough according to the instructions on pages 297–98. Roll into a ½-inch-thick square and cut into 2-inch strips. Roll the strips into coils. Let rise to double size. Sprinkle with sesame seeds and bake (coil side up) on a nonstick baking sheet at 400 °F. for 45 to 50 minutes.

⋖§ BREADSTICKS

Makes 36–40 6-inch breadsticks

- **3 cups lukewarm water**
- **2 packages active dry yeast**
- **2 tablespoons frozen apple-juice concentrate**
- **8 cups whole-wheat flour**
- **2 teaspoons baking powder**
- **1 teaspoon baking soda**

Prepare the dough according to the instructions on pages 297–98. For each breadstick, take ¼ cup dough and roll between hands to form a cylinder about 1 inch in diameter. Place the sticks on a nonstick baking sheet and bake for 15 minutes in a 400°F. oven, or until crisp and golden brown.

⊸§ BANANA BREAD

Makes 1 loaf

2 cups whole-wheat flour
1 tablespoon baking powder
2 teaspoons baking soda
1 teaspoon cinnamon
1 6-ounce can (¾ cup) evaporated skim milk
¾ cup nonfat milk
¾ cup frozen apple-juice concentrate
2 bananas, peeled and mashed
¼ cup raisins
¼ cup chopped canned chestnuts (optional)
¼ cup Grape-Nuts (optional)

Combine the flour, baking powder, soda, and cinnamon. Add both milks and the apple-juice concentrate, and mix thoroughly. Then add the bananas, raisins, and chestnuts (if used) and pour into a nonstick 9×5×4-inch loaf pan. Sprinkle with Grape-Nuts if desired. Bake 30 to 35 minutes in a 375°F. oven.

⊸§ CORN BREAD

This corn bread has a solid, hearty consistency, while the corn bread that follows is light and cake-like.

Makes 1 loaf

1 **cup cornmeal**
1 **cup whole-wheat flour**
1 **tablespoon low-sodium baking powder**
2 **teaspoons baking soda**
¾ **cup frozen apple-juice concentrate**
¾ **cup nonfat milk or buttermilk (strained)**

Combine all the dry ingredients in a mixing bowl. Then add the liquids. Mix thoroughly and bake in a nonstick loaf pan for 35 minutes in a 375°F. oven.

VARIATION: Add 1 cup grated carrot and ½ teaspoon cinnamon to the batter.

⊸§ CORN-BREAD MUFFINS

Makes approximately 24 muffins

1 **cup cornmeal**
1 **cup whole-wheat flour**
1 **tablespoon baking powder**
2 **teaspoons baking soda**
¾ **cup frozen apple-juice concentrate**
¾ **cup evaporated skim milk**
¾ **cup nonfat milk**

Combine all the dry ingredients in a mixing bowl. Then add the liquids. Mix thoroughly. Fill muffin tins ⅔ full of batter. Bake for 25 minutes in a 375°F. oven.

VARIATION: Add 1 cup grated carrot and ½ teaspoon cinnamon to the batter.

✒️ BLUEBERRY MUFFINS

Makes 12–14 muffins

2 cups whole-wheat flour
1 tablespoon baking powder
2 teaspoons baking soda
¾ cup nonfat milk
¾ cup frozen apple-juice concentrate
1 cup fresh blueberries *or* 1 cup frozen blueberries, thawed
    and drained

Combine all the dry ingredients in a mixing bowl. Add the milk and apple-juice concentrate and mix thoroughly. Then add the blueberries, folding them in gently. Fill a nonstick muffin tin ⅔ full. Bake 30 to 35 minutes at 375°F.

✒️ BRAN MUFFINS

Makes 12–16 muffins

1 cup whole-wheat flour
1 cup bran flakes
2 teaspoons baking powder
1 teaspoon baking soda
1 teaspoon cinnamon
a dash of nutmeg
¾ cup evaporated skim milk
¾ cup frozen apple-juice concentrate
1 teaspoon pure vanilla extract

In a mixing bowl, combine all the dry ingredients. Then add the liquids, mixing thoroughly. Fill muffin tins ⅔ full and bake for 20 minutes at 375°F.

⋖§ APPLE-BRAN MUFFINS

Makes 12–16 muffins

2 apples, peeled, cored, and diced
¾ cup frozen apple-juice concentrate
1 teaspoon lemon juice
1½ cups whole-wheat flour
1 cup bran
2 teaspoons baking powder
1 teaspoon baking soda
1 teaspoon cinnamon
a dash of nutmeg
1 cup evaporated skim milk
1 tablespoon pure vanilla extract
¼ cup black currants or raisins

Soak the apples in the frozen apple-juice concentrate and lemon juice for 1 hour. Combine the dry ingredients in a mixing bowl, then add the milk and vanilla. Mix thoroughly. DO NOT BEAT. Fold in the apples, along with the juice in which they have been soaking, and the raisins and bake in muffin tins for 20 minutes at 375°F. Fill the muffin tins only ⅔ full of batter to allow for rising.

✑§ DUTCH CRUNCH BREAD TOPPING

2 packages yeast
½ cup warm water
1 tablespoon frozen apple-juice concentrate
1 teaspoon whole-wheat flour

Dissolve the yeast in the warm water. Add the apple juice and the flour to the yeast mixture and mix thoroughly. Cover and let stand in a warm place for 10 to 15 minutes. The topping will be a heavy paste. Spread it like frosting over the tops of breads before baking. Delicious on Quick Whole-Wheat Bread (page 299) or Zucchini Bread (page 303).

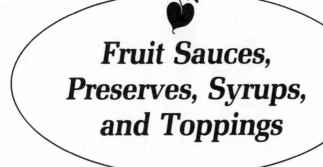

Fruit Sauces, Preserves, Syrups, and Toppings

Syrups without refined sugar? Preserves that aren't made "a cup to a cup"? Yes, it's all possible! You can make exquisite, even exotic spreads like pineapple preserves or peach syrup without adding so much as a grain of sugar, using frozen apple-juice concentrate as a safe and delicious substitute.

Note: Cooking brings out the natural sugar content of fruit, so people on severely sugar-restricted diets should use these recipes only in moderation.

✧ FRESH APPLESAUCE

Makes 1 pint

4 solid tart apples such as Granny Smiths, peeled, cored, and cut into chunks
1 tablespoon frozen apple-juice concentrate
1 teaspoon pure vanilla extract
2 tablespoons raisins (optional)
1 teaspoon arrowroot or cornstarch dissolved in 2 tablespoons water

Puree the apples with the apple-juice concentrate and vanilla in a blender. Place the puree in a saucepan and heat until it steams. Add the raisins if you are using them. Add the arrowroot or cornstarch mixture for thickening. Serve hot or cold.

✎§ KENNIE'S NATURAL APPLESAUCE

Because the skins are left on the apples, this applesauce has a hearty, up-country texture.

Makes 1 quart

> **8 solid tart apples, such as Gravensteins or Granny Smiths, cored and cut into chunks**
> **2 tablespoons frozen apple-juice concentrate**
> **¼ teaspoon cinnamon**
> **1 teaspoon grated orange rind (optional)**
> **1 teaspoon arrowroot or cornstarch dissolved in 2 tablespoons water**

Mix the apples, frozen apple-juice concentrate, cinnamon, and orange rind in a saucepan. Heat to a boil. Remove from the heat. Add the arrowroot or cornstarch mixture and stir. Cover and allow to stand 3 to 5 minutes. Chill and serve.

Note: This sauce will be equally tasty made with such other fruits as pears, apricots, or peaches.

✎§ FRESH CRANBERRY-FRUIT RELISH

This recipe is especially designed for the holiday season. Its vibrant color and zesty taste will add that cranberry-sauce sparkle to your Thanksgiving or Christmas dinner. At the same time, its refreshing fruitiness makes it a delightful complement for meals all through the year.

Makes 1 pint

1 pound fresh cranberries
1 orange, peeled and cut into ½-inch chunks
1 cup fresh pineapple *or* 1 small can water-packed crushed pineapple, drained
1 cup frozen apple-juice concentrate
1 teaspoon pure vanilla extract

Steam the cranberries in a 1½–2-quart pot for 10 minutes, until they are soft. Drain completely. In a large bowl, combine all the remaining ingredients; then add the cranberries and mix well. Chill and serve.

ᵉ§ BLUEBERRY PRESERVES

Makes 1 pint

2 6-ounce cans frozen apple-juice concentrate
3 cups fresh blueberries *or* 1 package frozen blueberries
1 tablespoon pure vanilla extract
2 teaspoons arrowroot powder or cornstarch, dissolved in 2 tablespoons cold water

In a saucepan, cook the apple juice for 15 minutes over medium-low heat until it is reduced by one half. Add the blueberries and vanilla, cover, and continue to simmer for 3 minutes. Add the arrowroot or cornstarch solution to thicken. Cool and place in jars.

Note: Any fruit can be substituted for the blueberries to make a delicious preserve.

✑ STRAWBERRY JAM

Makes 1 pint

2 6-ounce cans frozen apple-juice concentrate
3 cups fresh strawberries, washed and hulled *or* 1 package
frozen strawberries
2 teaspoons arrowroot powder or cornstarch, dissolved in 2
tablespoons cold water

In a saucepan, cook the apple juice for 15 minutes over medium-low heat until it is reduced by one half. Add the strawberries, cover, and continue to simmer for 3 minutes. Add the arrowroot or cornstarch solution to thicken. Put in a blender at medium speed. Remove and strain out seeds. Cool and put into jars.

✑ BRANDIED PEACH PRESERVES

Makes 1 pint

2 6-ounce cans frozen apple-juice concentrate
3 cups peeled and sliced fresh peaches *or* 1 package frozen
peaches
1 teaspoon brandy
2 teaspoons arrowroot powder or cornstarch dissolved in 2 tablespoons cold water

Follow the instructions for Blueberry Preserves, adding brandy at the same time as the fruit. Can also be made with pears, apricots, or plums.

◄§ PIÑA COLADA PRESERVES

Makes 1 pint

2 6-ounce cans frozen apple-juice concentrate
1 tablespoon frozen orange-juice concentrate
1 medium-size fresh pineapple *or* 3 6-ounce cans crushed
  pineapple (no sugar), drained with the liquid set aside
1 teaspoon pure coconut extract
2 teaspoons arrowroot powder or cornstarch dissolved in 2 tablespoons water

Combine the apple-juice concentrate, orange-juice concentrate, and pineapple juice (if you are using canned pineapple) in a saucepan. Cook over medium-low heat until the
liquid is reduced by half. Add the pineapple and the coconut
extract, cover, and simmer for 3 minutes. Stir in the arrowroot
or cornstarch mixture to thicken the preserves. Cool and put
into jars.

◄§ APPLE BUTTER

Makes 1 quart

2 pounds baking apples such as Jonathans or Winesaps,
  washed
1 cup frozen apple-juice concentrate
1 tablespoon apple-cider vinegar
¼ teaspoon cinnamon
a dash of ground cloves (optional)
1 teaspoon grated lemon rind

Peel and core the apples and cut them into quarters. Cook
in the apple-juice concentrate and vinegar for 20 to 25 minutes, adding the spices and lemon rind. Blend at medium
speed. Put into jars and chill.

✑ FRUIT SYRUPS

These syrups and compotes make great pancake toppings
or toppings for dessert crêpes (page 294).

STRAWBERRY SYRUP

Makes 1–1½ pints

6 cups fresh strawberries, washed and hulled *or* 2 packages
frozen strawberries, thawed
1 6-ounce can (¾ cup) frozen apple-juice concentrate
1 tablespoon pure vanilla extract
1 teaspoon arrowroot powder or cornstarch, dissolved in 2 tablespoons water

Puree the fruit in a blender with the apple-juice concentrate and vanilla. Pour the puree into a saucepan and heat
until it steams. Add the arrowroot or cornstarch solution to
thicken. Serve hot or cold.

Note: Almost any fruit can be substituted for the strawberries to make a delicious syrup.

BLUEBERRY COMPOTE

Makes 1–1½ pints

6 cups fresh blueberries, washed and any stems removed *or* 2
packages frozen blueberries (no sugar added), thawed
1 6-ounce can (¾ cup) frozen apple-juice concentrate
1 tablespoon pure vanilla extract
1 teaspoon arrowroot powder or cornstarch, dissolved in 2
tablespoons water

In a blender, puree ¾ of the fruit along with the apple-juice
concentrate and vanilla. Place this puree in a saucepan and

heat until it steams. Add the arrowroot or cornstarch solution to thicken. Add the rest of the fruit. Serve hot.

Note: Again, the fruit is a matter of choice.

BRANDIED APRICOT COMPOTE

Makes 1–1½ pints

- **6 cups peeled and sliced fresh apricots *or* 2 packages frozen (no sugar added)**
- **¾ cup (6 ounces) frozen apple-juice concentrate**
- **1 tablespoon pure vanilla extract**
- **1 tablespoon brandy**
- **2 teaspoons arrowroot powder or cornstarch, dissolved in 2 tablespoons of cold water**

In a blender, puree ¾ of the fruit with the apple-juice concentrate, vanilla, and brandy. Place the puree in a saucepan and heat until it steams. Add the arrowroot or cornstarch solution to thicken. Add the remaining fruit. Serve hot.

Note: Try this using other fruits too.

◄§ FRUIT TOPPINGS

Consider this an open-ended recipe, in that any fruit will substitute beautifully for the apples. Use the fruit topping on pancakes or blintzes, over Ice Cream (page 269), on muffins, even as a spread for toast. This "topping" is thicker than the preceding fruit syrups.

APPLE TOPPING

Makes 1 cup

2 cups apples, peeled, cored, and cut into chunks
1 tablespoon frozen apple-juice concentrate
1 teaspoon pure vanilla extract
1 teaspoon arrowroot powder or cornstarch, dissolved in 2 tablespoons cold water

Place the apples, apple-juice concentrate, and vanilla in a blender, and puree. Put the puree in a saucepan and heat until it steams. Stir the arrowroot or cornstarch solution into the steaming mixture until it is thickened. Serve hot or cold.

≈§ "WHIPPED CREAM" TOPPING

Whipped cream on a fat-free diet? Hard to believe, isn't it? In fact, I didn't really think it could be done. But I had to try, didn't I? Sure I did. This "whipped cream" actually has the same thick, stand-up texture as the fatty stuff, and you can use it in exactly the same ways: as a dessert topping, as a cake icing, or as a finishing touch for a fruit smoothie. In fact, combine it with 1 cup of fresh or frozen fruit and you can use it as a dessert all by itself!

Makes about 3 cups

3 cups nonfat dry milk
1 tablespoon pure vanilla extract
1 cup water
2 tablespoons frozen apple-juice concentrate

Put all the ingredients in a blender and blend at high speed until the mixture is smooth and thick.

✑ YOGURT CREAM TOPPINGS

Makes 3–3½ cups

Choose one of the fruit flavors below. Add 1 tablespoon frozen apple-juice concentrate and 1 teaspoon pure vanilla extract to the selected fruit; place in a blender and puree. Add 2 cups nonfat yogurt (page 72) and blend until smooth. Serve chilled. Eat it solo as a dessert in itself, as a topping for crêpes, or as a cold sauce for fresh fruit.

APPLE TOPPING

2 apples, peeled, cored, and cut into quarters

PEACH TOPPING

2 fresh peaches, peeled, pitted, and cut into quarters *or* 1 package frozen peaches

APRICOT TOPPING

6 fresh apricots, peeled, pitted, and cut into quarters *or* 1 package frozen apricots

STRAWBERRY TOPPING

1 basket fresh strawberries, washed, hulled, and cut in half *or* 1 package frozen strawberries

BLUEBERRY TOPPING

3 cups fresh blueberries *or* 1 package frozen blueberries

PAPAYA TOPPING

1 fresh papaya, cut in half lengthwise. Spoon out and discard the seeds, then spoon the fruit out of the skin.

Beverages

When it comes time for a beverage to complete the meal—or just to quench the thirst between meals—most of us run into a big health problem, perhaps without even realizing it. Our most popular beverage, for example, is coffee, which is high in caffeine, a stimulant which has been implicated in heart-damaging stress and even in breakdowns in the reproductive system. Many of the teas we drink have as much caffeine as coffee, and some even more. Milk has some definite nutritional value, but is dangerously high in fat.

So what's the answer? Well, decaffeinated coffee is a start, but one wants to know the process used in decaffeinating. If the beans are simply rinsed in water before roasting, that's okay. But if it's a chemical process, as is most commercial decaffeination, then it might be best to pass it by. Cereal-based coffee substitutes like Postum and Pero may actually be your best bets from a nutritional and health standpoint.

There are also a number of herbal teas which are entirely caffeine-free. Some of the best examples are Linden Flower Tea, Red Bush Tea (sometimes called Rooi Bush), chamomile, and peppermint. All these teas are commercially available; they can be found in the herb-tea section of supermarkets or in health-food stores.

The dangerous element in milk, of course, is the fat, and you can eliminate that by drinking the nonfat variety. If you want to liven up the flavor of this sometimes rather thin-tasting product, try stirring in a few tablespoons of any of the fruit syrups on page 316.

Of course, there's always the dieter's friend: fruit juice. Fresh fruit is the best, with frozen a second choice, followed by the canned dietetic variety. Try to make your juices out of the whole fruit so that you ingest some fiber with the natural sugar. If you're on a sugar-restricted diet—or even if you're not—use the fruit-containing recipes in this section only in moderation.

Now: a word about alcohol. Without going into a long treatise on its other dangers, let me just mention that alcohol is similar to sugar and honey in that its calories are "empty"—they have little or no nutritional value. I've included a few wine cocktail recipes for people who feel that life gets pale without a little liquor, but these drinks should be used no more than a few times a week, and then no more than two at a time—at the *most*.

✑ BASIC SMOOTHIE

In any of these Smoothies, fruit juice can be substituted for nonfat milk to provide a nondairy drink.

Keep some bananas in a plastic bag in your freezer, so you can have a smoothie whenever the spirit moves you.

Makes 1 glass

1½ bananas
  1 teaspoon pure vanilla extract
  1 tablespoon nonfat dry milk
  ½ cup nonfat milk
dash cinnamon (optional)

Peel the bananas and put them in a plastic bag in the freezer for about 2 hours or until frozen. Break them into 1-inch chunks and put them in a blender with the nonfat dry milk, nonfat milk, and vanilla extract and blend to a smooth, creamy milkshake. Serve immediately.

✑ STRAWBERRY SMOOTHIE

Makes 1 glass

1½ bananas, peeled
  ½ cup fresh or frozen strawberries
  ½ cup nonfat milk
  1 tablespoon nonfat dry milk
  1 teaspoon pure vanilla extract
  1 teaspoon pure strawberry extract

Place the bananas and fresh strawberries, if used, in a plastic bag and place in the freezer for about 2 hours or until frozen. Break the bananas into 1-inch chunks and put them in a blender with the strawberries, nonfat milk, nonfat dry milk, vanilla, and strawberry extract and blend to a smooth, creamy milkshake. Serve immediately.

❧ BLUEBERRY SMOOTHIE

Makes 1 glass

1½ bananas, peeled
½ cup fresh or frozen blueberries
½ cup nonfat milk
1 tablespoon nonfat dry milk
½ teaspoon pure almond extract

Place the bananas and fresh blueberries, if used, in a plastic bag in the freezer for about 2 hours or until frozen. Break the bananas into 1-inch chunks and put in a blender with the blueberries. Add the nonfat milk, nonfat dry milk, and almond extract and blend to a smooth, creamy milkshake. Serve immediately.

❧ PEACH SMOOTHIE

Makes 1 glass

1 banana, peeled
½ cup fresh or frozen sliced peaches
½ cup nonfat milk
1 tablespoon nonfat dry milk
1 teaspoon pure vanilla extract

Place the banana and fresh peaches, if used, in a plastic bag in the freezer for about 2 hours or until frozen. Break the banana into 1-inch chunks and put them in a blender with the peaches. Add the nonfat milk, nonfat dry milk, and vanilla extract and blend to a smooth, creamy milkshake. Serve immediately.

⋑ PIÑA COLADA SMOOTHIE

Makes 1 glass

1 banana, peeled
½ cup fresh or 1 small can dietetic crushed pineapple, drained
1 orange, peeled and cut into quarters *or* 1 tablespoon frozen orange-juice concentrate
½ cup nonfat milk
1 tablespoon nonfat dry milk
1 teaspoon pure coconut extract

Place the banana, pineapple, and fresh orange quarters, if used, in a plastic bag in the freezer for about 2 hours or until frozen. Break the banana into 1-inch chunks. Put it in a blender with the pineapple and orange quarters or orange-juice concentrate. Add the nonfat milk, nonfat dry milk, and coconut extract and blend to a smooth, creamy milkshake. Serve immediately.

⋑ LOW-SUGAR SODA POP

There's a little bit of kid in all of us, and that kid still loves a good soda pop once in a while. Well, here's a way to make your own, so that you can get the flavor without swallowing the sugar. And you may even find those here more flavorful than the commercial dietetic sodas. For variety, simply substitute orange, grape, grapefruit, or any other natural fruit concentrate. One caution: Many commercial soda waters are extremely high in salt content. Be sure to buy only those products which are labeled low-sodium.

Makes 1 glass

1 tablespoon frozen fruit-juice concentrate (apple, orange, grape, grapefruit, or any other that appeals to you)
Perrier water, Calistoga water, or any similar low-sodium carbonated water
a twist of lemon

Put the fruit-juice concentrate in an 8-ounce glass. Fill with carbonated water and stir. Add the twist of lemon. Serve chilled.

✎§ COCKTAILS

BLOODY MARY

6 ounces tomato juice
2 ounces sake or dry white wine
a dash of Tabasco
a dash of tamari
1 lime wedge

Pour the juice over ice and stir in the wine and the condiments, or shake together in a cocktail shaker.

SCREWDRIVER

6 ounces orange juice
2 ounces sake or dry white wine
1 teaspoon frozen apple-juice concentrate

Pour these ingredients over ice and stir, or shake together in a cocktail shaker.

PIÑA COLADA

    6 ounces pineapple juice
    2 ounces sake or dry white wine
    1 teaspoon pure coconut extract
    1 tablespoon frozen orange-juice concentrate

Pour these ingredients over ice and stir, or shake together
in a cocktail shaker.

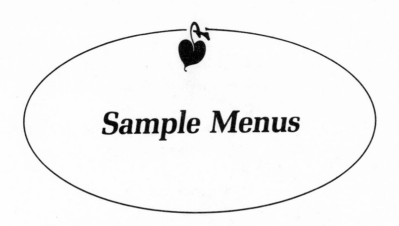

Sample Menus

A Sample Low-Calorie Menu for Three Days

The following menus are low in calories because they are high in vegetables that do not contain a large amount of starch. At the same time these menus are high in nutrition and contain a balance of all the nutrients required for energetic daily living. For maximum weight loss a person should avoid the use of tamari; it contains some salt, which will cause you to retain liquids, thus slowing the weight loss.

Day 1

Breakfast

½ grapefruit

Baked Egg Casserole (page 42)

chamomile tea

Lunch

Gazpacho (page 100)

Tangy Green Bean Salad (page 58)

a 6-ounce slice of Corn Bread (page 307)

peppermint tea

Dinner
Quick Vegetable Stew (page 148)
Fresh or frozen sweet corn
Glazed Carrots (page 216)
Mixed Green Salad with Italian Herb Dressing (page 77)
and cucumber slices
1 slice of fresh melon for dessert
chamomile tea

Day 2

Breakfast
1 orange
Seven-Grain Cereal (page 34) with nonfat milk
and sliced ½ banana
peppermint tea

Lunch
Artichoke Pâté Sandwich (page 51) on whole-wheat
or sourdough bread
Spanish Tomato Salad (page 67)
chamomile tea

Dinner
Delectable Vegetable Soup (page 104)
Zucchini Lasagne (page 155)
Basic Artichoke (page 211)
Baked Banana Squash à l'Orange (page 226)
1 slice of Apple Raisin Pie (page 276) for dessert
chamomile tea

Day 3

Breakfast
½ grapefruit
Date Granola (page 37) with sliced ½ banana and nonfat milk
chamomile tea

Lunch
Stir-Fry Italiana (page 231)
Garlic Toast (page 304)
Marinated Mushroom Salad (page 63)
peppermint tea

Dinner
Chinese Hot-and-Sour Soup (page 106)
Baked Spaghetti Squash (page 227)
Spicy Bell Peppers (page 222)
1 baked potato
chamomile tea
Fruit Ice Cream (page 269) with 2 Banana-Bran Cookies
(page 280) for dessert

The foregoing menus are suggested to give you a guideline
for what is possible in a weight-loss mode for the use of this
cookbook. The guidelines for weight loss are recipes that are
high in nonstarchy vegetables in soups, salads, and entrées. I
invite you to create your own menus from these examples.

A Sample Weight-Maintenance Menu for Three Days

Treat the following menus as an invitation to sample all the recipes in this book, with the only restriction being to avoid daily consumption of the recipes containing animal protein such as poultry or seafood.

Day 1

Breakfast
Banana-Raisin Pancakes (page 46) with Strawberry Topping
(page 317)

chamomile tea

Lunch
All-Bean Soup (page 92)

Carrot Delight (salad) (page 60)

Banana Bran Loaf (page 286)

peppermint tea

Dinner
Cornish Hens with Mandarin Glaze (page 208)

Casserole Potatoes (page 223)

Sautéed Brussels Sprouts (page 215)

Streusel Coffee Cake (page 284) for dessert

chamomile tea

Day 2

Breakfast
1 orange, quartered
Garden Omelette (page 41) with Mushroom Sauce (page 252)
whole-wheat or sourdough toast
peppermint tea

Lunch
Creamy Carrot-Apple Cheese Sandwich (page 52) with lettuce and tomato on whole-wheat or sourdough toast
Broccoli Floret Salad (page 59)
Oatmeal Cookies (page 282)
chamomile tea

Dinner
Stuffed Mushrooms Italiana (appetizer)
Lobster Dijon (page 177) over Wild and Brown Rice (page 243)
Steamed Green Beans (page 212)
Nouvelle Pie (page 278)
peppermint tea

Day 3

Breakfast
Oatmeal (page 33) with sliced ½ banana and nonfat milk
whole-wheat or sourdough toast with Peach Preserves
(page 314)
peppermint tea

Lunch
Split-Pea Soup (page 104)
Potato Pancakes (page 134)
Leona's Sour Cream (page 71) and fresh Applesauce
(page 311)
1 piece fresh fruit (such as peach or apple) in season
chamomile tea

Dinner
Egg Rolls (appetizer) (pages 127, 130) with mustard or
Sweet-and-Sour Sauce (page 129)
Lasagne (page 152)
Glazed Yams (page 231)
Simple Broccoli (page 214)
Carrot Cake (page 288) with Strawberry Yogurt Cream
Topping (page 319) for dessert
peppermint tea

The foregoing menus are a suggestion of how this book may be used. All the recipes will keep two or three days, so that meals may be created at your convenience.

A Thanksgiving or Christmas Holiday Menu

Creamy Cucumber Cheese with Chips (pages 52, 30)
Roast Turkey Breast with Turkey Gravy (page 205)
Fresh Cranberry Relish (page 312)
Corn-Bread Stuffing (page 206)
Glazed Yams (page 231)
Asparagus with Dill Sauce (page 210)

Glazed Fresh Beets (page 213)
Zucchini Balls (page 151)
Pumpkin Pie (page 273) or Pear-Apple-Peach Pie (page 275)

Fourth of July or Outdoor Menu

Vegetable Medallions (page 157) on Garlic Toast (page 304)
with Tomato Sauce (page 159)
Potato Salad (page 64)
Creamy Cole Slaw (page 66)
Cheesecake (page 291)
Fresh-Fruit Banana Ice Cream (page 269)
Carob Cookies (page 283)
Smoothies (pages 322–324)

Index